Handbook of
MEDIA ECONOMICS

Handbook of
MEDIA ECONOMICS

Volume 1B

Edited by

SIMON P. ANDERSON
Commonwealth Professor of Economics,
University of Virginia, Charlottesville, VA, USA

JOEL WALDFOGEL
Frederick R. Kappel Chair in Applied Economics,
Carlson School of Management,
University of Minnesota, Minneapolis, MN, USA

DAVID STRÖMBERG
IIES, Stockholm University, Stockholm, Sweden

ELSEVIER

Amsterdam • Boston • Heidelberg • London • New York • Oxford
Paris • San Diego • San Francisco • Singapore • Sydney • Tokyo
North-Holland is an imprint of Elsevier

North-Holland is an imprint of Elsevier

Radarweg 29, PO Box 211, 1000 AE Amsterdam, The Netherlands
The Boulevard, Langford Lane, Kidlington, Oxford OX5 1GB, UK

British Library Cataloguing-in-Publication Data
A catalogue record for this book is available from the British Library

Library of Congress Cataloging-in-Publication Data
A catalog record for this book is available from the Library of Congress

ISBN: 978-0-444-62721-6 (Vol. 1A)
ISBN: 978-0-444-63685-0 (Vol. 1B)

For information on all North-Holland publications
visit our website at http://store.elsevier.com/

Working together
to grow libraries in
developing countries

www.elsevier.com • www.bookaid.org

Publisher: Nikki Levy
Acquisition Editor: J. Scott Bentley
Editorial Project Manager: Joslyn Chaiprasert-Paguio
Production Project Manager: Nicky Carter
Designer: Alan Studholme

Typeset by SPi Global, India
Printed and bound in the UK

INTRODUCTION TO THE SERIES

The aim of the *Handbooks in Economics* series is to produce Handbooks for various branches of economics, each of which is a definitive source, reference, and teaching supplement for use by professional researchers and advanced graduate students. Each Handbook provides self-contained surveys of the current state of a branch of economics in the form of chapters prepared by leading specialists on various aspects of this branch of economics. These surveys summarize not only received results but also newer developments, from recent journal articles and discussion papers. Some original material is also included, but the main goal is to provide comprehensive and accessible surveys. The Handbooks are intended to provide not only useful reference volumes for professional collections but also possible supplementary readings for advanced courses for graduate students in economics.

Kenneth J. Arrow and Michael D. Intriligator

CONTENTS

Introduction		*xiii*
Contributors		*xvii*
Acknowledgment		*xix*
Dedication		*xxi*

Volume 1A

Part I.   Media Market Structure and Performance   **1**

1.   Preference Externalities in Media Markets   **3**
Simon P. Anderson, Joel Waldfogel

1.1.	Introduction	4
1.2.	Fixed Costs and Heterogeneous Preferences	6
1.3.	Theory	10
1.4.	Empirical Results: Facts Relevant to Predictions from Theory	28
1.5.	Technological Change, Fixed Costs, and Preference Externalities	36
	Acknowledgments	38
	References	38

**2.   The Advertising-Financed Business Model in Two-Sided
      Media Markets**   **41**
Simon P. Anderson, Bruno Jullien

2.1.	Introduction	42
2.2.	Cast of Characters	43
2.3.	Equilibrium Analysis of Single-Homing Viewers/Readers/Listeners/Surfers	47
2.4.	Multi-Homing Viewers/Readers	66
2.5.	Equilibrium Genre Choices	78
2.6.	Further Directions	86
	Acknowledgments	87
	References	87

**3.   Empirical Modeling for Economics of the Media:
      Consumer and Advertiser Demand, Firm Supply and
      Firm Entry Models for Media Markets**   **91**
Steven T. Berry, Joel Waldfogel

3.1.	Introduction	92
3.2.	Audience Demand	93
3.3.	Advertiser Demand	105

3.4. The Supply Side: Choice of Prices, Ad Quantity, and Other Continuous Characteristics   107
3.5. The Supply Side: Positioning and Entry   114
3.6. Future Challenges   118
References   119

4. **Advertising in Markets**   **121**
Régis Renault

4.1. Introduction   122
4.2. Search and Advertising   127
4.3. Product Advertising   143
4.4. Advertising as a Signal   166
4.5. Advertising Technology   176
4.6. Advertising that Might Not Inform   184
4.7. Closing Comments   198
Acknowledgments   200
References   200

5. **Recent Developments in Mass Media: Digitization and Multitasking**   **205**
Kenneth C. Wilbur

5.1. Recent Trends in Mass Media Consumption   207
5.2. Effects of Digitization   213
5.3. Effects of Media Multitasking   218
5.4. Discussion   221
Acknowledgments   222
References   222

6. **Merger Policy and Regulation in Media Industries**   **225**
Øystein Foros, Hans Jarle Kind, Lars Sørgard

6.1. Introduction   226
6.2. Price and Quantity Effects of Mergers in Two-Sided Markets   228
6.3. Mergers and Platforms' Choice of Genres   236
6.4. Merger Control in Media Markets   244
6.5. Concluding Remarks   258
Acknowledgments   261
References   261

Part II. Sectors   **265**

7. **The Economics of Television and Online Video Markets**   **267**
Gregory S. Crawford

7.1. Introduction   268
7.2. The Television Industry   270

7.3. A Simple Model of the Television Market   292
7.4. Extensions to the Simple Model: "The Four Bs"   302
7.5. Open Policy Issues in Television Markets   321
7.6. Online Video Markets   327
7.7. Conclusions   333
Acknowledgments   334
References   334

8.   Radio   **341**
Andrew Sweeting

8.1. Introduction   342
8.2. A Brief History of the Radio Industry in the United States   345
8.3. Data   352
8.4. The Effects of Industry Consolidation on Market Outcomes: Theoretical Considerations   356
8.5. Empirical Evidence on the Effects of Ownership Consolidation in Radio   359
8.6. Excess Entry   375
8.7. Strategies for Retaining Listeners   376
8.8. Non-commercial Radio and the Effects of Competition Between
         Non-commercial and Commercial Broadcasters   381
8.9. Effects of Radio on the Music Industry, and Cultural and Political Outcomes   384
8.10. Conclusions   391
Acknowledgments   392
References   392

9.   Newspapers and Magazines   **397**
Ambarish Chandra, Ulrich Kaiser

9.1. Introduction   398
9.2. An Overview of the Print Media Industry   401
9.3. Market Structure in Newspapers and Magazines   409
9.4. Newspapers and Magazines as Two-Sided Markets   416
9.5. Advertising in Newspapers and Magazines   422
9.6. Antitrust Issues in Newspapers and Magazines   427
9.7. Print Media and the Internet   433
9.8. Thoughts for Future Research and Conclusions   437
Acknowledgments   440
References   440

10. The Economics of Internet Media   **445**
Martin Peitz, Markus Reisinger

10.1. Introduction   446
10.2. Media and Advertising on the Internet: Some Facts   450
10.3. Providing Media Content   459

10.4.	Users Choosing Media Content	470
10.5.	Media Platforms Matching Advertising to Content	494
10.6.	Media Platforms Matching Advertising to Users	511
10.7.	Conclusion	525
	Acknowledgments	526
	References	526

Index	*531*

Volume 1B

11.   Privacy and the Internet   **541**
Catherine E. Tucker

11.1.	Introduction	541
11.2.	Economics of Privacy	542
11.3.	Privacy and Advertising	544
11.4.	Privacy and Social Media	552
11.5.	Privacy in a World of Infinitely Persisting Data: The Right to be Forgotten	554
11.6.	Privacy: Online Data Security	555
11.7.	Privacy and the Government	557
11.8.	Conclusion: Future Spheres of Privacy	558
	Acknowledgments	559
	References	559

12.   User-Generated Content and Social Media   **563**
Michael Luca

12.1.	Introduction	564
12.2.	The Impact of User-Generated Content	568
12.3.	The Quality of User-Generated Content	575
12.4.	Incentive Design and Behavioral Foundations	582
12.5.	Other Issues	584
12.6.	Discussion	588
	Acknowledgments	589
	References	590

Part III.   The Political Economy of Mass Media   **593**

13.   Media Coverage and Political Accountability: Theory and Evidence   **595**
David Strömberg

13.1.	Introduction	596
13.2.	Theory	596
13.3.	Evidence	608

13.4.	Conclusion	620
References		620

14. Media Bias in the Marketplace: Theory — **623**
Matthew Gentzkow, Jesse M. Shapiro, Daniel F. Stone

14.1.	Introduction	624
14.2.	What is Bias?	624
14.3.	Bias and Welfare	627
14.4.	A Model of the Market for News	628
14.5.	Supply-Driven Bias	630
14.6.	Demand-Driven Bias	633
14.7.	Conclusion	643
Acknowledgments		644
References		644

15. Empirical Studies of Media Bias — **647**
Riccardo Puglisi, James M. Snyder, Jr.

15.1.	Introduction	648
15.2.	Estimating Bias	649
15.3.	Factors Correlated with Bias	659
15.4.	Bias and Voter Behavior	662
15.5.	Conclusions	664
References		664

16. Media Capture and Media Power — **669**
Andrea Prat

16.1.	Introduction	669
16.2.	Media Capture	672
16.3.	Media Power	676
16.4.	Implications for Media Regulation	682
16.5.	Conclusions	685
References		685

17. Media Capture: Empirical Evidence — **687**
Ruben Enikolopov, Maria Petrova

17.1.	Introduction	688
17.2.	Evidence on Media Capture	689
17.3.	Determinants of Media Capture	693
17.4.	Media Effects in the Presence of Media Capture	694
17.5.	Limits of Media Capture	697

17.6.   Conclusion   698
References   699

18.   **The Role of Media in Finance**   **701**
Paul C. Tetlock

18.1.   Introduction   702
18.2.   Theory   703
18.3.   Media as a Reflection of the Information Environment   705
18.4.   Causal Role of Media   712
18.5.   Corporate Finance Applications   715
18.6.   Discussion and Directions for Future Research   716
Acknowledgments   717
References   718

19.   **Economic and Social Impacts of the Media**   **723**
Stefano DellaVigna, Eliana La Ferrara

19.1.   Introduction   724
19.2.   Methodological Issues   728
19.3.   Outcomes   731
19.4.   Policy and Conclusion   758
Acknowledgments   766
References   766

Index   *769*

INTRODUCTION

Media markets are special in many ways, and they take on an importance that is much larger than their accounting contribution to GDP. First, on the consumer side, is the astonishingly large fraction of leisure time devoted to them. Second, on the advertiser side, they provide a conduit for firms to get consumers to buy goods, which supports employment in the advertising industries and may foster economic growth by enabling innovations to be brought quickly and profitably to market and rewarding risk-taking. Third, the media plays a very special role in providing information on current events and politics. However, the media by necessity systematically filters and biases this information. How much and which information is transmitted is likely to affect wide range of political, economic, and social outcomes, including political accountability, corporate accountability, financial market performance, and educational and family choices. Because of these effects, the media is a particular industry that is specifically regulated in the constitutions of most democratic (and nondemocratic) countries.

Foremost, perhaps is the paramount role of informing the electorate, arising largely as an externality to news consumption. In terms of market performance, media markets may embody several key features that give rise to specific types of market failure. Many media have relatively high fixed costs and low marginal costs, and hence a paucity of equilibrium product offerings, leading to preference externalities in content provision whereby majority groups' tastes tend to be catered at the expense of minorities. This news bias also alters the trade-off in political competition and therefore introduces a bias in public policy against the interest of minority groups. Moreover, the business model of advertising finance is that of a two-sided market with media outlets (platforms) delivering eyeballs to sell to advertisers, which is a quite different market structure from traditional market interactions.

This volume (1A and 1B) contains 19 chapters on the state of the art on the economics of media. These chapters are divided broadly into three parts.

Part I. Media market structure and performance, covering theory and methodology.

Chapter 1 explores the implications of the high fixed costs and heterogeneous consumer preferences endemic to media markets and the ensuing preference externalities in media markets. Both the positive and the normative economics are developed through a suite of theoretical models that are then illuminated empirically.

Chapter 2 covers the theory of two-sided markets as it relates to media markets. Platforms realize a two-sided balance between the two sides, and in competition with each other. The extent of consumer (viewer) multihoming is a key driver of positive predictions. Advertising revenues ultimately underwrite programming content, and this feature impacts performance measures from static market efficiency through genre choice and equilibrium variety.

Chapter 3 reviews the techniques of empirical industrial economics most helpful for the study of media markets. The chapter includes an extensive discussion of demand modeling, as well as entry modeling. The chapter takes a more methodological approach than others in the volume.

Much of the media sector is dependent on advertising for revenue. Chapter 4 takes a detailed look (primarily theoretical) at the background to the economics of advertising. It develops various conceptual roles that advertising may take, and it draws out the consequences for evaluating the surplus associated to advertising. This is a key ingredient to evaluating the performance of ad-financed media.

Chapter 5 takes a primarily marketing perspective to describe audience behavior and consumer response to ads. It discusses recent innovations such as advertising avoidance, advertising targeting and personalization, and reviews how the landscape has changed over the last decade.

Chapter 6 explores merger policy and regulation of media industries. These industries require a dedicated analysis distinct from standard markets because of their two-sided nature and because of their pivotal place in providing information. The chapter exposits the extant theory, delivers some empirical evidence on the consequences of mergers, and discusses recent cases.

Part II. Industry sectors, covering the economics of particular media industries. The first three chapters of this part give historical background and empirical results on various pertinent aspects, with special emphasis on the US landscape. The last three chapters of this part address various facets of the economics of the Internet.

Chapter 7 surveys the economics of television, the dominant entertainment medium for most consumers. The chapter describes incentives for production and consumption of content, recent trends in television and online video markets, and the state of economic research on these industries. Topics emphasized include pay television, vertical relations, the role of public television, and growing online video.

Chapter 8 on radio pays special attention to the effects of recent consolidation in the United States. It also addresses the impact of the public sector and findings on the extent of overentry in the sector. Another contribution is to depict the interaction between the music and radio industries.

Chapter 9 on newspaper and magazines describes the history and structure of print markets in the United States. The chapter discusses these sectors in the context of two-sided markets. It includes discussions of whether or not advertising is a net nuisance to print media consumers, antitrust issues in print markets, and the effect of the Internet on these sectors.

Chapter 10 on media economics of the Internet is a primarily theoretical synthesis of recent key advances as applied to this emergent sector. The chapter includes discussion of such pertinent aspects as aggregators, search engines, and Internet service providers.

Chapter 11 covers the topic of privacy and the Internet, which has been an issue of much public concern and debate. A conceptual framework is developed and related to empirical estimates. Further topics include advertising, social networks, data security, and government surveillance.

Chapter 12 addresses user-generated content and social media. It covers an eclectic set of applications in a fast-moving sector, and pays particular attention to determining the quality of the content.

Part III: The political economy of mass media, covering the effects of media on political, economic, and social outcomes. Chapters 13–17 discuss the media's political coverage, bias and capture, and the resulting effects on political accountability. Chapter 18 covers effects in finance and Chapter 19 covers effects on social outcomes.

Chapter 13 presents a baseline model of how the information filtering caused by media coverage affects political accountability. It discusses the welfare consequences of private provision of news as well as regulation to solve the problem of underprovision of news. The model also supplies an array of testable implications, used to organize the existing empirical work. The key questions are: what drives media coverage of politics; how does this coverage influence government policy, the actions and selection of politicians, and the information levels and voting behavior of the public?

Chapter 14 discusses how bias may reduce the informativeness of media, undermining its positive role for political accountability. It surveys the theoretical literature on the market forces that determine media bias. A simple model is used to organize the literature on the determinants of bias, focusing first on supply-side forces such as political preferences of media owners, and then turning to demand-side forces working through consumer beliefs and preferences. The chapter defines bias, analyzes its welfare consequences and how these are affected by, for example, competition.

Chapter 15 surveys empirical studies of media bias, with a focus on partisan and ideological biases. The chapter discusses the methods used to measure media bias, the main factors found to be correlated with media bias and measures of the persuasive impact of media bias on citizens' attitudes and behavior.

Chapter 16 surveys models of media capture and media power. In both cases, media sources deliberately deviate from truthful reporting in order to affect electoral outcomes. The chapter speaks of media capture when the government has an active role in capturing the media, and media power when media organizations distort news reporting for political ends. The chapter discusses theories of when news manipulation is more likely to succeed and electoral outcomes are more likely to be distorted. It discusses how media regulation can reduce the extent of these two phenomena.

Chapter 17 surveys the empirical literature on the determinants and the consequences of media capture. It reviews the literature on the determinants of media capture. It discusses the methods used to control media, and examines the evidence on the effect of media capture on media content. Next, it presents evidence on the effects of captured media on the behavior of people, as well as the effects of independent media in captured environment. It concludes by discussing the factors that limit the effect of propaganda.

Chapter 18 reviews and synthesizes a rapidly growing subfield that analyzes the relation between media and financial markets. The chapter discusses theories of the role of information provided by media in financial markets. It describes new data and methods that have enabled powerful tests of theories and have the potential to address longstanding puzzles in finance, such as why trading volume and stock price volatility are so high. The chapter presents evidence on, for example, the effect of the volume and content of media coverage on market activity and stock prices.

Chapter 19 reviews the literature on the impact of media exposure on a wide net of social and economic outcomes: education, family choices, labor and migration decisions, environmental choices, health, crime, public economics, attitudes, consumption and savings, and development economics. It stresses five themes: (i) the key role of the demand for entertainment; (ii) the importance of crowding out of alternative activities (substitution effect); (iii) identification of causal effects—credible estimates are available for some topics and media but not for others; (iv) effects may differ by type of media; and (v) both the substitution effect and the demand for entertainment play an important role for the policy impacts.

Simon P. Anderson
Joel Waldfogel
David Strömberg

CONTRIBUTORS

Simon P. Anderson
Commonwealth Professor of Economics, University of Virginia, Charlottesville, VA, USA

Steven T. Berry
David Swensen Professor of Economics, Yale University, New Haven, CT, USA

Ambarish Chandra
Department of Management, University of Toronto at Scarborough and
Rotman School of Management, University of Toronto, Toronto, Ontario, Canada

Gregory S. Crawford
Department of Economics, University of Zürich, and CEPR, Zurich, Switzerland

Stefano DellaVigna
University of California, Berkeley and NBER, Cambridge, MA, USA

Ruben Enikolopov
Icrea-Barcelona Institute of Political Economy and Governance; Universitat Pompeu Fabra, Barcelona, Spain; Barcelona Graduate School of Economics, Barcelona, Spain, and The New Economic School, Moscow, Russia

Øystein Foros
NHH Norwegian School of Economics, Bergen, Norway

Matthew Gentzkow
Department of Economics, Stanford University, Palo Alto, CA, USA, and NBER, Cambridge, MA, USA

Bruno Jullien
Toulouse School of Economics, Toulouse, France

Ulrich Kaiser
Department of Business Administration, Chair for Entrepreneurship, University of Zurich, Zurich, Switzerland; Centre for European Economic Research, Mannheim, Germany; Centre for Industrial Economics at the University of Copenhagen, Copenhagen, Denmark, and Institute for the Study of Labor, Bonn, Germany

Hans Jarle Kind
NHH Norwegian School of Economics, Bergen, Norway

Eliana La Ferrara
Bocconi University and IGIER, Milan, Italy

Michael Luca
Harvard Business School, Boston, MA, USA

Martin Peitz
Department of Economics, University of Mannheim, Mannheim, Germany

Maria Petrova
Icrea-Barcelona Institute of Political Economy and Governance; Universitat Pompeu Fabra, Barcelona, Spain; Barcelona Graduate School of Economics, Barcelona, Spain, and The New Economic School, Moscow, Russia

Andrea Prat
Columbia University, New York, NY, USA

Riccardo Puglisi
Department of Political and Social Sciences, Università degli Studi di Pavia, Pavia, Italy

Markus Reisinger
Department of Economics, Frankfurt School of Finance & Management, Frankfurt, Germany

Régis Renault
PSL, Université Paris Dauphine, LEDa, Paris, France

Jesse M. Shapiro
NBER, Cambridge, MA, USA, and Department of Economics, Brown University, Providence, RI, USA

James M. Snyder Jr.
Department of Government, Harvard University, and NBER, Cambridge, MA, USA

Lars Sørgard
NHH Norwegian School of Economics, Bergen, Norway

Daniel F. Stone
Department of Economics, Bowdoin College, Brunswick, ME, USA

David Strömberg
IIES, Stockholm University, Stockholm, Sweden

Andrew Sweeting
Department of Economics, University of Maryland, College Park, MD, USA

Paul C. Tetlock
Columbia University, New York, NY, USA

Catherine E. Tucker
MIT Sloan School of Management and NBER, Cambridge, MA, USA

Joel Waldfogel
Frederick R. Kappel Chair in Applied Economics, Carlson School of Management, University of Minnesota, Minneapolis, MN, USA

Kenneth C. Wilbur
Rady School of Management, University of California, San Diego, CA, USA

ACKNOWLEDGMENT

Simon Anderson gratefully acknowledges the NSF for their support.

DEDICATION

We dedicate this Volume to our respective wives, children, and parents.

CHAPTER 11

Privacy and the Internet

Catherine E. Tucker
MIT Sloan School of Management, Cambridge, MA, USA
NBER, Cambridge, MA, USA

Contents

11.1. Introduction	541
11.2. Economics of Privacy	542
11.3. Privacy and Advertising	544
11.3.1 Privacy Concerns and Targeted Advertising	544
11.3.2 Privacy Concerns and Behavioral Pricing	546
11.3.3 Privacy Regulation and Targeted Advertising	547
11.3.4 Privacy and Market Structure	551
11.3.5 New Directions in Research on Privacy and the Advertising-Supported Internet	551
11.4. Privacy and Social Media	552
11.5. Privacy in a World of Infinitely Persisting Data: The Right to be Forgotten	554
11.6. Privacy: Online Data Security	555
11.7. Privacy and the Government	557
11.8. Conclusion: Future Spheres of Privacy	558
Acknowledgments	559
References	559

Abstract

This chapter summarizes the fundamental questions underlying the economics of privacy. It highlights the tension between the multifaceted concept of privacy as commonly used in policy debates and its conceptualization as part of a utility function. The chapter then sets out new challenges for the economics of privacy in a variety of online settings with particular reference to the media industry. These settings include advertising, social networks, data security, and government surveillance.

Keywords

Privacy, Economics of privacy, Public policy, Online advertising

JEL Codes

K20, L82

11.1. INTRODUCTION

Privacy is not a new concern for the media or for media economics. However, it is a concern whose emphasis has changed and whose importance has grown. Privacy used

Handbook of Media Economics, Volume 1B
ISSN 2213-6630, http://dx.doi.org/10.1016/B978-0-444-63685-0.00011-5

to be important for media economics as it related to well-known people, and what restrictions were appropriate for news outlets when reporting on their private lives. The earliest theory of privacy in US legal history was written on account of the media: Warren and Brandeis (1890) wrote their theory of privacy in response to changes in journalistic practices. They were prompted both by the growth of the popular media and by the advent of small portable cameras, and the fear that they could prove to be an intrusive technology if used by journalists to document the lives of the famous:

> *Instantaneous photographs and newspaper enterprise have invaded the sacred precincts of private and domestic life; and numerous mechanical devices threaten to make good the prediction that 'what is whispered in the closet shall be proclaimed from the house-tops.' For years there has been a feeling that the law must afford some remedy for the unauthorized circulation of portraits of private persons; and the evil of the invasion of privacy by the newspapers, long keenly felt, has been but recently discussed by an able writer.*

Even after cameras became available to the mass market, however, there were still fixed costs from surveillance, represented by investments in equipment and in time, that made intruding on the privacy of the individual an expensive proposition. In practice, the investment in fixed costs would only pay off for people whose image was worth something to magazines. However, the advent of digital photography and of digital data sharing and storage has now reduced the marginal cost of surveillance to very close to zero. In turn, this has greatly expanded the areas where privacy issues are a concern for media economics. This chapter focuses on these new spheres, highlighting initial work that has been done in this area and research opportunities for the future.

11.2. ECONOMICS OF PRIVACY

Economics has struggled to arrive at a unified theory of privacy.[1] One of the reasons why the economics literature may have struggled with conceptualizing a unified theory of privacy is the difficulty in grounding in economics the factor in an individual's utility function which drives the desire for privacy. To help unravel this, Farrell (2012) makes a useful distinction, which is whether economists should treat privacy as an intermediate good, that is a good whose value simply lies in the way it can moderate the achievement of another good, or as a final good, that is, a good that should be enjoyed and valued for its own sake. Farrell argues that many policymakers, and even economists, do consider privacy to be a final good where a distaste for others intruding on or gathering knowledge about an individual's personal domain is perfectly valid as an emotion and by association a driver of an individual's utility. However, in terms of setting up a formal economic model, it is inevitable that economists will analyze privacy as an intermediate good in order to add richness to the model.

---

[1] This is a common theme for most summary chapters on the economics of privacy—see, for example, Varian (1997), Hui and Png (2006), Solove (2008), and Evans (2009).

Early attempts to model privacy as a final good are perhaps emblematic of the issues that economists face when attempting to model privacy as a final good. For example, Posner (1981) sets out a classic view of privacy-seeking as a preference for secrecy. In this theory, some individuals are modeled as having a taste for secrecy which distorts information available to society as a whole. In other words, the desire for privacy in this viewpoint is the opposite of the desire for transparency. This taste for secrecy and the consequent distortion this had on the disclosure of information had costs which were borne by society as a whole. It is worth understanding the historical context for this work, as explained in Posner (1978); this work was inspired by recent regulations surrounding privacy and credit reporting agencies. This specific context lends itself to a viewpoint where citizens who have shaky financial habits have a desire to hide these shaky financial habits from financial institutions to the detriment of citizens who do not have shaky financial habits. However, the theory does not consider whether or not a citizen with exemplary financial habits may have other reasons to feel a distaste for sharing information about their financial transactions with others.

Indeed, this view of privacy, while unified, does not capture all that is encompassed by the term "privacy" when commonly used. In common with many scholars, Hirshleifer (1980) criticizes the secrecy-focused Posner model as too limited a view of the "privacy continent." It does not capture, for example, privacy as confidentiality, and without confidentiality it would be highly risky to engage in certain kinds of economic activity. Confidentiality of financial transactions can be interpreted as facilitating the existence of markets rather than purely as imposing social costs. Without confidentiality between a lawyer and their client, fair arbitration of commercial disputes becomes impossible. Neither does it capture the ways in which pervasive monitoring may inhibit the ability of entrepreneurs to innovate (Cohen, 2000), criminal offenders to obtain paid work, or the press to report the news accurately. Solove (2004) defines certain forms of privacy as "architectural," governing the distribution of power within society and setting the rules whereby "information is disseminated, collected and networked."

However, there are also efforts within economics to improve on Posner's formulation. Recent work grounded in behavioral economics has focused on the negative psychological reaction to perceived intrusion, or "creepiness," that individuals usually cite when explaining why online privacy is important to them. A good example of this research is Acquisti et al. (2013), who use a field experiment to investigate individual privacy valuations and find evidence of behavioral phenomena such as "endowment" and "order" effects.[2] They found that individuals assigned markedly different values to the privacy of their data, depending on whether they were asked to consider how much money they would accept to disclose otherwise private information, or how much they would pay to protect otherwise public information. Similarly, Acquisti et al. (2012) found

---

[2] A nice summary of some of the ideas in this sphere of research is given in Acquisti (2010).

that relative standards and herding behavior also affected disclosure propensity. Such findings highlight in real data how fungible consumer valuations of privacy are.

This fungibility has led to something called the "privacy paradox." The privacy paradox emphasizes that though individuals state in surveys that they care about their online privacy (essentially, considering it to be a "final good" with value in and of itself), consumers' economic behavior generally treats privacy as an intermediate good. Miltgen and Tucker (2014) provide some evidence from a field experiment conducted in France which helps illuminate why this occurs. They show that when money is not involved, people tend to behave in a privacy-protective way which is consistent with their stated privacy preferences. However, when pecuniary rewards are in play, consumers behave inconsistently with their stated privacy preferences. This is particularly true for consumers who have the most online experience, suggesting that perhaps consumers have learned to trade off their data privacy for pecuniary rewards online.

11.3. PRIVACY AND ADVERTISING

Digital data makes it cheap and easy for firms to collect large amounts of information about consumers' purchases, behavior, and tastes. Consequently, there has been a seismic shift in the media industry as advertising has moved from a paradigm where advertising was indiscriminately broadcast to all viewers (Anderson, 2005; Grossman and Shapiro, 1984), to a paradigm where each ad is individually targeted based on that specific consumer's behavior (Anderson and de Palma, 2009; Athey and Gans, 2010; Bergemann and Bonatti, 2011; Johnson, 2013; Levin and Milgrom, 2010).

Other chapters in this volume consider the role and efficacy of targeting online. This chapter focuses instead solely on the privacy concerns that this shift to targeted advertising engenders. It considers in turn how internal consumer privacy concerns affect the efficacy of targeted advertising and how the actions of external bodies concerned about consumer's privacy online may affect the efficacy of targeted advertising.

11.3.1 Privacy Concerns and Targeted Advertising

Since the advent of the newspaper, newspapers have depended on purchases, subscriptions, and advertising for revenue. A major factor in the reduced circulation of newspapers has been a fall in advertising revenue, as advertisers shift from the relatively untargeted advertising environment offered by newspapers to the highly targeted ads available online in connection with specific search terms (as with Google) or specifically stated consumer preferences (as with Facebook). However, the new targeted ads pose their own set of analytical problems relating to stated privacy concerns. Advertisers select, on an anonymous basis, the consumers who will receive an ad impression, based on the advertiser's information on that set of consumers' personal tastes and actions. Consumers' "click-streams," their click-by-click footprints as they navigate across the web, are utilized to construct detailed profiles that can be used to target advertising more accurately than ever before, and much of this data collection occurs without consumers' knowledge or permission.

Collecting advertising data online is often argued to be effectively harmless on an individual level because it typically involves a series of actions linked only by an IP address or otherwise anonymous cookie-ID number. Advertisers cannot garner much about an individual's web surfing habits, say, from a family computer shared by four people of different ages, genders, and tastes. However, attempts by advertisers to use such information has still met with resistance from consumers due to privacy concerns. In a well-publicized survey, Turow et al. (2009) found that 66% of Americans do not want marketers to tailor advertisements to their interests—and this holds true even in situations like Facebook where consumers have voluntarily and affirmatively disclosed things that they like and do not like. This customer resistance to tailored advertising is a major problem for advertisers. Fear that users may react unfavorably because of privacy concerns has led advertisers to limit their tailoring of ads. A recent survey suggested that concerns about consumer response have led advertisers to reduce the targeting of advertising based on online behavior by 75% (Lohr, 2010).

Therefore, early work on Internet advertising suggests that when asked their preferences, consumers spurn tailored advertising. However, when we turn from consumers' stated preferences to their empirically measured behavior, a more complex picture emerges.

Goldfarb and Tucker (2011a) investigate how consumer privacy concerns affect what kind of advertising techniques work and, more crucially, do not work. Faced with consumers who simply ignore online banner ads, the advertising industry developed two different techniques. First, advertisers improved their targeting of ads—for example, by making sure that ads matched the content that the web user appeared to be seeking. Second, advertisers developed obtrusive ad features using video and audio, including the ability to make an ad float above or take over content the user is seeking. We explore the effectiveness of these two techniques, both in isolation and in combination. To measure advertising effectiveness, the paper used a very large database of field tests for online display advertising campaigns. In isolation, these two techniques each significantly increase advertising effectiveness. However, surprisingly, attempts to combine both targeting and obtrusiveness nullify the positive effects that the two techniques have in isolation. The same obtrusive ad works far better on websites with irrelevant content than with relevant content. One potential explanation of this result is that both of these advertising techniques impinge on users' privacy. Even weak forms of targeting rely on advertisers collecting and using more data about the user and what they are looking at online than is the case for mass-media advertising. Intentionally obtrusive advertising—ads designed to compete with the content next to it—also intrudes on users' privacy by interrupting their online experience without permission. Privacy concerns appear to be the underlying behavioral driver in our results because the combination of obtrusiveness and targeting diminishes ad effectiveness more for privacy-sensitive items (such as healthcare and financial products) and for people who exhibit privacy-sensitive behavior while taking the survey. Acquisti and Spiekermann (2011) reinforce this finding by showing that obtrusive pop-up ads online negatively affect willingness to pay for the advertised goods. This again emphasizes that though much of the privacy debate may be focused on data-enriched ads, there are many other negative ways that advertising can intrude on users' privacy beyond behavioral targeting. A more comprehensive approach to user privacy would therefore consider how obtrusiveness also hinders the user experience, and how that can be traded off against non-obtrusive but personally targeted ads.

White et al. (2008) show that privacy concerns are greatest when advertising is most personalized. Expanding on this theme of personalized advertising, Lambrecht and Tucker (2013) examine one of the most data-intensive and personalized forms of online advertising—dynamic retargeting.[3] Dynamically retargeted ads display products that consumers have viewed previously on other external websites. The paper uses a field experiment conducted by a travel firm and finds, contrary to accepted marketing wisdom, that ads personalized using a consumer's previous product exploration are not usually effective. The only time when they become moderately effective is when a consumer's browsing history indicates that they have reached a stage in their purchase process where they are ready to buy.

Given this work, it is interesting to contemplate how users' ability to control what ads they see affects outcomes. In particular, it would seem likely that privacy concerns may give rise to advertising-avoidance tools (Hann et al., 2008). Johnson (2013) shows that the increasing ability of firms to target their ads influences market outcomes when consumers have access to advertising-avoidance tools. Consumers may gain by absorbing more-relevant ads; two negative consequences of improved targeting are that the number and obtrusiveness of ads received may increase, and rather counter-intuitively, that improved information accuracy may lead consumers to receive ads that they say they prefer less, like ads from niche firms when they say they would prefer an ad from the mainstream firm.

11.3.2 Privacy Concerns and Behavioral Pricing

Returning to Farrell (2012)'s taxonomy, one way in which we can model privacy as an intermediate good in the context of online advertising depends on the extent to which

---

[3] Another potential downside of the digital technologies which make such personalization possible is that in order to target efficiently using algorithms, advertising delivery needs to be automated. Goldfarb and Tucker (2014) investigate the effects of this process of standardization of ad formats on advertising effectiveness. The findings reveal a tradeoff between how standardized digital ad formats are and how effective they are at attracting viewers' attention—for most ads, recall of banner advertising declines the more ads conform to standard formats. This is especially the case for ads that focus on brand logos, and less so for ads designed by advertising agencies.

there is behavioral price discrimination such as coupons and discounts baked into online ads. Farrell argues that modeling privacy as an intermediate good protects information about a consumer's true willingness to pay which, if revealed, would cost the consumer substantially more. As set out by Acquisti and Varian (2005) and Fudenburg and Villas-Boas (2006), conditioning purchase prices on past browsing, can lead to welfare implications that consumers would rationally seek to avoid.

Behavioral price discrimination means that firms use past consumer actions to distinguish between customers who have low and high willingness to pay for their product and offer them low and high prices as a consequence. One example may be that firms may offer ads that offer discounted coupons to consumers whom they observed browsing their products but not purchasing the product, in order to provide a final incentive for that customer to buy the product. Therefore, consumers could be offered very different effective prices based on their click-stream data without their knowledge. This may be harmful, especially if it distorts consumer decisions—that is, consumers might strategically waste time exhibiting behavior (such as browsing a website and not purchasing a product) in order to attract a discounted ad. It might be thought that the Robinson–Patman Act of 1936, which requires "sellers treat all competing customers on the same basis, unless there is some recognized legal justification for different treatment," might be applicable here. However, as shown by Luchs et al. (2010), the Robinson–Patman Act is no longer in practice interpreted as applying in such settings. In this sense, behavioral price discrimination in the US is not meaningfully legally constrained, but it may still be perceived as inappropriate by consumers, and therefore cause reputational harm to firms that use it. For example, Staples implemented a model whereby consumers located nearer to a competing store got charged lower prices than consumers not located near a competing store, which in turn meant that richer areas got charged lower prices.[4] In this context, evidently, a setup where the Staples website did not collect geolocation information on the consumers browsing their site would have meant that Staples did not get into trouble for its price discrimination practices. Consumers, as in Farrell's example, did not explicitly consent to the disclosure of information about their (genuinely) higher aggregate willingness to pay.

Work such as Armstrong and Zhou (2010) has extended this analysis to reflect the fact that behavioral price discrimination may give rise to incentives to consumers to distort their browsing behavior to avoid being subject to behavioral price discrimination.

11.3.3 Privacy Regulation and Targeted Advertising

A more externally focused perspective is to try and understand how actions by outside bodies that try and protect consumer privacy might affect the new media industry.

---

[4] See "Websites Vary Prices, Deals Based on Users' Information," Wall Street Journal, December 24, 2012, accessed on August 7, 2014 at online.wsj.com/news/articles/SB100014241278887323377720457818 9391813881534.

The first legislation which addressed this issue was the European Union's "E-Privacy Directive," EC/2002/58. This legislation was predominantly targeted at the telecommunications sector. However, there were several provisions of the Privacy Directive that limited the ability of companies to track user behavior on the Internet. These changes made it more difficult for a specific advertiser, perhaps selling cruises, to collect and use data about consumers' browsing behavior on other websites to decide whether or not they could potentially be in the market for a cruise. The interpretation of this EC/2002/58 directive has been somewhat controversial as it relates to behavioral targeting. For example, the extent to which a provision that requires companies who use invisible tracking devices such as web bugs to use them only with the "knowledge" of consumers is not clear, meaning that companies need explicitly to obtain opt-in consent. This is one of the reasons why, in the recent "Telecoms Reform Package," the EU amended the current regulation to require a user's explicit consent before placing a cookie on a computer. However, in general the limitations current EU regulation impose on data collection by online advertisers are widely seen as stricter than those in the United States and elsewhere. For example, Baumer et al. (2004, p. 410) emphasize that the privacy laws that resulted from the Privacy Directive are far stricter than in the US and that "maintaining full compliance with restrictive privacy laws can be costly, particularly since that adherence can result in a loss of valuable marketing data." In 2009, EC/2002/58 was amended by Directive 2009/136/EC. The most crucial change was the requirement of consent for storage or access to information stored on a subscriber or user's terminal equipment, in other words a requirement to obtain consent for cookies and similar technologies. There are signs that the US may move to more stringent privacy regulation. FTC (2010) in particular suggested that the US should move to a policy of implementing a "Do Not Track" policy that would allow consumers to enable persistent settings on their web browsers preventing firms from collecting click-stream and multiple bills currently under discussion in the US Congress.

In general it seems likely that such privacy regulation may have costs. As described by Evans (2009) and Lenard and Rubin (2009), there is a tradeoff between the use of online customer data and advertising performance. Goldfarb and Tucker (2011b) examined responses of 3.3 million survey takers who had been randomly exposed to 9596 online display (banner) advertising campaigns to explore how strong privacy regulation, in the form of the European Union's E-Privacy Directive, has influenced advertising effectiveness. The papers find that display advertising became 65% less effective at changing stated purchase intent after the laws were enacted relative to other countries. Although some argue this might simply reflect changes in European consumer attitudes toward advertising, there was no change in ad effectiveness on Europeans who looked at non-EU websites after the regulation was passed.

Goldfarb and Tucker (2011b) find that the E-Privacy Directive disproportionately affected ads that did not have additional visual or interactive features. One interpretation is that plain banner ads' effectiveness depends on their ability to be appropriate and interesting to their audience. Therefore, the laws curtailing the use of past browsing behavior to identify a target audience for the ads would affect plain banner ads disproportionately. The paper also finds that the Privacy Directive affected ads that had a small footprint on a webpage more than those with a large footprint. Crucially, the paper also found that websites that had general content unrelated to specific product categories (such as news and media services) experienced larger decreases in ad effectiveness after the laws passed than websites that had more specific content (such as travel or parenting websites). Customers at travel and parenting websites have already identified themselves as being in a particular target market, so it is less important for those websites to use data on previous browsing behavior to target their ads.

Together, these findings have important implications for how privacy regulation will affect the development of the scope of the advertising-supported Internet and related media industries. There is evidence that the protection will limit its scope. However, it also crucially suggests that the type of content and service provided on the Internet may change. There is also the potential for the type of advertising that is shown on the Internet to change. In particular, without targeting it may be the case that to maintain revenues, publishers and advertisers will be forced to switch to more intentionally disruptive, intrusive, and larger ads. Content publishers may find it more necessary to adjust their content to be more easily monetizable. For example, rather than focusing on investigative journalism, they may focus on travel or parenting news, where the target demographic is more obvious. If adjustment is not possible and a sharp reduction in revenue for free advertising-supported websites results, it is natural to deduce that fewer free websites will be available. This in turn suggests that a general equilibrium model of privacy would also have to effectively factor in the efficiency and welfare gains from the availability of a wide variety of free online content.

This helps to explain the greater emphasis that has emerged in the last few years on "click-bait" journalism. "Click-bait" journalism occurs when a headline such as "Ten ways you are destroying your childrens' lives" is used to entice parents to a site, despite the fact that the content of the article itself may be superficial or trite or even only barely related to the title. Such charges have been levied against websites like the Huffington Post and Buzzfeed, and the critiques have often been virulent. For example, Silver (2014) described such sites as "silly, manipulative, least-common-denominator." It appears troubling that privacy regulation which is intended to help protect consumers online may contribute to a degradation of the quality of journalism consumers are exposed to. As a counterweight to this development, niche journalism websites like ProPublica and Wikileaks are set up on a donations model rather than pursuing revenues from advertising.

These unintended effects would suggest that an approach most likely to foster the health of mainstream, high-quality news websites would be to eschew explicit regulation in favor of empowering users to control what information is used, thereby reducing potential harm to the online advertising industry. Focusing on user-centric controls, rather than government mandated controls, Tucker (2014b) investigates how Internet users' perception of control over their personal information affects how likely they are to click on advertising. I use data from a randomized field experiment that examined the relative effectiveness of personalizing ad copy to mesh with personal information on Facebook. Facebook gave users more control over their personally identifiable information in the middle of the field test, though it did not change how advertisers used anonymous data to target ads. After this change, users were twice as likely to click on personalized ads but there was no change in the effectiveness of ads that did not signal that they used private information for targeting. The increase in effectiveness was more pronounced for ads that used more unusual private information and for users who were more likely to use their privacy controls. This suggests that creating the perception of more control over consumer private information can be an effective strategy for advertising-supported websites.[5] This builds on research such as Brandimarte et al. (2012), which illustrates how perceptions of control influence privacy concerns in general. The precise nature of privacy protection can be expected to matter a lot for the direction of innovation: It is not clearly a matter of a simple binary choice to have privacy protection or not.

Another important approach for guiding regulators is to try and estimate directly or predict the effect of different types of privacy protection on consumer welfare. Johnson (2014) estimates the financial effect of privacy policies on the online display ad industry by applying an empirical model to an auction dataset. This highlights the fact that much online advertising is now sold in real-time using auctions. He uses structural analysis to interpret the price premium paid by advertisers to reflect the information profile of the consumer. He uses this structural model to evaluate three privacy policies that vary by the degree of user choice. My results suggest that online publisher revenues drop by 3.9% under an opt-out policy, 34.6% under an opt-in policy, and 38.5% under a tracking ban. Total advertiser surplus drops by 4.6%, 43.9%, and 45.5%, respectively. This paper is very useful for understanding the effect on publishers (rather than simply advertisers) of privacy regulation. What is striking in this chapter is the stark difference between an opt-out policy and an opt-in policy. This seems plausible given that this has been the central nexus of many debates over privacy regulation. It is also striking that there is little real difference in outcomes between a complete tracking ban and an opt-in policy, suggesting that an opt-in policy in effect has similar real consequences to simply banning tracking altogether.

This analysis is related to earlier theoretical work by Hermalin and Katz (2006), who return to the original arguments of Posner (1981) and Stigler (1980), and explore whether

---

[5] Tucker (2012) compares this result with work that suggests there may be benefits from addressing consumer privacy concerns.

indeed privacy regulation necessarily comes at the expense of allocative efficiency. What is striking about their paper is that, perhaps because it predates the advent of the current controversy about targeted advertising, their model is evocative of a labor market where there is potential information out there to inform employers about the employees' potential quality. Their paper finds that privacy can be efficient even when there is no taste for privacy present. They also explore the related argument that privacy regulation is not needed if property rights can be convincingly established for data. Their model suggests that an effective privacy policy may need to ban information transmission or use, rather than simply assigning individuals' control rights to their personally identifiable data.

11.3.4 Privacy and Market Structure

It is tempting to think that one advantage of privacy regulation is that it might have pro-competitive effects in industries such as the media industry. This is because data-intensive operations can lead to natural economies of scale. Regulation designed to curb the use of data might therefore be thought to decrease tendencies toward monopolization of industries, as large tracts of data offer less of a competitive advantage. However, in Campbell et al. (2015), we show that this intuition may not always hold true. This is because privacy regulations typically require firms to persuade their consumers to give consent, which in turn imposes a cost on the consumer. As pointed out in their study of privacy policies, McDonald and Cranor (2008) assert that even the time taken to read a privacy policy online itself represents a large cost. Firms that have more to offer in the way of content, for example, may find it easier to persuade consumers to give this consent. Therefore, though privacy regulation imposes costs on all types of media firms, it is actually small media and new media firms who are disproportionately affected because it is harder for them to obtain consent under the regulation.

One potential consequence of privacy regulation is that it will lead to a return to "walled gardens" or information silos on the Internet. An archetypal walled garden is a website such as the *New York Times*. Because the *New York Times* is considered an essential website, it is likely that even with government privacy protections in place, consumers would explicitly consent to give the *New York Times* control of their data. However, websites that take a siloed approach control all data and encourage users to expand their Internet usage within the confines of the website. As such, privacy protection may once again restrict the entry of new media firms, but as yet there has been little empirical work on this issue to assess the importance of such arguments.

11.3.5 New Directions in Research on Privacy and the Advertising-Supported Internet

Though the focus of this chapter is on Internet privacy, it is important to remember that when it comes to advertising there are also important offline privacy issues (Petty, 2000).

Varian et al. (2005), for example, give a nice summary of the role of the federally sponsored "Do Not Call" list in preventing potentially intrusive direct sales calls.

An open question is whether the ability to use data to enrich advertising leads not just to ineffective advertising but also to negative welfare outcomes. This is an important question because one of the critiques often made about the new digital economy is that it leads to information silos, where Internet users are compartmentalized and consequently not exposed to potentially welfare-improving information. Gentzkow and Shapiro (2011) find that while online news consumption is more segregated than offline consumption of local news, it is almost as much less segregated than offline national news, and is also significantly lower than the segregation of face-to-face news-related interactions with neighbors, coworkers, and family members. They find no evidence that Internet news consumers are becoming more segregated into information silos over time. Indeed, they observe that the most conservative news consumers online are more likely than less conservative news consumers to have visited nytimes.com, and similarly that the most liberal news consumers online are more likely than less liberal news consumers to have visited foxnews.com. Exposure, then, is not necessarily a good instrument of moderation; but, in fact, exposure to contrary information can often harden your own opinions (Nyhan and Reifler, 2010).

This suggests that, at the very least, it is far from settled that the shift to Internet news has aggravated information silos, and that therefore it would not be appropriate to mount regulatory intervention to decrease such silos on the Internet.

In general, we know little about how advertising works (Percy and Rossiter, 1992; Vakratsas and Ambler, 1999), so it is not a surprise that at the moment there are many open questions when it comes to how privacy moderates the effectiveness of targeted advertising. For example, we do not know if active self-selection into forms of targeted advertising such as the True View platform on youtube.com can actually increase advertising effectiveness. Similarly, we do not yet know whether there are ways of explicitly anonymizing data which may reassure media readers exposed to personalized advertising.

11.4. PRIVACY AND SOCIAL MEDIA

Chapter 12 by Michael Luca in this handbook describes the rise of social media and user-generated content and its increasing societal importance. Much of the early empirical work on privacy in online settings focused on social networks (e.g., Acquisti and Gross, 2006; Bonneau and Preibusch, 2010; Dwyer et al., 2007; Gross and Acquisti, 2005). This reflects that social networks are important advertising venues (Zubcsek and Sarvary, 2011) and consequently subject to heightened concerns about targeted advertising. Instead, the type of content that appears on such websites itself gives rise to privacy concerns. In turn this attracted the attention of computer scientists who were faced with a new challenge, which was how to make a social networking site give appropriate privacy protections when the entire reason that such websites exist is to allow consumers to reveal private information and then make money off that information.

Echoing this technical challenge, in general the most interesting economic questions surrounding privacy and social media appear to be to try to understand the tension between network effects and privacy concerns. To illustrate this, from a network perspective, as a user I benefit the more people who can see my profile. But as more people see my profile, privacy concerns themselves in turn increase. At some point it seems reasonable to think that the latter effect will overwhelm the former effect. This is perhaps illustrated by the fall of early social networks such as Friendster—one of the attractions of the newer social networks such as Facebook was the potential to exclude some of the potential audience from your profile. It is also illustrated by the regular "friend purge" efforts users mount on Facebook to limit their circle of friends to people whose updates and tastes are actually interesting to them, and whom users want to have information on their updates.

The tension can also be seen in the fact that, in such venues, advertisers can explicitly use a consumer's social network to improve advertising performance. Aral and Walker (2011) show that advertising on social networks faces a problem of a lack of ability to engage or co-opt social networking users. They analyze a field experiment on Facebook where a Facebook application randomized whether or not a message was pushed to an adopter's friends and contrasted it with a situation where the user had the opportunity to personalize and choose whether to broadcast the message. Forcing users to broadcast ended up being far more effective, despite the lack of personalization or control.

Tucker (2014a) uses field experiment data to study the use of an individual's social network on Facebook to enhance advertising. In social advertising, ads are targeted based on underlying social networks and their content is tailored with information that pertains to the social relationship. The paper explores the effectiveness of social advertising using data from field tests of different ads on Facebook. Social advertising is effective, mainly from the ability of targeting based on social networks to uncover similarly responsive consumers. However, social advertising is less effective if the advertiser explicitly states they are trying to promote social influence in the text of their ad. This suggests that advertisers must avoid being overt in their attempts to exploit social networks in their advertising.

Privacy issues on social media are broader than merely advertising, and deal with what can best be described as "failures in the wall." If Facebook presents itself as a "walled garden" in which people can express themselves freely, there is an implicit norm violation when information disclosed only on Facebook generates adverse consequences in the world outside Facebook. Acquisti and Fong (2013) conduct a field experiment to study how employers use information on social networks to filter the suitability of employees. They find considerable use of social networking sites for potentially discriminatory purposes. In the United States, several state legislatures have introduced bills that would prevent employers from requiring access to employees' social media passwords as a condition of employment. Without such legislation, employers have a stronger hand than before social media in regulating the non-work activities of employees in such a way as to reflect well on the employer—female grade school teachers seem to have been a particularly common target of such regulation. In this sense, the development of social media inhibits the individual's power of self-(mis)representation to different audiences.

Similarly, the use of facial recognition technology on social networks including Facebook decreases user control by placing the persistent assignation of an identity to an image outside the control of that user. Social media make reputation management more difficult even if you do not use a social network site yourself because an (embarrassing?) photo of you can be tagged in Facebook by someone you know and then digitally distributed across the Internet without limit and without the practical ability to "recall" it.

11.5. PRIVACY IN A WORLD OF INFINITELY PERSISTING DATA: THE RIGHT TO BE FORGOTTEN

In theory, there is no reason why data, once digitized and placed somewhere online, should not infinitely persist. The Internet Archive is the custodian of the Wayback Machine (https://archive.org/web/), which preserves for posterity the vast majority of websites as they appeared on every date since their inception.[6]

This means that data can be revealed about you online at a time when you did not understand the consequences of revealing it, and then can be used against you reputationally or legally at an age when your wiser self would not have taken the decision to reveal that information. It does not appear, contrary to public perception, that "the younger generation" will grow up not caring about privacy; instead, it appears to be the case that they care relatively less than older people do about privacy because they have less experience of reputational harms, and that they will care more as they get older, rather than their privacy preferences remaining stable over time Goldfarb and Tucker (2012). This means that, on average, every person can be considered to have intertemporal instability that may well result in adverse effects on consumer welfare in a world where data potentially persists for a lifetime. However, this is largely an area for future research because social media have barely existed for long enough to enable longitudinal comparison of the same subjects at different levels of maturity.

One current controversy, however, acutely foregrounds the topic of intertemporal privacy preferences. Recently, the European Court of Justice (ECJ) ruled[7] that Google must honor individuals' requests to be removed from search results. This principle has come to be referred to as the "right to be forgotten." It is an attempt to address the challenge of infinitely persisting data—the tendency of information in digital format to last for a very long time regardless of its accuracy. In the analog era, if a telephone directory listed

---

[6] In practice, "link rot" somewhat constrains the persistence of such data, just as changes in format from CDs to .mp3s result in the loss even of digital data.
[7] *Google Spain* v. *AEPD and Mario Costeja Gonzalez* (2014), Court of Justice of the European Union.

a number incorrectly, the result would be missed calls and wrong numbers until a new directory was published a year later. But in the digital world, wrong information gets repeated again and again, often showing up long after the original mistake was made. While digital technology can perpetuate the mistakes others make about us, it also has the same effect on the mistakes we make ourselves when younger.

It seems unlikely on the face of it that regulators are correct to tackle this weighty problem by focusing on Google. Google may be a handy scapegoat, especially in Europe where it is especially dominant in search. However, the American search giant is far from the only source of digital data that threatens the right to be forgotten. Information persists in government records, online newspapers, and social media, as well as in other search engines. To rein in Google while leaving other major information sources unimpeded will not unring the bell. Second, the ECJ's actions ignore the nature of search engines. They work so well because they are automated. The combination of sophisticated algorithms, high-speed networks, and the Internet's vast stores of data is what produces Google's instantaneous and usually on-target results. Introduce humans into this formula via requests to be forgotten, and Google's performance will inevitably be damaged with respect to searches for individuals. A third problem with the ECJ's approach is that the process of approving requests to be forgotten can have precisely the opposite effect of what the architects of the policy intended. When someone asks to be removed from search results, say a politician concerned about rumors of an illicit affair, the request itself sparks interest. In the case of the politician combating damaging rumors, reports of a request to be forgotten prompt new speculation and more rumors, even if the politician is not mentioned by name. In the case that sparked the ruling, Mario Gonzalez's property had been sold to pay social security debts; he is now the most famous person in Spain to have had his property seized in this way.

The right to be forgotten, if applied more broadly, would also challenge the reliability of the news media, the practice of history, and the stability of the law. A truly effective right to be forgotten would enable Mr. Gonzalez to remove the report of the seizure of his property retrospectively from the Spanish newspaper Google linked to, *La Vanguardia*, and also from Spanish governmental records. This would give every private citizen the power of Orwell's "memory hole."

In a sense, the right to be forgotten is a more general application of an older debate regarding the effectiveness of laws allowing the expungement of juvenile and (in some countries) adult criminal records to facilitate their re-entry into paid work.

11.6. PRIVACY: ONLINE DATA SECURITY

One of the most challenging aspects when studying privacy as an economist is the conflation in the public's mind between Internet privacy and Internet security. However, from an economics perspective, modeling the economics of security is far more straightforward.

Indeed, it is helpful for understanding the ambiguity over modeling the economics of privacy by contrasting it with the relatively more clear-cut case of the economics of information security. Standard economic models of moral hazard and the principal-agent problem (Anderson and Moore, 2006) define three agents: an external malicious actor, a consumer, and a firm. As with many public goods problems, the consumer desires that the firm invests in data information security protection, such as encryption or user access controls, to protect the consumer's data from the external threat. However, the firm has few incentives to actually invest in information data security protection, and the consumer's ability to monitor the firm is imperfect Gordon and Loeb (2002).

A good example of this work is Gal-Or and Ghose (2005), who use game theory to develop an analytical framework to investigate the competitive implications of sharing security information and investments in security technologies. We find that security technology investments and security information sharing act as "strategic complements" in equilibrium. Their analysis suggests that information sharing is more valuable when product substitutability is higher, implying that such sharing alliances yield greater benefits in more competitive industries rather than uncompetitive ones.

In general, it seems reasonable to think that most data used in the advertising-supported Internet poses less of a security risk than other customer data. First, most data stored for online advertising is attached to an anonymous profile attached to a particular IP address. It is far harder for an external party to tie such data back to a specific individual user than the kind of data used for product personalization discussed in this section, which has the explicit purpose of linking online data to a real person and their actions. Second, the majority of online advertising data is stored for a short time. Indeed, the IAB suggested in 2010 that such data collection could be limited to a 48-h window (htt://www.theregister.co.uk/2010/10/04/iab_cookie_advice/). Though this met with some controversy, it is indicative of the extent to which the utility of data for advertising is short-lived. Purchase decisions occur relatively quickly, so prior browsing behavior quickly becomes irrelevant to predicting whether a customer will buy. However, customer data for operational purposes tends to stored for longer. For example, currently there is a large debate over whether search engines should be able to store user search profiles for 18 months in the EU as they currently do (Kirk, 2010). One of the risks of longer storage time frames is that it enables a fuller and more widespread profile of a user's habits to emerge, which could more adversely affect a consumer if used for surveillance or malicious purposes.

In general, customer data in the media sector (as opposed to the advertising sector) tends to be focused toward operational efficiency. As such, this data has tended to not attract privacy concerns as much as in other sectors. However, in some sense the storage of this data represents a larger potential privacy risk to individuals than advertising data. Data like this tends both to be stored for longer than data used for advertising purposes and to be more easily tied back to an individual. Furthermore, someone's online reading habits, when matched with their financial and demographic information, could potentially pose a far bigger information security threat. This threat may increase with the increasing use of paywalls and potentially micropayments for information content (Chiou and Tucker, 2013). Therefore, though much of the discussion on privacy has focused on advertising, it seems likely that there may in the future need to be far greater discussion about the economics of information security rather than privacy in the media context.

11.7. PRIVACY AND THE GOVERNMENT

A more recent issue is how government surveillance of its citizens affects Internet and media firms. This is an area which has attracted the interest of legal scholars and, outside of the United States, an entire subfield of "surveillance studies," but as yet it has not attracted the attention of economists as a major issue for analysis.

In particular, it has become important to ask how government surveillance, prompted by national security concerns and facilitated by new digital technologies, affects economic outcomes. Again, as with other research analyzing privacy, there is plenty of survey data to suggest that the surveillance revelations of 2013 caused users to self-report that they meaningfully changed their online behavior, and there are anecdotal reports of substantial negative impacts to the exports of American tech firms such as IBM, Cisco, and even Boeing. However, there is a significant need for empirical research quantifying actual changes to user behavior and systematic analyses of impacts on the American economy. Marthews and Tucker's (2014) "Government Surveillance and Internet Search Behavior" examines how Internet search behavior changed after the Snowden surveillance revelations of June 2013. The surveillance revelations represent a shock in information about how closely users' Internet searches were being monitored by the US government. The analysis uses data from Google Trends on search volume for a panel of search terms across 11 different countries. These search terms were independently rated for their degree of privacy sensitivity along multiple dimensions. In the US, the main subset of search terms that were negatively affected were search terms that users believed would get them into trouble with the US government. However, internationally there was also a drop in traffic for search terms that were rated as personally sensitive. Overall, the surveillance revelations caused a drop of around 5% in Google traffic on privacy-sensitive search terms that was not meaningfully offset by increased searching on other search engines. These results have implications for policymakers, in terms of quantifying chilling effects on search behavior of disclosures relating to the scale of government surveillance on the Internet.

There are three new avenues for future research in media economics in this area:

First, it is not clear whether the results of Marthews and Tucker (2014) are limited to search behavior or whether they have a broader effect. For example, are Internet users less likely to visit more controversial news sites, or news sites in foreign languages, in the wake of revelations about government surveillance—in other words, does it constrain users' search for differing perspectives?

Second, are journalists themselves chilled in their use of sources, or forced toward more expensive and burdensome means of secure communication in order to pursue their craft without fear of legal repercussions? Does surveillance compound the effects discussed above, that already encourage mainstream news outlets to substitute toward less controversial and less general-interest news?

Third in this field would be the welfare implications of "Open Data"—government initiatives to release large datasets to the public for analysis and reuse. In Acquisti and Tucker (2014), "Guns, Privacy and Crime," we investigate an attempt by a regional newspaper to provide value to readers by digitizing and printing government datasets (in this case, a Memphis database of gun permit holders). The publication of the database drew political criticism from gun owners, and also measurably affected criminal behavior. The empirical analysis suggests both displacement and deterrent effects on burglaries. Related to this is Acquisti and Gross (2009), who show that using public data online, it is possible to predict an individual's social security number. Increasingly, news media and even private citizens will find value in aggregating and publicizing already-public information in unexpected ways that may antagonize people who do not expect public data to be that public.

11.8. CONCLUSION: FUTURE SPHERES OF PRIVACY

When thinking about how online privacy issues will develop in the next decade, it is helpful to think of other spheres of life where digitization will happen on a broad scale and consequently create privacy issues. To highlight future avenues for research, this chapter points to three spheres where privacy issues are likely to grow in the next decade. It is important to emphasize that at the moment these spheres are somewhat removed from traditional issues of media economics. This chapter does not attempt to draw tenuous links, as generally futurology and economics are not the same. However, from the standpoint that media convergence is likely to continue and that media ubiquity is likely to increase, there are several spheres where we can expect to see significant privacy discussions occurring.

The first is the so-called Internet of things. As everyday objects such as thermostats, door locks, webcams, televisions, alarms, garage openers, power outlets, sprinklers, and scales start generating large amounts of digital data, new privacy issues will emerge. What is crucial about this is not the items themselves, which are generally mundane, but instead the idea of hyperconnectivity. By measuring how a user interacts with each of these "things," external outsiders and data analysts will be able to gain a far fuller and more complete picture of the user's behavior. Into this category of concerns falls also more advanced technologies such as Google Glass, which undoubtedly will generate huge amounts of both useful and potentially controversial data.

The second is the digitization of bio-information. There has been substantial research on the effect of privacy regulation and concerns on the digitization of medicine (Miller and Tucker, 2009, 2011; Westin, 2005). However, so far this arena has not yet really impinged on media economics. However, the emergence of genetic testing (Miller and Tucker, 2014) can be considered as a special case of the infinitely persistent data problem described above. The lack of our ability to change our genetics is the source of both the exceptional utility of genetic data and its exceptional potential, when released and interpreted by an outsider, to reduce our privacy regarding our susceptibility to medical conditions.

The third sphere is in the digitization of location. Xu et al. (2012), Teo et al. (2012) present some initial research on locational privacy. As we have seen in the discussion above, retailers' data on users' location has grown steeply in complexity. The development (or re-emergence) of hyperlocal media is an effect of having geolocation information on users. Your location can be tracked over time using mobile devices, and the metadata associated with those movements can reveal a great deal about you, even if largely unintentionally. This has huge implications for consumer behavior and welfare.

In general, the aim of this chapter has been to highlight some of the research done on the economics of privacy as it relates to media economics and in some sense to emphasize the large gaps in our knowledge. There remains remarkable scope for researchers to grapple with significant privacy questions in this field, and the rapid pace of technological advance means that this is likely to continue to be true once our current questions have been answered.

ACKNOWLEDGMENTS

I thank Alex Marthews for valuable assistance. All errors are my own.

REFERENCES

Acquisti, A., 2010. The economics to the behavioral economics of privacy: a note. In: Kumar, A., Zhang, D. (Eds.), Ethics and Policy of Biometrics. In: Lecture Notes in Computer Science, Springer, Heidelberg.

Acquisti, A., Fong, C.M., 2013. An Experiment in Hiring Discrimination via Online Social Networks. CMU working paper.

Acquisti, A., Gross, R., 2006. Imagined communities: Awareness, information sharing, and privacy on the Facebook. In: 6th Workshop on Privacy Enhancing Technologies, pp. 36–58.

Acquisti, A., Gross, R., 2009. Predicting social security numbers from public data. Proc. Natl. Acad. Sci. 106, 10975–10980.

Acquisti, A., Spiekermann, S., 2011. Do interruptions pay off? Effects of interruptive ads on consumers' willingness to pay. J. Interact. Mark. 25, 226–240.

Acquisti, A., Tucker, C., 2014. Guns, Privacy and Crime. MIT Sloan working paper.

Acquisti, A., Varian, H.R., 2005. Conditioning prices on purchase history. Mark. Sci. 24 (3), 367–381.

Acquisti, A., John, L.K., Loewenstein, G., 2012. The impact of relative standards on the propensity to disclose. J. Mark. Res. 49, 16–174.

Acquisti, A., John, L.K., Loewenstein, G., 2013. What is privacy worth? J. Leg. Stud. 42 (2), 249–274.

Anderson, S.P., 2005. Market provision of broadcasting: a welfare analysis. Rev. Econ. Stud. 72 (4), 947–972.

Anderson, S.P., de Palma, A., 2009. Information congestion. RAND J. Econ. 40 (4), 688–709.

Anderson, R., Moore, T., 2006. The economics of information security. Science 314 (5799), 610–613.

Aral, S., Walker, D., 2011. Creating social contagion through viral product design: a randomized trial of peer influence in networks. Manag. Sci. 57 (9), 1623–1639.

Armstrong, M., Zhou, J., 2010. Conditioning Prices on Search Behaviour: Technical Report MPRA Paper 19985. University Library of Munich, Germany.

Athey, S., Gans, J.S., 2010. The impact of targeting technology on advertising markets and media competition. Am. Econ. Rev. 100 (2), 608–613.

Baumer, D.L., Earp, J.B., Poindexter, J.C., 2004. Internet privacy law: a comparison between the United States and the European Union. Comput. Secur. 23 (5), 400–412.

Bergemann, D., Bonatti, A., 2011. Targeting in advertising markets: implications for offline versus online media. RAND J. Econ. 42 (3), 417–443.

Bonneau, J., Preibusch, S., 2010. The privacy jungle: on the market for data protection in social networks. In: Moore, T., Pym, D., Ioannidis, C. (Eds.), Economics of Information Security and Privacy. Springer, New York, NY, pp. 121–167.

Brandimarte, L., Acquisti, A., Loewenstein, G., 2012. Misplaced confidences: privacy and the control paradox. Soc. Psychol. Personal. Sci. 4, 340–347.

Campbell, J.D., Goldfarb, A., Tucker, C., 2015. Privacy regulation and market structure. J. Econ. Manag. Strateg 24 (1), 47–73.

Chiou, L., Tucker, C., 2013. Paywalls and the demand for news. Inf. Econ. Policy 25 (2), 61–69.

Cohen, J.E., 2000. Examined lives: informational privacy and the subject as object. Stanford Law Rev. 52, 1373–1438.

Dwyer, C., Hiltz, S., Passerini, K., 2007. Trust and privacy concern within social networking sites: a comparison of Facebook and MySpace. In: AMCIS 2007 Proceedings, p. 339.

Evans, D.S., 2009. The online advertising industry: economics, evolution, and privacy. J. Econ. Perspect. 23 (3), 37–60.

Farrell, J., 2012. Can privacy be just another good. J. Telecommun. High Technol. Law 10, 251.

FTC, 2010. Protecting Consumer Privacy in An Era of Rapid Change. Staff Report.

Fudenburg, D., Villas-Boas, J.M., 2006. Behavior based price discrimination and customer recognition. Handbooks in Information Systems, vol. 1 Emerald Group Publishing, Bradford, United Kingdom, pp. 377–435 (Chapter 7).

Gal-Or, E., Ghose, A., 2005. The economic incentives for sharing security information. Inf. Syst. Res. 16 (2), 186–208.

Gentzkow, M., Shapiro, J.M., 2011. Ideological segregation online and offline. Q. J. Econ. 126 (4), 1799–1839.

Goldfarb, A., Tucker, C., 2011a. Online display advertising: targeting and obtrusiveness. Mark. Sci. 30, 389–404.

Goldfarb, A., Tucker, C.E., 2011b. Privacy regulation and online advertising. Manag. Sci. 57 (1), 57–71.

Goldfarb, A., Tucker, C., 2012. Shifts in privacy concerns. Am. Econ. Rev. Pap. Proc. 102 (3), 349–353.

Goldfarb, A., Tucker, C., 2014. Standardization and the effectiveness of online advertising. Manage. Sci. (forthcoming).

Gordon, L.A., Loeb, M.P., 2002. The economics of information security investment. ACM Trans. Inf. Syst. Secur. 5 (4), 438–457.

Gross, R., Acquisti, A., 2005. Information revelation and privacy in online social networks. In: Proceedings of the 2005 ACM Workshop on Privacy in the Electronic Society. ACM, pp. 71–80.

Grossman, G.M., Shapiro, C., 1984. Informative advertising with differentiated products. Rev. Econ. Stud. 51 (1), 63–81.

Hann, I.-H., Hui, K.-L., Lee, S.-Y.T., Png, I.P., 2008. Consumer privacy and marketing avoidance: a static model. Manag. Sci. 54 (6), 1094–1103.

Hermalin, B., Katz, M., 2006. Privacy, property rights and efficiency: the economics of privacy as secrecy. Quant. Mark. Econ. 4 (3), 209–239.

Hirshleifer, J., 1980. Privacy: its origin, function, and future. J. Leg. Stud. 9 (4).

Hui, K., Png, I., 2006. Chapter 9: the economics of privacy. Economics and Information Systems. Handbooks in Information Systems, vol. 1 Elsevier, Amsterdam, The Netherlands.

Johnson, J.P., 2013. Targeted advertising and advertising avoidance. RAND J. Econ. 44 (1), 128–144.

Johnson, G., 2014. The impact of privacy policy on the auction market for online display advertising. SSRN Electron. J. Available at SSRN 2333193, University of Rochester Working Paper.

Kirk, J., 2010. Europe Warns Search Companies Over Data Retention. PC World Business Center.

Lambrecht, A., Tucker, C., 2013. When does retargeting work? Information specificity in online advertising. J. Mark. Res. 50 (5), 561–576.

Lenard, T.M., Rubin, P.H., 2009. In Defense of Data: Information and the Costs of Privacy. Technology Policy Institute Working Paper.

Levin, J., Milgrom, P., 2010. Online advertising: heterogeneity and conflation in market design. Am. Econ. Rev. 100 (2), 603–607.

Lohr, S., 2010. Privacy Concerns Limit Online Ads, Study Says. Technical report.

Luchs, R., Geylani, T., Dukes, A., Srinivasan, K., 2010. The end of the Robinson-Patman act? Evidence from legal case data. Manag. Sci. 56 (12), 2123–2133.

Marthews, A., Tucker, C., 2014. Government Surveillance and Internet Search Behavior. MIT Sloan Working Paper.

McDonald, A.M., Cranor, L.F., 2008. Cost of reading privacy policies. ISJLP 4, 543.

Miller, A., Tucker, C., 2009. Privacy protection and technology adoption: the case of electronic medical records. Manag. Sci. 55 (7), 1077–1093.

Miller, A., Tucker, C., 2011. Can healthcare information technology save babies? J. Polit. Econ. 2, 289–324.

Miller, A., Tucker, C., 2014. Privacy Protection, Personalized Medicine and Genetic Testing. MIT Sloan Working Paper.

Miltgen, C., Tucker, C., 2014. Resolving the Privacy Paradox: Evidence from a Field Experiment. MIT Sloan Working Paper.

Nyhan, B., Reifler, J., 2010. When corrections fail: the persistence of political misperceptions. Polit. Behav. 32 (2), 303–330.

Percy, L., Rossiter, J.R., 1992. Advertising stimulus effects: a review. J. Curr. Issues Res. Advert. 14 (1), 75–90.

Petty, R.D., 2000. Marketing without consent: consumer choice and costs, privacy, and public policy. J. Public Policy Market. 19 (1), 42–53.

Posner, R.A., 1978. Privacy, Secrecy, and Reputation. Technical report.

Posner, R.A., 1981. The economics of privacy. Am. Econ. Rev. 71 (2), 405–409.

Silver, S., 2014. False is the New True: Fake News Clickbait, Blood Feud and Why the Truth Stopped Mattering. Technology Tell.

Solove, D.J., 2004. The Digital Person: Technology and Privacy in the Information Age. New York University Press, New York, NY.

Solove, D., 2008. Understanding Privacy. Harvard University Press, Cambridge, MA.

Stigler, G.J., 1980. An introduction to privacy in economics and politics. J. Leg. Stud. 9 (4), 623–644.

Teo, H.-H., Tan, B.C.Y., Agarwal, R., 2012. Research note–effects of individual self-protection, industry self-regulation, and government regulation on privacy concerns: a study of location-based services. Inf. Syst. Res. 23 (4), 1342–1363.

Tucker, C., 2012. The economics of advertising and privacy. Int. J. Ind. Organ. 30 (3), 326–329.

Tucker, C., 2014a. Social Advertising. Working paper at MIT Sloan Cambridge, MA.

Tucker, C., 2014b. Social networks, personalized advertising, and privacy controls. J. Mark. Res. 51 (5), 546–562.

Turow, J., King, J., Hoofnagle, C.J., Bleakley, A., Hennessy, M., 2009. Americans Reject Tailored Advertising and Three Activities that Enable It. Berkeley.

Vakratsas, D., Ambler, T., 1999. How advertising works: what do we really know? J. Mark. 63 (1).

Varian, H., 1997. Economic Aspects of Personal Privacy. Available at http://people.ischool.berkeley.edu/~hal/Papers/privacy/.

Varian, H., Wallenberg, F., Woroch, G., 2005. The demographics of the do-not-call list. IEEE Secur. Priv. 3 (1), 34–39.

Warren, S.D., Brandeis, L.D., 1890. The right to privacy. Harv. Law Rev. 4 (5), 193–220.

Westin, A.F., 2005. Testimony of Dr. Alan F. Westin, professor of public law & government emeritus, Columbia University. In: Hearing on Privacy and Health Information Technology, NCVHS Subcommittee on Privacy, Washington, D.C.

White, T., Zahay, D., Thorbjornsen, H., Shavitt, S., 2008. Getting too personal: reactance to highly personalized email solicitations. Mark. Lett. 19 (1), 39–50.

Xu, H., Teo, H.-H., Tan, B.C.Y., Agarwal, R., 2012. Effects of individual self-protection, industry self-regulation, and government regulation on privacy concerns: a study of location-based services. Inf. Syst. Res. 23. Available at http://people.ischool.berkeley.edu/~hal/Papers/privacy/.

Zubcsek, P., Sarvary, M., 2011. Advertising to a social network. Quant. Mark. Econ. 9, 71–107.

CHAPTER 12

User-Generated Content and Social Media

Michael Luca

Harvard Business School, Boston, MA, USA

Contents

12.1. Introduction	564
12.2. The Impact of User-Generated Content	568
12.2.1 Data and Identification Challenges	568
12.2.1.1 Cross-Platform Comparisons	*570*
12.2.1.2 Platform Quirks	*570*
12.2.1.3 Field Experiments	*570*
12.2.2 Impact of UGC on Demand: Data, Methods, and Results	571
12.2.3 Social Effects of Social Media	573
12.2.4 Other Findings and Open Questions	574
12.3. The Quality of User-Generated Content	575
12.3.1 Promotional Content	575
12.3.2 Self-Selection	579
12.3.3 Peer Effects and Social Influence	581
12.3.4 Other Issues	581
12.4. Incentive Design and Behavioral Foundations	582
12.5. Other Issues	584
12.5.1 Business Models	584
12.5.2 Competition and Network Effects	585
12.5.3 Digital Exhaust, Property Rights, and Privacy	586
12.5.4 Information Aggregation	587
12.5.5 Welfare Effects	588
12.6. Discussion	588
Acknowledgments	589
References	590

Abstract

This chapter documents what economists have learned about user-generated content (UGC) and social media. A growing body of evidence suggests that UGC on platforms ranging from Yelp to Facebook has a large causal impact on economic and social outcomes ranging from restaurant decisions to voting behavior. These findings often leverage unique datasets and methods ranging from regression discontinuity to field experiments, and researchers often work directly with the companies they study. I then survey the factors that influence the quality of UGC. Quality is influenced by factors including promotional content, peer effects between contributors, biases of contributors, and self-selection into the decision to contribute. Non-pecuniary incentives, such as "badges" and social status on a platform, are often used to encourage and steer contributions. I then discuss other issues including business models, network effects, and privacy. Throughout the chapter, I discuss open questions in this area.

Keywords

User-generated content, Social media, Economics of information, Design economics

JEL Codes

D8, L1, L86

12.1. INTRODUCTION

Imagine that a hypothetical employee at an encyclopedia company in the year 1980 pitches the following idea to her boss:

> *I think we can cut most of our expenses and produce more content than ever before. All we have to do is allow anyone to visit our office and write encyclopedia entries on the topics they think know something about. Forget about the experts we typically hire. We can validate the content by having other unvetted visitors correct their entries and hope that it all comes out in the wash. Don't worry, we can still have editors. The best contributors can become editors, but here's the beauty: let's not pay any of them. Let them volunteer to write encyclopedia entries. Oh, and I think we should stop selling encyclopedias and just run on donations.*

It's safe to say that, in 1980, this employee would likely not have been long for her job. Situated in a different time and place, the conceptual framework of one of the most popular social media sites of the early twenty-first century seems like an absurd proposition. Yet that site, Wikipedia, has thrived, even as traditional encyclopedias (produced with content generated and edited by paid professional writers and editors) have sped toward obsolescence.

The concept of user-generated information has spread well beyond encyclopedias. Consumers now turn to Yelp to find new restaurants, TripAdvisor to plan a vacation, Rotten Tomatoes to find a movie, AngiesList for contractors, ZocDoc to check on physicians' reputations, and Amazon reviews when purchasing anything ranging from a book to a vacuum cleaner to cat food. With the click of a button, consumers can share experiences, information, and recommendations about product quality for nearly any product imaginable. Table 12.1 provides a sample of popular platforms covering different industries as of 2014.

The sheer number of products that consumers, relative to other information sources, are able to review is striking. To take one example, Figure 12.1 shows the percentage of restaurants covered by different review systems in selected urban areas. The consumer review website Yelp contains reviews of 70% of the restaurants in Seattle, while Zagat covers roughly a 5% sample of Los Angeles restaurants (Jin and Leslie, 2009). *The Seattle Times*, the local newspaper, contains even fewer restaurants, and *Food & Wine* magazine

Table 12.1 Sample platforms with user reviews (as of 2014)

Industry	Sample platforms with UGC	Most popular (unique monthly visitors)[a]
Restaurants	Yelp, Zagat, Urbanspoon, OpenTable, Chowhound	Yelp (52 million)
Movies	Rotten Tomatoes, Yahoo! Movies, IMDB, Metacritic	Rotten Tomatoes (400,000)
Hotels and Rooms	TripAdvisor, Expedia, Orbitz, Hotels.com, Airbnb, HomeAway	TripAdvisor (10.8 million)
Physicians	Healthgrades, ZocDoc, Vitals, RateMDs	Healthgrades (4.9 million)
Consumer goods	Amazon, eBay, Target, Walmart, Target	Amazon (80 million)

[a]These figures are obtained from the most recent month with data available on Quantcast. All figures are from 2014.

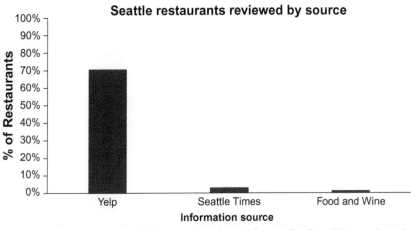

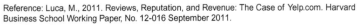

Reference: Luca, M., 2011. Reviews, Reputation, and Revenue: The Case of Yelp.com. Harvard Business School Working Paper, No. 12-016 September 2011.

Figure 12.1 Restaurant coverage by media outlet.

reviews even fewer. Looking at numbers like these, it is clear that online consumer reviews and recommendations have become important sources of information.

The way consumers receive news has changed just as quickly. People read news and commentary via blogs and tweets, which supplement—and in some cases replace—more traditional media. Even the fabric of our day-to-day interactions is changing, with online social networks such as Facebook, LinkedIn, and WhatsApp complementing, and at times replacing, offline networks. Clearly, in the digital age, how we interact with friends and family, learn about products, services, and jobs, and think about news, politics, and religion are dramatically changing.

Social media platforms such as YouTube, Wikipedia, Yelp, WhatsApp, and Twitter enable users to interact with each other through the generation and sharing of content. The common thread across these platforms is that they contain *user-generated content* (UGC). UGC is material that a platform sources from its own end-users. Part of the crowdsourcing movement, UGC ranges from videos on YouTube to posts on Wikipedia to reviews on Yelp. All social media platforms contain UGC. However, not all UGC is contained on traditional social media platforms. Virtually all online platforms—ranging from online newspapers to online marketplaces—rely to some extent on UGC. UGC is dramatically transforming the media landscape. In addition to producing unprecedented amounts of information, UGC raises a variety of new intellectual and practical questions and challenges.

UGC has grown dramatically over the past 10 years. From 2001 to 2006, a number of major social media platforms sprang up, including Wikipedia (2001), LinkedIn (2003), MySpace (2003), Facebook (2004), Yelp (2004), YouTube (2005), and Twitter (2006). UGC now spans a vast swath of the Internet, from user-provided pictures to videos to comments on news stories and blogs. Table 12.2 presents an overview of different types of UGC and a sampling of prominent platforms that display it, including the world's largest social network (Facebook) and the world's most trafficked video site (YouTube).

There are several types of actors on any given UGC platform. First, there are contributors who provide content. Second, there are consumers of content. In traditional media, these are typically two different sets of actors. A novel feature of UGC is that a platform's end-users are both contributors and consumers. Because *users* are producing

Table 12.2 Popular user-generated content platforms

Types of user-generated content	Prominent platforms
Pictures	Instagram, Pinterest, Snapchat, Flickr
Personal updates and networking	Twitter, FourSquare, Facebook, LinkedIn
Reviews for products and services	Yelp, Rotten Tomatoes, ZocDoc, Amazon
Encyclopedia and reference sites	Wikipedia, Wikia
Videos	YouTube, Vine
Comments on news articles	NY Times Online, WSJ Online
Crowdfunding	Crowdrise, Kickstarter, IndieGoGo
Sharing platforms	Uber, Airbnb, Couchsurfing
Social payments	Venmo, Square
Discussion/question and answer	Reddit, Quora, StackOverflow
Blogs	Tumblr, WordPress

content, the amount of content and its value to any given user depends on the number of total users. There are significant network effects on all UGC platforms, and the value of the platform depends on the number of users. Of course, some users will primarily produce, while others will primarily consume. You may prefer to watch YouTube videos, for example, yet have a friend who posts them but rarely watches them.

A third set of actors is the set of *advertisers*—people and organizations that are trying to reach users. For example, Facebook earns four billion dollars per year through advertising,[1] with major clients including Ford, Disney, Walmart, and Microsoft. Advertising is also a central source of revenue for Yelp and many other UGC platforms. In addition to advertisements that are displayed on UGC webpages, advertisers sometimes use other channels to influence content. For example, there have been reports of staffers being paid to maintain Wikipedia pages for politicians.

Fourth, UGC platforms have *bystanders*—people or organizations that are essentially the subjects of content. A person being discussed on Twitter is a bystander, as is a restaurant being reviewed on Yelp. Bystanders may or may not be users, and in some cases are not allowed to be. They are sometimes advertisers as well, and may more generally try to shape the content users create—through both legitimate and illegitimate means.

Finally, every UGC platform has a *designer* who sets the rules that shape contributions and interactions on the platform. Ultimately, the designer decides which users are allowed to interact on the platform and the incentives the users will face. The designer creates the market for advertisements to be sold, and decides whether the platform should intervene at the request of a bystander. Ultimately, these choices determine the impact and quality of UGC.

While social media platforms and the content generated on them will continue to evolve, a set of principles and intellectual questions underlies UGC platforms. A growing body of research investigates the ways in which social media and UGC platforms are affecting the world around us. The goal of this chapter is to summarize the main areas of this research and to identify areas in which this emerging field can progress, focusing on issues such as why people provide content, the degree to which this content matters in making decisions, and the information design challenges and choices that platform designers face.

The chapter proceeds as follows. Section 12.2 surveys the effect of UGC on user and market behavior. Section 12.3 discusses these challenges to the quality of content and mechanisms that improve quality. Section 12.4 discusses incentive design for UGC. Section 12.5 provides a brief discussion of several related issues. Section 12.6 offers a conclusion.

---

[1] http://www.businessinsider.com/the-30-biggest-advertisers-on-facebook-2012-9.

12.2. THE IMPACT OF USER-GENERATED CONTENT

According to Wikipedia, the 2010 edition of the Encyclopedia Britannica—the last to be printed—was "written by about 100 full-time editors and more than 4000 contributors, including 110 Nobel Prize winners and five American presidents." While there is a certain irony to this Wikipedia entry, it raises a question that is central to the study of UGC: How will UGC affect existing media markets and the economy more generally?

In contrast with the Encyclopedia Britannica, Wikipedia (and other UGC platforms) have a self-organizing authority and do not rely on the standard institutional arrangements for assigning authority, such as credentialing or restrictions on resources. Critics often argue that the grass roots, unvetted nature of UGC leads to content that is too unreliable to meaningfully change the world, beyond perhaps the case of Wikipedia. In this view, platforms such as Yelp and TripAdvisor (which consist of a non-representative sample of amateur reviews, with no way to eliminate all fake reviews) might have limited impact on the market as a whole. Comments on news articles may simply be entertainment for a small niche of readers with no discernible influence on how news is produced or digested. Similarly, YouTube videos of cats riding Roombas may simply be procrastination material for bored students, posing little threat to traditional media.

Yet, an alternative possibility is that UGC participants amount to millions of Davids, relative to the small number of Goliaths in competing media outlets. According to this view, UGC might influence markets despite its challenges. This would have the potential to reshape the way media is consumed and produced on a mass scale.

A priori it is unclear which of these views is more representative of the world we inhabit, and under which conditions each is more likely to dominate. In this section, we survey the literature on the impact of UGC. After discussing the unique data and challenges involved in this area of research, we look at how UGC influences the behavior and structure of markets, and highlight potential areas for future research. Ultimately, estimates of the extent and types of impact UGC has on markets offer important insights for policymaking, strategic decisions of UGC and traditional media outlets, design of online platforms, and welfare calculations.

12.2.1 Data and Identification Challenges

Data is a central challenge to the study of UGC. Most of the papers cited in this chapter began with a researcher (or team of researchers) constructing a novel dataset that had not previously been analyzed. For papers that study phenomena happening within a UGC platform, researchers often gather data on their own, working directly from the platform. More recently there has been a movement toward researchers working directly with companies, including Yelp, Facebook, Airbnb, eBay, and oDesk. This trend gives researchers greater access to data, as well as the ability to run field experiments.

Data from a given UGC platform alone is sometimes insufficient to measure the impact of UGC on a market. For example, suppose that a researcher wants to study the impact of Facebook posts on demand for Diet Coke. One option would be to look at the number of users who "like" Diet Coke's Facebook page and/or read its posts. Yet this method would provide an incomplete picture of Facebook's overall impact on Diet Coke demand. An approach of potentially greater value would be to obtain sales data from Diet Coke—which Facebook would not have to estimate the effect of UGC on sales. At the same time Coca-Cola would not have all of the data that Facebook would have—which highlights that partnerships between multiple organizations might be valuable in this situation.

When studying UGC, there are two key barriers to constructing the optimal dataset. The first is data collection, which can be difficult due to the proprietary nature of much of the data in this realm. One challenge to this is that many for-profit companies consider their data to be a competitive advantage and choose not to share it for research. Others view sharing as a strategic choice. Still others attempt to be generally open with data. I expect partnerships between companies and researchers to grow in this area on academic research papers that produce findings that are valuable for the partner companies. While this is valuable in many situations, researchers should consider the extent to which their objective aligns with those of the firm when choosing a data collection strategy. There are times when *not* partnering with an organization is the optimal strategy, even if the organization is interested in cooperating.

The second data challenge involves the actual merging and preparation of datasets. In this field, datasets are often large (consider, for example, the number of words written on Wikipedia), and hence unwieldy and time-consuming to analyze. In contrast with merging different pieces of a carefully constructed survey with unique identifiers, two datasets from different field sources are almost certain to have different labels and formats. While this problem is typically surmountable, it can be complicated, requiring researchers to make subjective decisions about which data to keep and which to drop. In many settings, a match rate of 85–90% is considered very high.

Once data are in hand, there are a variety of identification challenges to understanding the impact of UGC. For example, consider a researcher who wishes to estimate the impact of a movie's Rotten Tomatoes rating on ticket sales. The researcher may begin by regressing the movie's ticket sales on its Rotten Tomatoes rating. But note that while social media content can influence demand (the topic of this section), it can also *reflect* demand. Buzz can make movies popular, but popular movies also tend to generate more buzz. Because of the reflection problem (Manski, 1993), it is difficult to interpret this type of regression as being causal.

Researchers have implemented a variety of empirical approaches to support a causal interpretation in this context, ranging from difference-in-differences across platforms to regression discontinuity taking advantage of platform quirks to pure field experiments.

Next, I briefly describe the three distinct types of methodologies discussed throughout the rest of the chapter.

12.2.1.1 Cross-Platform Comparisons

One approach to identifying an outcome of interest on a particular platform is to compare outcomes across platforms, as done by Chevalier and Mayzlin (2006), Wang (2010), Zhu and Zhang (2010), and Mayzlin e al. (2014). Essentially, each of these papers looks at institutional features or content on a given platform that is different on other platforms, and uses this as variation in the feature or content of interest.

Properly implemented, this would represent a difference-in-differences approach—with variation across platforms representing one of the differences. For example, Mayzlin et al. (2014) compare the difference between ratings for hotels with a single unit and hotels with multiple units (first difference) across TripAdvisor and Expedia (second difference).

There are empirical challenges to implementing this flavor of identification strategy. The key conceptual challenge is detecting whether other factors could be driving the same outcome. One important econometric challenge is deciding on the unit of observation and how to cluster standard errors. In particular, researchers may run into the issue of a small number of clusters; see Bertrand et al. (2004) for a discussion of standard errors in difference-in-differences estimation.

12.2.1.2 Platform Quirks

A second approach has been to exploit institutional details within a single UGC platform, or essentially to look for platform "quirks." For example, Luca (2011) and Anderson and Magruder (2012) exploit the fact that ratings on Yelp are rounded before they are displayed to users, which creates exogenous variation between the true rating and the displayed rating. This idiosyncratic institutional detail allows the researchers to estimate the causal effect of ratings on their outcome of interest. This approach has now been used on other platforms such as TripAdvisor (Ghose et al., 2012).

Many platforms have the feature of rounded ratings, but one can imagine a variety of similar approaches by identifying and exploiting unique features across UGC platforms. Leveraging this type of platform quirk achieves two goals. First, it allows researchers to better understand the causal impact of UGC. Second, it provides insight into the behavioral foundations of how people behave on a platform. For example, in the average rating case, it is clear that readers are very inattentive, paying attention to coarse summaries of existing information. This could potentially be used to inform the large literature on limited attention. Other identification strategies would likely yield other behavioral insights.

12.2.1.3 Field Experiments

A third approach has been to run experiments directly on platforms, as Bond et al. (2012) and Aral and Walker (2012) did in field experiments on Facebook. A powerful tool, field experiments on online platforms are becoming increasingly common, allowing researchers and organizations to answer questions in a simple, straightforward manner. In fact, the main challenge to implementing a field experiment may be finding areas of mutual interest between the organization and the researchers. As discussed above, one challenge is that a firm's goals and a researcher's goals do not overlap entirely. Thus far, some firms have been open to researchers pursuing topics outside of the narrow short-run needs of the firm. Other firms with privacy concerns, such as Google, restrict access to data. Others with strategic concerns, such as Amazon, also restrict access.

12.2.2 Impact of UGC on Demand: Data, Methods, and Results

An abundance of evidence now reinforces a causal link between user-generated reviews and product demand in areas ranging from book sales (Chevalier and Mayzlin, 2006) to restaurants (Luca, 2011) to hotels (Ghose et al., 2012). As briefly introduced in the previous section, three types of approach have been used to causally identify the impact of reviews on sales.

The first approach, first offered by Chevalier and Mayzlin (2006), is to look at reviews across two different platforms to determine the effect of a review on both sites' sales. Using Amazon and Barnes & Noble's platforms, the authors show the differences in a book's sales following three points in time at which a review was posted on one of the company's websites. By using this difference-in-differences approach, the authors can isolate the effects of the review on one site by assuming parallel book sale trends absent the review. They find that, depending on the specification, many review-related variables influence book sales, including the number of reviews, average review rating, fraction of one-star reviews, and fraction of five-star reviews. Looking at only one platform, it is easy to imagine that an OLS regression of sales on review variables would be biased due to the omission of unobservable product and firm-level quality variables, which affect both sales and reviews. The difference-in-differences method of Chevalier and Mayzlin (2006) allows them to include book–time fixed effects, and book–site fixed effects, enabling them to isolate the causal effect of reviews on sales.

The second approach, which has been used by Luca (2011), Anderson and Magruder (2012), and Ghose et al. (2012), leverages a common institutional detail of review platforms. These papers exploit the fact that many review platforms choose to round the rating that they display to users. For example, consider two restaurants on Yelp—one with 3.24 stars and the other with 3.25 stars. The 3.24 star restaurant will be displayed as 3 stars, while the 3.25 star restaurant will be displayed as 3.5. This variation in displayed ratings is unrelated to underlying quality and other market forces that could be driving demand. These papers then implement regression discontinuity designs around these rounding thresholds.

Combining restaurant ratings from Yelp with sales data for every restaurant that operated in Seattle over a 6-year span, Luca (2011) shows that a one-star increase in Yelp rating leads to roughly a 5% increase in sales for an independent restaurant, but has no impact for chains. This result is consistent with the idea that consumers have more information about chains, and hence learn less about them through Yelp. Applying the same general approach to restaurant reservation data from Opentable, Anderson and Magruder (2012) show that increases in Yelp ratings increase the probability that a restaurant will be fully booked on a given night. Ghose et al. (2012) also follow this general approach to identify the causal effect of TripAdvisor ratings on hotel bookings.

The third approach involves using UGC platforms as a field site for randomized controlled trials. For example, Aral and Walker (2012, 2014) use a Facebook application to send notifications of a user's "like" of an app to a random selection of his or her peers and measure the subsequent adoption of the app. Using this approach to determine the contagion of the "like," the authors found that final demand for the product increased 13% relative to the initial adopter cohort.

Every element of a business's online presence—from the length and distribution of reviews to the emotional content of tweets—contains information. Identifying the factors that customers use is of direct managerial relevance and provides further evidence of the behavioral foundations of how users process information.

Ghose et al. (2012) also develop a structural model for estimating hotel demand based on hotel characteristics, as well as Travelocity and TripAdvisor review characteristics. Collecting review text and measures of review length, they use machine learning to assess readability, complexity, and subjectivity. The authors find that longer, easy-to-read reviews are associated with higher demand while word complexity and spelling errors are associated with lower demand. Though they do not make causal claims about review characteristics, they argue that since ratings influence demand (using the regression discontinuity approach discussed above), it seems plausible that these other factors are also causal. One novel feature of this paper is its use of machine learning and text analysis.

Similarly, Chevalier and Mayzlin (2006) find that one-star reviews affect book sales more than five-star reviews. This may be because a large majority of reviews are five-star such that consumers expect books to have several five-star reviews and thus perceive five-star reviews to provide less new information than one-star reviews. This phenomenon is akin to reputation models, in which one piece of negative news is enough to ruin a good reputation.

The identity of the writer of a review may also matter. Through a laboratory experiment simulating online book reviews, Huang and Chen (2006) find that peer reviews affect subjects' book choices more than expert reviews. Looking at the impact of Yelp reviews on sales, Luca (2011) finds that reviews written by those with "elite" status (awarded by Yelp for high-quality reviews) are more influential than other reviewers.

Another widely studied review system is that of eBay, the popular auction website that tallied 115 million unique visitors in September 2014.[2] On this site, the main item

---

[2] This figure is available on Quantcast.

of interest in reviews is the reliability of each party, not the quality of a good. Reliability ratings are conveyed through the numbers of positive and negative feedback reports that a user has received. The most documented effect of this review regime is the impact of a seller's overall rating (given by buyers) on the sale price. One particular challenge to estimating this effect is that goods sold on eBay vary in their condition, and in small (but significant) characteristics that are difficult to observe by the econometrician. For example, books of the same title might be heavily used, lightly used, or brand new; they might be a domestic or international edition; they might have highlighter marks or dog-eared pages. Looking at data from auctions of mint condition $5 US gold coins (which are plausibly undifferentiated), Melnik and Alm (2002) find that seller ratings are significantly correlated with final price. Lucking-Reiley et al. (2007) obtain the same qualitative result. Looking at the dynamics of reputation, Cabral and Hortaçsu (2010) show that once a seller on eBay receives negative feedback, subsequent negative feedback arrives 25% more rapidly.

An alternative approach to observational data is to run a field experiment on eBay, with different seller characteristics. Resnick et al. (2006) worked with an established eBay user to sell a pair of matched postcards, offering them either on the seller's highly rated main account or on one of the seller's recently created accounts with few ratings. On average, buyers were willing to pay 8.1% more for a postcard from the established, highly rated account. While some of the effect may be attributed to the difference in ages between the user's main account and the accounts generated for the experiment, this supports the causal effect of ratings on prices.

12.2.3 Social Effects of Social Media

Thus far, I have focused on the impact of social media on market outcomes such as purchases. However, there are a variety of behaviors—from education to public health to voting—that can be influenced by social media and UGC.

Bond et al. (2012) examine the effect of different types of messages sent to more than 61 million adult Facebook members visiting the site on November 2, 2010, the date of the US midterm elections, on each member's probability of voting that day. The authors find that those who received a social message (one showing friends who had voted) were 2 percentage points more likely to click an "I voted" button than those who were merely shown an informational message about Election Day. Of course, the ultimate goal of this study is to look at voting behavior. Because voting records are public, the authors were able to merge voting records with data from Facebook on users. Looking at roughly six million records, the authors find that members who were sent a social message voted 0.39 percentage points more often than those who were shown an informational message or no message at all. The authors estimate that the direct and indirect effects of the Facebook messages increased the 2010 voter turnout by roughly 340,000 votes.

Facebook could potentially influence a variety of other behaviors as well. For example, in 2012 Facebook began allowing users to include an indicator for whether they were organ donors as part of their profiles. During the rollout of this, users were provided a link to their state donor registries; moreover, status updates were sent to friends of donors. Cameron et al. (2013) show that on the first day of this campaign, roughly 13,054 people registered as organ donors—relative to the baseline daily average of 616 per day. This suggests a role for Facebook in contributing to the social good. One can imagine social media playing an important role in advancing a variety of public health goals such as increasing childhood vaccination rates, and more generally in areas ranging from education to savings.

12.2.4 Other Findings and Open Questions

There are many open areas for future research on the impact of UGC. One possible direction is to investigate the impact of UGC on market structure. For example, Clemons et al. (2006) argue that information provided in reviews can help to grow demand for products with more differentiated products by increasing the quality of the match, and find generally consistent evidence when looking at reviews for beer and growth in demand. Bar-Isaac et al. (2012) theoretically show that introducing new information into a market will lead to a higher degree of product differentiation in markets. This suggests that the existence of platforms such as Yelp and TripAdvisor may lead to a greater variety of restaurants and hotels. Online reviews may also create incentives for businesses to change prices, as modeled by Li and Hit (2010), where the pricing incentives depend on whether the reviews take into account only quality or price and quality.

Second, UGC has the potential to displace more traditional media content. Much as Wikipedia has supplanted traditional bound encyclopedias, YouTube may replace traditional television content, Yelp may replace the professional restaurant critic, and blogs may replace traditional news media outlets. In addition to competing on content, one can imagine contributors aspiring to work at traditional media outlets. There are prominent examples of this, such as Nate Silver transitioning from his start as an anonymous blogger to a prominent employee at the New York Times and then ESPN. An important area for future research is to explore these types of career dynamics.

Beyond direct competition in content, there are a variety of ways in which UGC platforms may affect more traditional media platforms. For example, there can be competition in advertising markets. Apartment and job listings on Craigslist directly compete with local advertisements in online newspapers (Kroft and Pope, 2014). This, in turn, generates a reduced value from additional content (Seamans and Zhu, 2014). See Chapter 9 for further discussion on this. A fruitful area for future research would be to further investigate these effects, as well as the extent of competition and cooperation between traditional media and UGC platforms.

More generally, an important direction for future research would be to investigate the limits of UGC. For example, research has shown the value of Yelp and TripAdvisor for restaurants and hotels. Will user reviews become the norm for doctors and cars as well? The potential for reviews to proliferate in different industries likely depends on factors such as the number of products or services being evaluated and the extent to which specialized knowledge is required to evaluate that product or service. There may also be areas where UGC will never be feasible.

In addition, an important intersection between UGC and social goods has been under-examined. While the areas of voting and organ donation are clearly important, virtually every action we take is now potentially influenced by social media platforms. It is possible that UGC data will have effects on outcomes such as improving high school graduation rates, reducing teen pregnancies, and reducing bankruptcy rates.

12.3. THE QUALITY OF USER-GENERATED CONTENT

Because UGC creates a positive externality, underprovision of content is a standard prediction of models of UGC (Avery et al., 1999; Miller et al., 2005). Because network effects are central to social media platforms (Zhang and Zhu, 2011), this can be exacerbated in new platforms and in areas where UGC is not yet popular. Theoretically, this can lead to multiple equilibria, in which some platforms are filled with excellent content and other equally good platforms are virtual ghost towns. In a world with little to no payment for content, generating an optimal *quantity* of content is a major challenge in the digital age. Che and Hörner (2014) theoretically demonstrate that it can be optimal to over-recommend a product early after its release in order to encourage more experimentation. One productive area for research is to further explore mechanisms to solve the underprovision problem as well as factors that cause one platform to succeed and another—often very similar—platform to fail.

Even when incentives are put in place to generate a high quantity of content, it is also important to understand the quality of content. Overall, there is evidence that online reviews are generally consistent with expert reviews (Cao et al., 2015; Dobrescu et al., 2013). However, every type of media and information source has unique challenges and biases to the quality of content.[3] This section highlights several main challenges to the quality of content that are especially important in the UGC context.

12.3.1 Promotional Content

Celebrities such as Khloe Kardashian and Jared Leto reportedly earn $13,000 for writing a single sponsored tweet (Kornowski, 2013). Bloggers often link to each other in an

---

[3] For example, see Chapter 16 for a discussion on media capture.

implicit *quid pro quo*, gaining additional viewers for both blogs in the process (Mayzlin and Yoganarasimhan, 2012). Businesses often leave reviews about themselves or competitors (Luca and Zervas, 2015; Mayzlin et al., 2014). Politicians, including Vice President Joe Biden, have been known to have their paid staff edit their Wikipedia pages to make them more favorable (Noguchi, 2006). These are all attempts by businesses or individuals to promote themselves using social media or UGC. While there is a small literature beginning to emerge on these issues, the extent and implication of this type of content across different UGC platforms is largely an open question.

There are many methods of promoting a business online, such as advertising, maintaining a business profile, or responding to customer comments. Many of these are honest attempts to provide information and incentives to customers. Yet there are also misleading (and sometimes illegal) approaches to promoting a business online. For example, due to the semi-anonymous convention of online handle names, businesses can attempt to create promotional content that will blend in with the general population of non-promotional contributors in a misleading way.

Perhaps the most frequently cited concern about UGC platforms is that they could become overrun by fraudulent or misleading operators seeking to boost their own reputations or plug their own products. After all, with the click of a button, virtually anyone can leave an anonymous review, post a video, write a Wikipedia entry, or indicate that they "like" a product or service. Promotional content arises in virtually every form of UGC.

The remainder of this section discusses the literature on promotional reviews (a term coined by Mayzlin et al., 2014). The focus on reviews reflects the fact that promotional content has been an especially salient issue in this area, and also the fact that there has been relatively more research in this area relative to other types of promotional content.

Concerns abound about firms providing fake positive reviews to boost their own reputations and providing fake negative reviews to harm their competitors' reputations. Noting that reviews influence demand, neoclassical economists might be tempted to suggest that promotional content will litter social media sites. However, behavioral economists and social psychologists have documented the fact that people are generally uncomfortable with lying, even when they can get away with it (Fischbacher and Föllmi-Heusi, 2013; Gneezy, 2005; Hurkens and Kartik, 2009). Moreover, as quickly as businesses find ways to manipulate content, platforms find ways (discussed below) to mitigate these concerns. Hence, the extent of fake reviews and promotional UGC is *a priori* unclear.

Consider a business that is managing its online reputation. Because it has the potential to increase revenue by leaving fake reviews, it has high-powered incentives to game the system. To blend in with authentic reviewers, the artful fake reviewer will try to disguise his or her review as an outside observer's true experience. For example, here are two reviews—one fake and the other real—for dental services:

Review A

"I was in need of teeth whitening and my friend referred me to Southland Dental. Pain or no pain, it was very much worth it. I can't stop staring at my bright smile in the mirror."

Review B

"Lorna Lally's office does a great job with cleanings and treatments. The staff is also friendly and they send reminders before each appointment."

While there are potential red flags with both reviews—for example, neither mentions specific details about the business and the information given could easily pertain to most dental offices—it is difficult to determine which is real. Here, the first is fake and the second is real. The difficulty of telling the difference highlights the empirical, managerial, and policy challenges of fake reviews and promotional content.

It is hard to empirically separate legitimate from promotional content. To identify potential false reviews, a computer science literature has emerged designing algorithms to analyze review characteristics, such as text patterns and reviewer social networks (e.g., Akoglu et al. (2013)). One approach (taken by Ott et al., 2011) is to create a "gold standard" of known fake reviews by hiring workers from Amazon Mechanical Turk to write reviews about places they haven't been to. The researchers then compare the features of these reviews to features of reviews found on TripAdvisor, which are likely to include both real and fake reviews. Using machine learning, they then construct an algorithm that helps to identify the reviews that are most likely to be fake given these features that often include text, ratings, and characteristics of reviewers.

These classifiers allow companies to identify which reviews should be trusted the most and least. In practice, companies typically create their own algorithms using markers for promotional content such as the content's origins, the patterns of contributions, and whether they can verify the content. For example, Yelp's automated software places filtered reviews in a separate category that does not contribute to the aggregate star rating, whereas TripAdvisor adapts credit-card-detection algorithms used in the financial services world and uses them to scan for fake hotel, airline, and car rental reviews on its site (Williams, 2013).

How many fake reviews are there? Estimates inherently hinge on the analyst's ability to identify a fake, and are hence noisy. Investigating 316,415 reviews for 3625 Boston-area restaurants, and using an algorithm developed by Yelp to identify suspicious reviews, Luca and Zervas (forthcoming) find that Yelp identified 16% of restaurant reviews submitted to the site as being flagged as suspicious. Per Yelp's filing, roughly 20% of reviews overall across categories and markets are filtered by its spam detection algorithm. Using the text of Yelp reviews, Ott et al. (2012) classify roughly 4% of reviews on Yelp as fake. Several factors may be contributing to these differences. First, Yelp has considerably more information about the reviews being written than researchers do, and hence, given an algorithm, it can more easily classify reviews as real or fake. For example, Yelp knows where a review has been written and the reviewers' detailed patterns of behavior on the platform. Second, it could be that Yelp prefers to be cautious and err on the side of removing a higher proportion of suspicious reviews. Third, there is an upward trend in suspicious reviews submitted over time (Luca and Zervas, forthcoming) and the data used by Ott et al. (2012) was from an earlier period.

What does a fake review look like? As discussed above, this is difficult to identify due to the fact that fake reviews are typically not directly observed. However, the literature using algorithmically identified fake and suspicious reviews has some insights into this question. For example, Ott et al. (2012) find that a disproportionate amount of fakes are written by first- and second-time reviewers. Comparing suspicious (as identified algorithmically) and legitimate reviews submitted to Yelp, Luca and Zervas (forthcoming) find that suspicious reviews are more extreme than real ones, and are more likely to be written by reviewers with little social capital on Yelp. Ott et al. (2011) note reviews that algorithmically identified suspicious reviews on TripAdvisor tend to have positive textual descriptions in addition to high ratings. As these algorithms are developed, fake reviewers may learn to write reviews that won't be identified by the algorithm, highlighting the game theoretic nature of fake reviews.

While the computer science literature has primarily focused on markers of fake reviews, a small economics literature has focused on investigating the economic incentives and welfare effects of leaving fake reviews. Dellarocas (2006) develops a theoretical model of strategic manipulation of content and shows that although manipulation leads to a rat race and leads to wasted resources by all firms, the informational content may increase or decrease, depending on the relationship between the cost of manipulation and the true quality of firms.

To empirically investigate this question, Mayzlin et al. (2014) compare hotel reviews written on Expedia to those written on TripAdvisor. Because Expedia identifies people who have booked a hotel through its platform and then left reviews, it is more difficult to leave a fake review on Expedia than on TripAdvisor, which cannot verify whether users have actually stayed in a given hotel. Comparing the distribution of reviews within a hotel across the two platforms, the authors show that independent hotels (which have stronger incentives than chains to game the system) tend to have a higher proportion of five-star ratings on TripAdvisor relative to Expedia. Moreover, hotels that are near an independent hotel tend to have a higher proportion of one-star reviews on TripAdvisor. Overall, this suggests that businesses with the strongest incentive to leave a promotional review are doing so, and that these reviews are concentrated on platforms where it is easier. Consistent with this, Ott et al. (2012) find that Expedia–Orbitz has a lower rate of promotional content relative to TripAdvisor, using an algorithm to estimate the prevalence of promotional content.

Table 12.3 Examples of mechanisms to prevent fraudulent content

Platform	Any verification?	Reviewer reputation?	Fraud algorithm?
Yelp	Yes	Yes	Yes
Rotten Tomatoes	Yes	Yes	Yes
TripAdvisor	Yes	Yes	Yes
Expedia	Yes	No	No
Amazon	Yes	Yes	Yes
Angie's List	Yes	Yes	Yes
Wikipedia	Yes	Yes	Yes

Looking at restaurant reviews on Yelp, Luca and Zervas (forthcoming) show that a restaurant is more likely to commit review fraud when it experiences a negative shock to its reputation. Moreover, restaurants are more likely to receive fake negative reviews after a competitor opens up. Consistent with Mayzlin et al. (2014), this paper also finds that independent businesses are more likely to commit review fraud. Overall, this research stream suggests that review fraud involves an element of cost–benefit analysis that is influenced by economic incentives.

Review platforms employ a variety of mechanisms to prevent review fraud. As discussed, Expedia's decision to verify whether the reviewer made a purchase makes it more difficult to leave a fake review. This allows Expedia not only to reduce the amount of fraudulent contributions to the platform but also to reduce legitimate content. For example, if a hotel review platform only allows verified customers to review, it would eliminate many legitimate reviews by people who have stayed at the hotel but booked through a different platform—suggesting that these types of mechanisms present an important tradeoff for the platform designer.

Other mechanisms for screening fake reviews include allowing reviewers to build a reputation on the site (hence making it more difficult to leave a fake review), developing an algorithm to flag and remove fake reviews, and allowing the community to flag and investigate fake reviews. Table 12.3 illustrates some of the anti-fraud mechanisms used by a sampling of popular platforms.

12.3.2 Self-Selection

The types of survey datasets that social scientists frequently use and rely on attempt to be representative at the state or national level (e.g., the Census, National Longitudinal Survey of Youth, and General Social Survey). UGC is clearly quite different. One of its central features is that contribution is voluntary, and no attempt is made to create a representative sample of the population. Thus it is difficult to assume that the UGC on a site (or in aggregate) exactly reflects the sentiment or preferences of the underlying population of readers. In the case of user reviews, there are two levels of self-selection.

First, the potential reviewer selects whether to purchase a given product. Second, the potential reviewer decides whether or not to leave a review.

Because people are more likely to purchase a product if they think they will like it (e.g., Star Wars fans are most likely to see the series' final installment), people who buy a product will rate the product more highly, on average, than those who don't. This can lead to an upward bias in its review. Moreover, early buyers may be systematically different from late buyers. For example, if early buyers are the biggest fans—which Hitt and Li (2008) find to be the case for most books on Amazon—the upward bias will be exacerbated.

The second source of selection bias is the decision to leave a review after purchasing. The impact of this decision on the final content depends on the factors that drive someone to review. We might assume that people are most likely to review when their opinions are extreme, but they also might want to leave a review to promote a product they consider to be relatively obscure. Clearly, the first type of motivation would lead to a different type of bias than the second.

Empirically, Hu et al. (2009) note that most Amazon products have a J-shaped (asymmetric bimodal) distribution with more positive than negative reviews, which they take as evidence of self-selection into the decision to review. According to the authors, self-selection has two major drivers: under-reporting among customers with moderate views and purchasing bias (as described above). By contrast, the distribution of ratings on Yelp is not J-shaped (Dai et al., 2013, which I return to later). In their sample, the modal review is four with fewer reviews at the extremes. Purchase selection may be leading to the high average rating. However, the single peak and lack of extremes suggests that review selection is less central on this platform. The selection function may vary with the type of product, among other factors. For example, Dellarocas et al. (2010) show that very obscure movies and major blockbusters are most likely to be reviewed (as a percentage of people who have seen the movie). More generally, there are many different factors causing people to contribute content, and this heterogeneity ultimately shapes the content.

Self-selection is an issue of other types of UGC as well. Readers of news blogs may gain a very incomplete picture of current events. Bloggers tend to link to other blogs with similar views (Adamic and Glance, 2005; Hargittai et al., 2008). Looking at the *consumption* of online news, Gentzkow and Shapiro (2011) find that ideological segregation is larger online than offline, but still relatively small in absolute terms—suggesting that reading across platforms helps to limit the extent of bias. This type of mechanism is theoretically explored in Mullainathan and Shleifer (2005).

In a parallel series of papers, Greenstein and Zhu (2012, 2014) investigate bias on Wikipedia, which tends to be more left leaning than Encyclopedia Britannica. Within an article, having more authors and edits tends to reflect less bias, suggesting that simply having more people look at and edit content can serve as a bias-reducing mechanism. Overall, their findings are consistent with a mechanism in which "opposites attract."

In other words, the reduction in bias and slant over time is consistent with a mechanism in which conservative edits attract revisions and contributions that make an article more liberal or balanced, and vice versa. Most articles, however, have relatively few edits and do not deviate much from their initial slant.

Overall, the selection of contributors is a key determinant of the content offered on a platform. People who contribute may be different from the population at large. People who contribute a lot may be different from occasional contributors. An important area for future research would be to investigate the many different motivations to contribute content and the extent and types of bias that emerges across different types of UGC. For example, to the extent to which contributors lean toward people with particular preferences (e.g., video games) or a particular demographic (e.g., male), the content of UGC platforms can become skewed toward those preferences or set of customers even if each contributor is perfectly well-intentioned.

12.3.3 Peer Effects and Social Influence

A third determinant of the quality of UGC is the fact that later content may be influenced by earlier content. UGC, including Yelp reviews, Wikipedia posts, tweets, Facebook posts, comments on news articles, and YouTube videos, is not created in a vacuum. Rather, each contributor decides what to contribute taking into account all other contents that they see. This type of social influence can influence the final content generated.

To investigate social influence, Muchnik et al. (2013) ran an experiment on an undisclosed news aggregator that, similar to Reddit, allows users to vote articles up or down. They find that seeding an article with an up vote increased the likelihood of receiving future up votes by 32%. Social influence is also an important component in platforms such as Twitter. Bakshy et al. (2011) find that large cascades in retweets on Twitter tend to originate with very influential users. Kwak et al. (2010) find that over 85% of retweeted topics relate to current events, highlighting the blurry lines between Twitter as a social network and as a news platform.

While social influence can distort content, it can also be a positive force. For example, in the Wikipedia editing process described in the previous section, people may try to adjust their contributions in order to improve the final content taking into account previous content. Similarly, social influence may drive higher rates of contribution. Many open questions about social influence remain—such as the extent to which it exists in popular online markets, the factors that moderate it, and its welfare implications.

12.3.4 Other Issues

The aforementioned list of challenges to the quality of content is not exhaustive. One issue that has come up in the context of online marketplaces is that sellers often review buyers and buyers review sellers. This can lead to strategic incentives for upward biased reporting if reviewers fear retaliation. For example, even if a renter on Airbnb has a bad experience, she might be hesitant to leave a bad review if the landlord were to see the review before leaving feedback for her. There are several possible solutions to this type of reciprocal reviewing. For example, a platform can simply withhold ratings until both sides have left a review. Reciprocal reviewing has been explored in settings such as eBay (Bolton et al., 2013) and Airbnb (Fradkin et al., 2014).

In conclusion, understanding and improving the quality of UGC is an important question both for policymakers and for platform designers. From a policy perspective, each of the issues described above will influence the amount of welfare that is being created from UGC. From a platform's perspective, these issues should shape the design choices that the platform makes. The quality and slant of content will determine outcomes such as the number and types of users and contributions, the value of advertising to businesses, and the amount of value that the platform is creating. An important direction for future research is to explore these factors and develop mechanisms to improve the quality of content.

12.4. INCENTIVE DESIGN AND BEHAVIORAL FOUNDATIONS

Consider the hotel review platform TripAdvisor.com. The website is the largest provider of information about hotels in the world, hosting more than 170 million reviews related to travel services (hotels, destinations, tours, etc.)—all of them provided for free. If the company offered, say, a penny per review, many users would probably be so offended that they would not review at all. Any reasonable level of payment for reviews (for example, $15 for a thoughtful review) would be financially unsustainable. In this sense, perhaps the most surprising aspect of platforms such as TripAdvisor is the simple fact that they exist and are viable.

In a world where contributors do not typically receive financial compensation, why do people contribute at all? This is a fundamental question about the existence of UGC. After all, it takes time and effort to contribute meaningful content. In practice, there are many factors that cause people to contribute. One important factor is that although *financial* incentives are rare, *non-pecuniary* incentive design is a core function of a platform designer. For example, Yelp and AngiesList provide incentives to elicit reviews for services, with an emphasis on both the quantity and quality of content. YouTube provides incentives to encourage users to generate videos that viewers will find interesting. Facebook and Twitter encourage users to post information that others will read. In this section, I discuss the main non-pecuniary incentives driving production of content—incentives largely grounded in ideas from behavioral economics—and the choices that designers make to create these incentives.

There is significant heterogeneity in the way that different platforms design incentives for contributors. For example, some platforms—such as Yelp and Wikia—have personnel who manage the contributing communities and engage directly with prolific contributors. Other platforms are more passive. Still others send heavy-handed messages reminding people to contribute content. Across all platforms, the design of the platform creates incentives that determine whether there will be more or less, and better or worse content.

One popular incentive used by platforms is to allow users to develop a reputation. User reputation systems come in two flavors. The first is a top-down system, typically in the form of badges or other outward-facing rewards from the platform. For example, Yelp provides "elite" status to reviewers who have written many high-quality reviews (as identified by Yelp); TripAdvisor, Amazon, and many other platforms have similar systems. The second type of social status is peer provided. UGC platforms often offer ways for other users to evaluate contributions, such as Yelp's "cool," "funny," and "useful" ratings, Amazon's "useful" rating, and Stack Exchange's "upvotes." Designers often enhance peer reputation by making it salient through titles and badges.

Easley and Ghosh (2013) analyze the role of badges as incentives for content creation. For example, Amazon and Yahoo! Answers award top-contributor titles to the users who produce the highest amounts of useful content. StackOverflow gives users badges for completing certain actions, such as voting on answers 300 or more times. Badges are clearly effective sources of motivation: there are entire discussion communities dedicated to becoming and staying top Amazon and Yahoo! Answer contributors. Empirically, Anderson et al. (2013) find that StackOverflow users participate more actively as they get closer to attaining certain badges. A growing literature is now beginning to investigate the effects and optimal design of these types of incentives. Once a platform has chosen an incentive system such as a badge or leaderboard, it must decide what someone should have to do to receive a reward. For example, Miller et al. (2005) propose a scoring rule based on a comparison of the posterior beliefs implied by a user's rating and the rating of a reference user.

Looking at the entire review ecosystem, rather than the behavior of individual reviewers, Wang (2010) analyzes differences between the reviews and reviewers of three popular websites: Citysearch, Yahoo Local, and Yelp. Although Yelp entered into an already existing online review market in which Citysearch was popular, Wang observes that Yelp has received a higher number of prolific reviewers than either Citysearch or Yahoo Local. He argues that the primary distinction between Yelp and the two incumbents is that Yelp provides social image incentives, suggesting that the reputational motivation must be a stronger driver of review provision than the intrinsic motivation. If reviewers were primarily motivated by altruism, the difference between the number of reviews on Yelp and the number of reviews on other websites might be smaller, since review readers benefit from reviews regardless of where they read them. While the study does not isolate the causal effect of social image, it suggests a potentially important role of social image in UGC.

Another important behavioral component of UGC is users' beliefs about the impact and quality of their contributions. Looking at Chinese government blocks of Wikipedia as exogenous shocks to the size of content readership, Zhang and Zhu (2011) show that the size of readership has a causal effect on contributions. The incentive to contribute increases with the size of the readership, suggesting that prosocial motivations underlie contribution decisions. A related factor pertains to a contributor's beliefs about the quality of her contribution. Zhang and Zhu (2006) show that Wikipedia contributors are less likely to contribute content after their earlier content has been edited or corrected, perhaps because this feedback suggests to them that their contributions are inferior. In a field experiment on MovieLens, Chen et al. (2010) show that providing information about how many ratings a median user has contributed leads to a large increase in contribution rates for low-frequency users and a drop in contribution rates for high-frequency users—suggesting that social norms guide the rates of contribution.

There are two main directions for future research in this area. First, UGC platforms create rich empirical contexts for testing behavioral theories. Second, the optimal design of incentives at the platform level, given the preferences of platforms users, remains a largely open question.

12.5. OTHER ISSUES

This section broaches several other important issues related to UGC. These issues serve as potentially fruitful areas of future research concerning UGC.

12.5.1 Business Models

Looking across UGC platforms, there are three main ways that UGC platforms generate revenue.

The first—and most common—way to generate revenue is to sell advertising, which is the approach taken by Facebook, Twitter, Yelp, and many others. One benefit of this approach is that UGC platforms often know a lot about contributors and users, including what they are interested in (for example, Yelp knows when users are searching for Thai food). However, advertising sales can also lead to policy and legal issues ranging from privacy (what data Facebook should be allowed to use to target ads) to fairness (how many advertisements should be shown in a newsfeed, relative to organic content). Advertising can also create incentives for contributors to alter their content. For example, Sun and Zhu (2013) find that after the introduction of an advertising revenue-sharing program on a Chinese portal, bloggers altered their content in order to receive more viewers.

Another related research question pertains to the optimal way to sell ads. One option is to use an auction, as Google and other platforms commonly do. By contrast, Yelp (like several other major platforms) has a large sales team that interacts with businesses to sell advertisements at a fixed price. Platforms that sell advertisements are then often able to offer content to users without a separate charge.

The second approach to revenue generation is to sell subscriptions to users who want to access the content. For example, AngiesList charges an annual membership fee to users. While this approach can eliminate some of the challenges of relying mainly on advertisements, it can also restrict the number of contributions (since fewer people will view the content) and ultimately the reach of the platform.

The third main approach to revenue generation is to sell analytics and data. For example, Facebook can presumably predict fashion trends across the country better than most other organizations can, by studying changes in user behavior and network data. Similarly, Yelp can presumably predict food trends better than other organizations. Such analyses could potentially change the way that businesses optimize their operations.

A fourth alternative is not to pursue profit at all. Some UGC platforms—such as Wikipedia—have opted to pursue a non-profit approach, relying on donations and fundraising drives to stay afloat.

There are many open questions in this area. For example, do Facebook advertisements work? Do they create a conflict of interest with the business's dedication to protecting privacy? To what extent does a paywall (such as AngiesList's) reduce content? Does a paywall reduce usage by making the profit motive salient to customers? Does an advertising-based model lead platforms to obscure the difference between paid and unpaid content, as suggested by Edelman and Gilchrist (2012)?

More generally, there are several main research topics related to business models and UGC: (1) the optimal pricing of these services, (2) the measurement of their efficacy, (3) identification and quantification of the unintended consequences, and (4) the conditions under which each business model is optimal.

12.5.2 Competition and Network Effects

The value of social media sites such as Facebook, Yelp, Twitter, LinkedIn, and YouTube to a given user depends on who else is using it. As mentioned earlier, this network effect is a feature of all UGC, such that the value of a UGC platform increases with the number of users. This helps to explain why investors often consider the number of users a site has in addition to its revenue. Network effects are also a natural source of market power. When Facebook has a large network, the value to each user goes up, making it harder for a competitor to capture users.

Despite the importance of network effects, there have been important examples of large UGC platforms that have been overtaken by competitors. Facebook was not the first popular online social network; Myspace preceded it. Similarly, Citysearch predated Yelp as a popular online review platform. In these cases, strong entrants with improved technology overcame the network-effects barrier. While considerable work documents social media networks and investigates influence within a network (see Sections 12.2 and 12.3.3 above, or Jackson and Yariv, 2011), many open questions remain about the role of network structure in online social networks. Important directions for future research include quantifying the value of network effects in these platforms, estimating the extent to which they provide market power, and exploring the factors that allow a competitor to overcome the network-effects barrier. For example, it could be that there is a tipping point at which users move en masse from one platform to another.

A related element of competition occurs between social media and more traditional media outlets. Wikipedia competes with traditional encyclopedias, blogs with newspapers, Yelp with the Michelin Guide, etc. A fruitful area for future research is to explore the extent and implications of this type of competition.

12.5.3 Digital Exhaust, Property Rights, and Privacy

Every Facebook post, every "like," every tweet, every Yelp review, every Instagram picture, and every Foursquare check-in leaves a trace on the web, a trail of what is sometimes referred to as *digital exhaust*.

Digital exhaust provides valuable new data. Bollen et al. (2011) show that the public mood, as assessed from tweets, predicts stock market outcomes. Kang et al. (2013) find that text from Yelp reviews predicts restaurant hygiene violations, thus suggesting that reviewers can help health inspectors decide which restaurants to inspect. Glaeser et al. (forthcoming) collaborate with Yelp and the City of Boston to explore the creation and implementation of a Boston-specific algorithm. Digital exhaust can be used for social good—for example, a city government might use Facebook networks to predict college dropout decisions or tweets to predict crime.

However, digital exhaust leads to issues of property rights. In particular, who owns the massive amounts of data that you are providing to these platforms? UGC platforms frequently sell data about users to enhance advertisers' ability to identify potential customers. Reducing the amount of user data platforms can sell may reduce the ability of advertisers to target consumers. Examining the effects of EU regulation on the amount of data online advertisers can collect, Goldfarb and Tucker (2011) find that advertising effectiveness, measured by participation on a five-point "likelihood of purchase" scale, fell by 65% in Europe relative to the rest of the world after this restriction was introduced. However, Tucker (2014) finds that social media users are more likely to click on personalized advertisements when they believe they have control over their personally identifiable information.

Digital exhaust also raises issues related to privacy and anonymity. What are the welfare effects of contributor anonymity? Facebook, for example, has many different privacy levels for profiles, pictures, and posts, based on user preference. A contributor to Yelp, Wikipedia, YouTube, TripAdvisor, or most other platforms has the ability to post material fairly anonymously (or to choose to make him- or herself public). Allowing anonymous contributions may improve content—especially in sensitive areas—but may also increase self-dealing (or, as discussed in Section 12.3.1, promotional content). In ways that may be good or bad, depending on the situation, anonymous users may also feel more comfortable violating social norms.

Public contributions give contributors social capital that provides incentives to generate high-quality content and also deters fraudulent content. In settings where a designer may want to deter certain types of conversations—such as limiting hate speech or bullying on a discussion board—requiring contributions to be public may be an important tool.

However, there is a tradeoff because public contributions may restrain users from contributing important content for fear of stigma or retribution. In some situations, forbidding anonymous complaints can backfire; for example, the fear that the police could identify contributors to a site could suppress complaints or tips to the police. For further discussion on the economic of privacy in media outlets, see Chapter 11.

To empirically investigate the role of anonymity on Wikipedia, Anthony et al. (2009) distinguish between registered editors and anonymous editors. While registered users provide more content, content by unregistered users is more likely to be retained over time, and hence may be more reliable.

In sum, understanding the growing tradeoffs surrounding privacy and anonymity in UGC is an important area for future research.

12.5.4 Information Aggregation

Consider a town with two hypothetical hotels: the Hotel California and the Hotel Yorba. Both hotels are quite popular on TripAdvisor, obtaining an average of 3.5 stars from hundreds of reviewers. On the surface, the two hotels seem similar. Yet as you look closer, you see that most of the favorable reviews for the Hotel California were from a long time ago and that the reputation has gone downhill from there. By contrast, Hotel Yorba has received a lot of favorable ratings over the last couple of years. Which hotel would you pick? Most likely, you would choose the Hotel Yorba.

Taking this hypothetical a step further, what overall rating should TripAdvisor display for the two hotels to its users to provide an estimate for the true quality of the hotel, and what order should they be listed in? As noted above, the arithmetic average rating for each hotel is 3.5 stars. Yet, it is only under very restrictive assumptions that an arithmetic average is the optimal way to aggregate this information. For example, an average might be optimal if each review were an independent and identically distributed draw of quality with no peer effects, quality changes, or heterogeneity in quality of reviews.

A question faced by UGC platforms is then how to aggregate this information. Looking at Yelp reviews, Dai et al. (2013) provide one structural approach to aggregation of UGC. Their model allows for peer effects in content, changes in restaurant quality, and reviewer heterogeneity, among other factors. Their results derive an optimal aggregation of Yelp ratings, which endogenously provides more weight to later reviews, and to elite reviewers, among other factors.

At the opposite extreme of arithmetic averages is the approach of finding "bad" content and removing it all together. Platforms that use algorithms to identify and remove content thought to be fake use this approach, as do spam detection algorithms (for example, in Ott et al., 2011). As with the case of arithmetic averaging, the approach of removing content altogether is only optimal under very restrictive assumptions, as it assumes that the removed content contains no useful information. Taking a step back from this specific application, it seems that, given some model of reviewer behavior, it should be possible to derive the optimal way to aggregate information to provide to users. To the extent that users have different preferences, it is then possible to customize content based on preferences of customers. In practice, information may literally be reweighted and displayed to customers. An alternative is that platforms can use these insights when deciding the order in which to display results.

12.5.5 Welfare Effects

TripAdvisor creates value for society by increasing the amount of information available to people who are choosing a hotel. Quantifying this welfare gain is complicated, as it requires data and assumptions about where people would go in the absence of TripAdvisor as well as the value people receive from going to different hotels. This is complicated further because new information can influence the diversity and quality of hotels in the market.

LinkedIn creates value by allowing people to connect with each other in an employment-focused setting, which could potentially reduce unemployment and lead to better job matches. Yet, computing this value is complicated because of the endogenous nature of connections, including the simple decision of whether to join LinkedIn as well as the difficulty in estimating the value of a connection.

Similar challenges arise when quantifying the welfare gains for virtually any type of UGC. This quantification remains an open direction for future research. Beyond the overall gain from new information, there are likely quite heterogeneous effects for consumers. For example, while AngiesList is tailored to customers who are willing to pay for it, Yelp is tailored to a broader audience. Similarly, online news conveyed through blogs and tweets may be very different from coverage on the *New York Times*. Future research can help to understand more about the winners and losers among customers, workers, and businesses.

12.6. DISCUSSION

Virtually every industry is touched by UGC. Every online interaction has a social element to it, and every type of media is incorporating, competing with, or being replaced by

UGC. Describing much of the current research being done in this area, this chapter has focused on the impact of UGC on behavior, the unique biases and challenges to the quality of content that these platforms face, and the design of incentives to generate sufficient high-quality content, among other issues.

Several themes have arisen throughout the chapter. One is methodological. Much of the frontier of this field involves finding the correct method to study a given problem. In many cases, this means identifying strategies to pinpoint causal effects that go beyond descriptive work and associations. There is also scope for pure prediction problems in cases where UGC may help to predict and target a variable of interest. But it is important to be clear about whether a paper is moving toward a causal claim, or trying to predict an outcome. Much of the current empirical work in this area lacks emphasis on causality, and often focuses on associations, with several notable exceptions. With an abundance of data and the growing feasibility of running experiments with companies, moving more toward causal estimates is a productive area for future research.

A second theme concerns the role of the economist. One important practical advance within economics has been the development of the idea of the economist as engineer (Roth, 2002). In this context, economists not only study UGC but also help to design UGC platforms. As described by Roth, this shift in the economist's role has necessitated a deeper understanding of the contexts we study and greater attention to assumptions and institutional details. This is reflected both in the work on incentive design (where practical new mechanisms are developed to encourage high-quality content) and information design (where new approaches are taken to aggregating and presenting material to users).

A third related theme has been a focus on the phenomenon. The field of economics often prides itself on abstraction and removing itself from the confines of a particular context. By contrast, research on UGC has focused considerably more on phenomena, potentially in part because of closer ties between organizations and researchers. Although this difference is appealing in many ways, the emerging literature on UGC might benefit from a heavier reliance on theory. For example, the theoretical literature on networks could be brought more directly into empirical studies of influence in social networks.

Ultimately, UGC platforms are a rapidly growing field, both in practice and in research, creating a unique feedback loop. There are ample opportunities for future research to develop new theories and analyses of how UGC is shaping the world around us, how UGC platforms currently work, and how they should work.

ACKNOWLEDGMENTS

I am grateful to the editors, as well as Duncan Gilchrist, Shane Greenstein, and Scott Kominers for helpful comments. Janet Lu and Patrick Rooney provided excellent research assistance.

REFERENCES

Adamic, L., Glance, N., 2005. The political blogosphere and the 2004 U.S. election: divided they blog. In: Proceedings of the 3rd International Workshop on Link Discovery. Association for Computing Machinery, New York, NY, pp. 36–43.

Akoglu, L., Chandy, R., Faloutsos, C., 2013. Opinion fraud detection in online reviews by network effects. In: The 7th International AAAI Conference on Weblogs and Social Media. The AAAI Press, Palo Alto, California, pp. 2–11.

Anderson, M., Magruder, J., 2012. Learning from the crowd: regression discontinuity estimates of the effects of an online review database. Econ. J. 122 (563), 957–989.

Anderson, A., Huttenlocher, D., Kleinberg, J., Leskovec, J., 2013. Steering user behavior with badges. In: Proceedings of the ACM International Conference on World Wide Web (WWW). Association for Computing Machinery, New York, NY, pp. 95–106.

Anthony, D., Smith, S., Williamson, T., 2009. Reputation and reliability in collective goods the case of the online encyclopedia wikipedia. Ration. Soc. 21 (3), 283–306.

Aral, S., Walker, D., 2012. Identifying influential and susceptible members of social networks. Science 337 (6092), 327–341.

Aral, S., Walker, D., 2014. Tie strength, embeddedness & social influence: a large scale networked experiment. Manag. Sci. 60 (6), 1352–1370.

Avery, C., Resnick, P., Zeckhauser, R., 1999. The market for evaluations. Am. Econ. Rev. 89 (3), 564–584.

Bakshy, E., Hofman, J.M., Mason, W.A., Watts, D.J., 2011. Everyone's an influencer: quantifying influence on twitter. In: Proceedings of the 4th ACM International Conference on Web Search and Data Mining, Hong Kong. Association for Computing Machinery, New York, NY, pp. 65–74.

Bar-Isaac, H., Caruana, G., Cuñat, V., 2012. Search, design, and market structure. Am. Econ. Rev. 102 (2), 1140–1160.

Bertrand, M., Duflo, E., Mullainathan, S., 2004. How much should we trust differences-in-differences estimates? Q. J. Econ. 119 (1), 249–275.

Bollen, J., Mao, H., Zeng, X., 2011. Twitter mood predicts the stock market. J. Comput. Sci. 2 (1), 1–8.

Bolton, G., Greiner, B., Ockenfels, A., 2013. Engineering trust: reciprocity in the production of reputation information. Manag. Sci. 59 (2), 265–285.

Bond, R., Fariss, C., Jones, J., Kramer, A., Marlow, C., Settle, J., Fowler, J., 2012. A 61-million-person experiment in social influence and political mobilization. Nature 489 (7415), 295–298.

Cabral, L., Hortaçsu, A., 2010. The dynamics of seller reputation: evidence from eBay. J. Ind. Econ. 58 (1), 54–78.

Cameron, A., Massie, A.B., Alexander, C.E., Stewart, B., Montgomery, R.A., Benavides, N.R., Fleming, G.D., Segev, D.L., 2013. Social media and organ donor registration: the Facebook effect. Am. J. Transplant. 13 (8), 2059–2065.

Cao, R., Ching, A., Ishihara, M., Luca, M., 2015. Can the Crowd Predict Roger Ebert's Reviews? Working Paper.

Che, Y., Hörner, J., 2014. Optimal Design for Social Learning. Working Paper.

Chen, Y., Harper, M., Konstan, J., Li, S., 2010. Social comparisons and contributions to online communities: a field experiment on MovieLens. Am. Econ. Rev. 100 (4), 1358–1398.

Chevalier, J., Mayzlin, D., 2006. The effect of word of mouth on sales: online book reviews. J. Mark. Res. 43 (3), 345–354.

Clemons, E., Gao, G., Hitt, L., 2006. When online reviews meet hyperdifferentiation: a study of the craft beer industry. J. Manag. Inf. Syst. 23 (2), 149–171.

Dai, W., Jin, G., Lee, J., Luca, M., 2013. Optimal Aggregation of Consumer Ratings: An Application to Yelp.com. Working Paper.

Dellarocas, C., 2006. Strategic manipulation of internet opinion forums: implications for consumers and firms. Manag. Sci. 52 (10), 1577–1593.

Dellarocas, C., Gao, G., Narayan, R., 2010. Are consumers more likely to contribute online reviews for hit products or niche products? J. Manag. Inf. Syst. 27 (2), 127–158.

Dobrescu, I., Luca, M., Motta, A., 2013. What makes a critic tick? connected authors and the determinants of book reviews. J. Econ. Behav. Organ. 96, 85–103.

Easley, D., Ghosh, A., 2013. Incentives, gamification, and game theory: an economic approach to badge design. In: Proceedings of the 14th ACM Conference on Electronic Commerce. Association for Computing Machinery, New York, NY, pp. 359–376.

Edelman, B., Gilchrist, D., 2012. Advertising disclosures: measuring labeling alternatives in internet search engines. Inf. Econ. Policy 24 (1), 75–89.

Fischbacher, U., Föllmi-Heusi, F., 2013. Lies in disguise—an experimental study on cheating. J. Eur. Econ. Assoc. 11 (3), 525–547.

Fradkin, A., Grewal, E., Holtz, D., Pearson, M., 2014. Bias and Reciprocity in Online Reviews: Evidence from Field Experiments on Airbnb. Working Paper.

Gentzkow, M., Shapiro, J., 2011. Ideological segregation online and offline. Q. J. Econ. 126 (4), 1799–1839.

Ghose, A., Ipeirotis, P., Li, B., 2012. Designing ranking systems for hotels on travel search engines by mining user-generated and crowdsourced content. Mark. Sci. 31 (3), 493–520.

Glaeser, E., Hillis, A., Kominers, S., Luca, M., 2015. Crowdsourcing city government: using tournaments to improve inspection accuracy. Amer. Econ. Rev. (forthcoming).

Gneezy, U., 2005. Deception: the role of consequences. Am. Econ. Rev. 95 (1), 384–394.

Goldfarb, A., Tucker, C., 2011. Privacy regulation and online advertising. Manag. Sci. 57 (1), 57–71.

Greenstein, S., Zhu, F., 2012. Is Wikipedia biased? Am. Econ. Rev. 102 (3), 343–348.

Greenstein, S., Zhu, F., 2014. Do Experts or Collective Intelligence Write with More Bias? Evidence from Encyclopaedia Britannica and Wikipedia. Working Paper.

Hargittai, E., Gallo, J., Kane, M., 2008. Cross-ideological discussions among conservative and liberal bloggers. Public Choice 134 (1–2), 67–86.

Hitt, L., Li, X., 2008. Self-selection and information role of online product reviews. Inf. Syst. Res. 19 (4), 456–474.

Hu, N., Zhang, J., Pavlou, P., 2009. Overcoming the J-shaped distribution of product reviews. Commun. ACM 52 (10), 144–147.

Huang, J., Chen, Y., 2006. Herding in online product choice. Psychol. Mark. 23 (5), 413–428.

Hurkens, S., Kartik, N., 2009. Would I lie to you? On social preferences and lying aversion. Exp. Econ. 12 (2), 180–192.

Jackson, M., Yariv, L., 2011. Diffusion, strategic interaction, and social structure. Handb. Soc. Econ. 1, 645–678.

Jin, G., Leslie, P., 2009. Reputational incentives for restaurant hygiene. Am. Econ. J. Microecon. 1 (1), 237–267.

Kang, J., Kuznetsova, P., Luca, M., Choi, Y., 2013. Where not to eat? Improving public policy by predicting hygiene inspections using online reviews. In: Proceedings of the Conference on Empirical Methods in Natural Language Processing. Association for Computational Linguistics Stroudsburg, PA, USA, pp. 1443–1448.

Kornowski, L., 2013. Celebrity Sponsored Tweets: What Stars Get Paid For Advertising in 140 Characters. The Huffington Post.

Kroft, K., Pope, D., 2014. Does online search crowd out traditional search and improve matching efficiency? Evidence from craigslist. J. Labor Econ. 32 (2), 259–303.

Kwak, H., Lee, C., Park, H., Moon, S., 2010. What is Twitter, a social network or a news media? In: Proceedings from the 19th International Conference on World Wide Web. Association for Computing Machinery, New York, NY, pp. 591–600.

Li, X., Hitt, L., 2010. Price effects in online product reviews: an analytical model and empirical analysis. MIS Q. 34 (4), 809–831.

Luca, M., 2011. Reviews, Reputation, and Revenue: The Case of Yelp.com. Working Paper.

Luca, M., Zervas, G., 2015. Fake it till you make it: reputation, competition, and Yelp review fraud. Manage. Sci. (forthcoming).

Lucking-Reiley, D., Bryan, D., Prasad, N., Reeves, D., 2007. Pennies from eBay: the determinants of price in online auctions. J. Ind. Econ. 55 (2), 223–233.

Manski, C., 1993. Identification of endogenous social effects: the reflection problem. Rev. Econ. Stud. 60 (3), 531–542.

Mayzlin, D., Yoganarasimhan, H., 2012. Links to success: how blogs build an audience by promoting rivals. Manag. Sci. 58 (9), 1651–1668.

Mayzlin, D., Dover, Y., Chevalier, J., 2014. Promotional reviews: an empirical investigation of online review manipulation. Am. Econ. Rev. 104 (8), 2421–2455.

Melnik, M., Alm, J., 2002. Does a seller's ecommerce reputation matter? Evidence from eBay auctions. J. Ind. Econ. 50 (3), 337–349.

Miller, N., Resnick, P., Zeckhauser, R., 2005. Eliciting informative feedback: the peer-prediction method. Manag. Sci. 51 (9), 1359–1373.

Muchnik, L., Aral, S., Taylor, S., 2013. Social influence bias: a randomized experiment. Science 341 (6146), 647–651.

Mullainathan, S., Shleifer, A., 2005. The market for news. Am. Econ. Rev. 95 (4), 1031–1053.

Noguchi, Y., 2006. Wikipedia's Help from the Hill. The Washington Post.

Ott, M., Choi, Y., Cardie, C., Hancock, J., 2011. Finding deceptive opinion spam by any stretch of the imagination. In: Proceedings of the 49th Annual Meeting of the Association for Computational Linguistics. Association for Computational Linguistics Stroudsburg, PA, USA, pp. 309–319.

Ott, M., Cardie, C., Hancock, J., 2012. Estimating the prevalence of deception in online review communities. In: Proceedings of the 21st International Conference on World Wide Web (WWW). Association for Computing Machinery, New York, NY, pp. 201–210.

Resnick, P., Zeckhauser, R., Swanson, J., Lockwood, K., 2006. The value of reputation on eBay: a controlled experiment. Exp. Econ. 9 (2), 79–101.

Roth, A., 2002. The economist as engineer: game theory, experimentation, and computation as tools for design economics. Econometrica 70 (4), 1341–1378.

Seamans, R., Zhu, F., 2014. Responses to entry in multi-sided markets: the impact of craigslist on local newspapers. Manag. Sci. 60 (2), 476–493.

Sun, M., Zhu, F., 2013. Ad revenue and content commercialization: evidence from blogs. Manag. Sci. 59 (10), 2314–2331.

Tucker, C., 2014. Social networks, personalized advertising, and privacy controls. J. Mark. Res. 51 (5), 546–562.

Wang, Z., 2010. Anonymity, social image, and the competition for volunteers: a case study of the online market for reviews. B.E. J. Econom. Anal. Policy 10 (1), 1–35.

Williams, C., 2013. TripAdvisor Borrows Anti-Fraud Techniques from Finance Industry. The Telegraph Online.

Zhang, M., Zhu, F., 2006. Intrinsic motivation of open content contributors: the case of Wikipedia. In: Workshop on Information Systems and Economics (WISE), Chicago, IL.

Zhang, M., Zhu, F., 2011. Group size and incentives to contribute: a natural experiment at Chinese Wikipedia. Am. Econ. Rev. 101 (4), 1601–1615.

Zhu, F., Zhang, M., 2010. Impact of online consumer reviews on sales: the moderating role of product and consumer characteristics. J. Mark. 74 (2), 133–148.

PART III

The Political Economy of Mass Media

CHAPTER 13

Media Coverage and Political Accountability: Theory and Evidence

David Strömberg
IIES, Stockholm University, Stockholm, Sweden

Contents

13.1. Introduction	596
13.2. Theory	596
13.2.1 The Role of Information in Politics	597
13.2.2 Market Provision of News	600
13.2.2.1 Total Coverage of Politics	600
13.2.2.2 Coverage Across Issues and Multitasking	604
13.2.3 Optimal Regulation and Public Provision of News	605
13.3. Evidence	608
13.3.1 Volume of Coverage	610
13.3.2 Voters	611
13.3.2.1 Information	611
13.3.2.2 Responsiveness	613
13.3.2.3 Political Participation	614
13.3.3 Politicians	615
13.3.4 Policy	616
13.3.4.1 Who Gets the News?	616
13.3.4.2 Volume and Focus of Political Coverage	617
13.3.5 Multitasking	618
13.3.5.1 Audience Share Bias	618
13.3.5.2 Media Access Bias	619
13.3.5.3 Newsworthiness Bias	619
13.3.5.4 Target Group Bias	620
13.4. Conclusion	620
References	620

Abstract

This chapter investigates how media coverage filters information and how this affects political account-ability and policy. I first present a baseline model of media coverage and its effect on political account-ability. The model is used to discuss the welfare consequences of private provision of news. It shows how media regulation and public broadcasting may correct market failures, notably the under-provision of news. The model also supplies an array of testable implications, used to organize the exist-ing empirical work. The key empirical questions are: what drives media coverage of politics; how does this coverage influence the information levels and the voting behavior of the general public, the actions and selection of politicians and government policy?

Keywords

Media, Regulation, Information, Political accountability, Policy, Voting

JEL Codes

D03, D72, H5, L82

13.1. INTRODUCTION

This chapter investigates how media coverage filters information and how this affects political accountability and policy. Because information gathering and transmission are costly, information frictions are unavoidable. By transmitting information to mass audiences, the media will lower these frictions. How much they will lower the frictions may depend on factors such as the degree of media competition, the size of the market, demand for advertising, and delivery costs. This chapter will provide theory and evidence of how media coverage depends on these factors, and what the effects of this are. The chapter models news media that do not conscientiously lie or distort information. Capture and ideological bias are discussed in Chapters 14–16, this volume. This chapter focuses on political accountability effects. It does not cover how the degree and direction of information filtering by news media affect economic outcomes such as investor attention (Merton, 1987) and price stickiness (Sims, 2003). This is discussed in Chapter 18, this volume.

This chapter first presents a baseline model of how informative media affect political accountability. The model is used to discuss the welfare consequences of private provision of news and how media regulation and public broadcasting may correct market failures, notably the under provision of news. The model also supplies an array of testable implications, used to organize the existing empirical work. The key empirical questions are: what drives media coverage of politics; how does this coverage influence the information levels and the voting behavior of the general public, the actions and selection of politicians and government policy?

13.2. THEORY

In the standard model of how informative media affect political accountability and policy, there are three classes of actors: voters, politicians, and the media. Voters try to elect politicians who will give them most utility, politicians try to get re-elected and perhaps enjoy political rents, and the mass media select political coverage to maximize profits. The model contains two building blocks: the first analyzes the role of information in politics and the second analyzes how media's news selection affects information levels. This setup has been used in a number of papers (e.g., Besley and Burgess, 2001, 2002; Besley and Prat, 2006; Prat and Strömberg, 2013; Strömberg, 1999, 2001, 2004a,b).

13.2.1 The Role of Information in Politics

The first building block describes how information from media influences policy. The key role of media is to provide political information. This information increases the responsiveness of votes to the quality and effort of politicians, which improves political selection and incentives, and eventually policy and welfare.

In these models, the specific type of information provided by media varies. To cast the right vote, citizens need to know who proposes, or is responsible for, what policies, and to what effect. Media matter because they transmit information to voters about any of these facts. In Strömberg (1999), they carry information about who proposes, or is responsible for, what policy. In other models, this is instead information about the incumbent's type with respect to, e.g., altruism (Besley and Burgess, 2002), quality— good or bad (Besley and Prat, 2006), or competence (Prat and Strömberg, 2013).

I will use a slightly modified version of the model in Prat and Strömberg (2013) as a basis for the discussion. Rather than restating the full model with these marginal changes, I will here only describe these changes and explain how they modify the results.

The timing of the model is the following. In the first period, nature selects the incumbent politician's type (competence), which remains unknown. The incumbent selects effort, which together with the incumbent's type affects the quality of government policy. Media cover the policy outcome. Voters use information from the media to guide a private action and their voting decision. In the second period, the elected political candidate selects effort and the second-period policy is determined.

I make three modifications to the model of Prat and Strömberg (2013). First, I assume that there is a continuum of voters of size n that all belong to one group. The model of Prat and Strömberg (2013) allows for many groups. The present model is thus a special case of their model. This is because I first want to focus on the total amount of political news coverage rather than the distribution across groups.

Second, I add a parameter a that affects the demand for public spending. The voters' utility from policy derives from their public goods consumption, given by

$$g = a(\theta + e), \tag{13.1}$$

where θ is the innate ability (type) of the incumbent. This θ is drawn from a uniform distribution with mean zero. The variable e is the amount of government resources spent per capita on the public good by the incumbent. The added parameter a measures the need for spending. This parameter is included in, e.g., Strömberg (1999, 2004a,b) and Besley and Burgess (2002). It is needed to show how government responsiveness is affected by media coverage.

Third, I let the utility from the private action be realized before the election, rather than after as in Prat and Strömberg (2013). The media inform voters of the level of public goods provision, g. This information has a private value for voters because they select a private action whose optimal value depends on government policy. If voters set their private action α equal to the actual level of the public good g, they realize the value T. Otherwise, they receive no utility from the action. If this is realized after the election, then media coverage creates an incumbency advantage. I do not want to focus on this here, and assume that T is realized before the election.

In this model, the political effects are driven by the share s of voters who are informed by the media about the policy outcome g. The following three equations (corresponding to equations 2–4 in Prat and Strömberg, 2013) describe the equilibrium. The vote share of the incumbent is

$$v^I = \frac{1}{2} + s(g - ae^*) = \frac{1}{2} + sa(\theta + e - e^*). \tag{13.2}$$

The baseline vote share is one-half. However, politicians who are more competent than average $(\theta > 0)$, or who exert more effort than expected $(e > e^*)$, receive a higher vote share. The voting choices of better-informed voters react more to differences in effort, e, and competence, θ, of politicians. In consequence, the electoral outcome becomes more responsive to these differences the larger is the share of informed voters, s.

This increased responsiveness improves political incentives and selection. It can be proven that in a pure-strategy sincere equilibrium, the incumbent selects effort

$$e^* = Bsa, \tag{13.3}$$

where B is the marginal voter density. The expected competence of re-elected politicians is

$$E[\theta|s] = sa\frac{\overline{\theta}^2}{12}. \tag{13.4}$$

Both politician effort and competence are hence increasing in the share of informed voters, s.

Voters receive utility from the private action and from public goods consumption. Only the share s of informed voters realizes the value from the private action. Hence, aggregate voter welfare from the private action is nsT. Public goods consumption depends on effort and competence as shown by Equation (13.1). However, the expected public good consumption in period 1 is simply effort, e^*, because the expected competence in that period is zero. In contrast, the expected public good consumption in period 2 only depends on competence, $E[\theta|s]$. This is because it is a dominant strategy for the incumbent to keep all resources in the second period and set effort to zero. Consequently, voter welfare is

$$nsT + n(e^* + E[\theta|s]). \tag{13.5}$$

We will rewrite this as

$$ns(W + T) = ns\theta, \tag{13.6}$$

where

$$W = a\left(B + \frac{\overline{\theta}^2}{12}\right),$$

from Equations (13.3) and (13.4) and $\theta = T + W$. Importantly, voter welfare is increasing in the share s of voters informed by mass media.

I finally specify how the share of informed voters s is affected by media consumption and coverage. Let x be the share of media consumers. The probability ρ that a consumer finds the information about g is assumed to be increasing in the amount of media coverage devoted to politics, q. Hence, the share of informed voters is the share x that consumes the media, multiplied by the share $\rho(q)$ that finds the news, conditional on consuming,

$$s = x\rho(q). \tag{13.7}$$

Proposition 13.1 summarizes the effect of informative media on politics.

Proposition 13.1
An increase in
(a)   the share of media consumers, x, or
(b)   the media coverage of politics, q, causes an increase in
   (i)   the share of informed voters, s,
   (ii)   the responsiveness of votes to perceived competence,
   (iii) the effort (spending) and expected competence of politicians,
   (iv)   the responsiveness of government effort to need, a,
   (v)   and a fall in political rents.

The letters (a) and (b) distinguish the type of media variation, consumption, and coverage that causes the media effects. The numbers (i)–(v) describe the affected outcomes. Part (i) follows directly from Equation (13.7), part (ii) follows from Equation (13.2), parts (iii) and (iv) follow from Equations (13.3) and (13.4), and part (v) follows from part (iii) since rents are decreasing in effort.

The proposition explains how the media improve political accountability. The letters (a) and (b) distinguish the type of media variation and the numbers (i)–(iv) the affected outcomes. The proposition states that (a) who gets the news and (b) what issues are covered matter for voter information. Informed voters are more responsive to differences in competence across politicians. This improves political incentives and selection and, eventually, the quality of policy.

13.2.2 Market Provision of News

The second building block of the model opens up the black box of information demand and supply. A first question to be answered is why voters demand news about politics. Some political news may be read for entertainment, such as scandals and personal details. Other news may be of interest because it influences the individuals' private actions and welfare, for example the building of a new road, the placement of a new military installation, or the introduction of a school voucher system. Finally, voters may require the information because it helps make the right voting choice. The private action motive is probably most commonly used (e.g., Anderson and McLaren, 2012; Strömberg, 1999, 2004b), followed by the voting motive (e.g., Chan and Suen, 2008; Larcinese, 2007).

Our model contains both a private and a social value of information. More exact news about future policies makes it more probable that the reader will take the right private and electoral action. However, the voter only internalizes the private value T. Since there is a continuum of voters, the social value, W, from improved political accountability is not internalized at all.

The expected probability of finding the news, $\rho(q)$, is a function of media coverage, q. Coverage can be increased at a cost. To save on notation, we will analyze the problem directly in terms of ρ, and its associated cost, rather than in terms of q. The expected private value of ρ is $T\rho$, while the expected social value is $(T + W)\rho = \theta\rho$.

A reader's valuation of a newspaper also depends on other pieces of news, and some characteristics that the newspapers cannot change by assumption. This other news is omitted from the analysis.[1] The fixed characteristics include, for example, the paper's editorial stance and the name and logotype of the newspaper. Voter j buys the newspaper if

$$T\rho + \gamma_j \geq p, \tag{13.8}$$

where γ_j captures individual j's valuation of the exogenous aspects of the newspaper and p is the newspaper price. We assume that $-\gamma_j$ is distributed with the cumulative distribution function $G(\cdot)$ and density function $g(\cdot)$. The share who buys the newspaper is then $G(T\rho - p) = x$. Let the inverse demand curve be $p(\rho, x) = T\rho - G^{-1}(x)$.

13.2.2.1 Total Coverage of Politics

Having specified the demand for newspapers, we now turn to their costs. News production is an increasing returns to scale industry. Once the fixed "first-copy" cost of gathering the news, writing and editing of the news stories has been borne, the variable cost of producing an additional copy is just the cost of reproducing and distributing the newspaper (Reddaway, 1963; Rosse, 1967). We will write the cost function as additively

---

[1] If voters' utility from other news were additively separable from news on election platforms, the equations below would still characterize news coverage of the subset of news on election platforms.

separable in the first-copy cost of news coverage, ρ, and a per-copy distribution and delivery cost, d. We will assume that it becomes increasingly costly to inform an increasingly larger share of the voters, more precisely, that the cost is quadratic in ρ. The distribution cost is assumed to be linear in the number of copies sold, nx. The costs are

$$c(\rho, x) = \frac{1}{2}\rho^2 + dnx.$$

13.2.2.1.1 Monopoly Media

A monopoly newspaper chooses news coverage and output (price) so as to maximize the expected profits,

$$\max_{x,\rho} \ p(\rho, x)nx - c(\rho, x).$$

Assuming concavity, its maximum is characterized by the first-order conditions,

$$p^m = d + xg^{-1}(x), \tag{13.9}$$

$$\rho^m = nxT. \tag{13.10}$$

The first equation is the classical Lerner formula. The monopoly price is above the marginal cost and more so the less elastic is demand (the smaller is $g(x)$). The second equation shows that news coverage is increasing in audience size and in the private value of news.

To get a closed-form solution, suppose that G is a uniform distribution on $[-1/2, 1/2]$. Then

$$x^m = \left(\frac{1}{2} - d\right)\frac{1}{2 - nT^2}, \tag{13.11}$$

$$\rho^m = \left(\frac{1}{2} - d\right)\frac{nT}{2 - nT^2}. \tag{13.12}$$

The second-order conditions imply that $1 > n/2T^2$.

This simple model makes clear a couple of basic but important points. First, the provision of political news is increasing in market size, n. This is because news production is an increasing returns to scale industry in the sense that the first-copy cost is fixed. This is a general point related to quality choice with quality-dependent fixed costs (Shaked and Sutton, 1987). The political implications are that large countries, and large political jurisdictions within countries, will have higher-quality political reporting, thus leading to better informed voters and better political selection and incentives. Second, news provision is falling in news delivery costs.

Third, news provision is increasing in the private value of news, T. While this is exogenous in our model, Strömberg (2004b) endogenizes the private value of news and finds that it is higher for policy issues where the variance in need is larger. The model of

Strömberg (2004b) also predicts that politicians will distort policy to manage publicity. They will focus increases in spending on a few projects that attract the attention of the media, and finance this by making many small cutbacks, each of which is not newsworthy.

Advertising can easily be included in our framework. Strömberg (2004b) also includes informative advertising and pricing in two-sided markets. Voters can buy an advertised good. Advertising informs consumers of their value of the good and consumers who are made aware that their valuation is high will purchase the good. This has the effect of lowering the monopoly media's subscription price to attract consumers.

Importantly, advertising improves political accountability by increasing news coverage and newspaper sales. To see this in our simplified model, suppose that the media is a price taker in the advertising market, and advertising prices are p_a per media subscriber. This has the same effect as reducing the cost of delivering the newspaper from d to $d - p_a$. Equations (13.11) and (13.12) continue to hold, but with d replaced by $d - p_a$. Hence, advertising revenues increase political coverage and media consumption.

13.2.2.1.2 Competition

The effect of media competition on voter information is theoretically unclear. Competition may increase the share of informed voters by reducing subscription prices and hence increasing the consumption of news. On the other hand, competition may reduce political news coverage because of the increasing returns caused by the fixed first-copy cost.

To see this, consider the duopoly case where media A and B compete. Suppose that there is no multi-homing so that consumers subscribe to one of the two media at most. The problem of selecting quality and price in a duopoly setting with a quality-dependent fixed cost has been studied by, e.g., Anderson et al. (1992). In general, there exist both symmetric and asymmetric equilibria. Here, we just want to highlight a few features and, for this reason, focus on the pure-strategy, symmetric equilibria, and suppose that consumers first decide whether to buy a newspaper (based on their expectation of media prices and coverage) and then which newspaper to buy.

Suppose that consumers first choose whether to consume a media product based on expected quality and price. As in the monopoly case, this is decided by Equation (13.8). A share x of consumers is in the market for media. A consumer who has decided to buy a newspaper chooses newspaper A if

$$T\left(\rho^A - \rho^B\right) - \left(p^A - p^B\right) \geq \varepsilon,$$

where the parameter ε describes consumer preferences for exogenous and fixed media features, and where ε has a cumulative distribution function $H(\varepsilon)$ and a density function $h(\varepsilon)$. The inverse demand of firm A is then

$$p^A = T\left(\rho^A - \rho^B\right) + p^B - H^{-1}\left[\frac{x^A}{x}\right].$$

Both duopoly firms simultaneously choose news coverage and output (price) so as to maximize the expected profits. Firm A's problem is to maximize

$$\max_{x,\rho} \; np^A x^A - C\left(\rho^A, x^A\right).$$

Given our functional form assumptions, the first-order conditions evaluated at the symmetric equilibrium are

$$p^d = d + \frac{x^d}{2} h^{-1}\left(\frac{1}{2}\right), \tag{13.13}$$

and

$$\rho^d = n\frac{x^d}{2} T. \tag{13.14}$$

Total demand is determined by

$$x^d = G\left(T\rho^d - p^d\right).$$

Equation (13.13) is the Lerner formula, where the markup over the marginal cost depends on the demand elasticity. It seems likely that the demand elasticity between media A and B is higher than that between the monopoly media and the outside good. In this case, the duopoly price will be lower than the monopoly price. However, because of the increasing returns to scale caused by the fixed cost of increasing coverage, political coverage may be higher or lower. Comparing Equations (13.10) and (13.14), it is clear that for political coverage to increase, total demand must double.

The positive welfare effect through accountability depends on the share of informed voters that both consumes media and is exposed to news ($s = \rho x$), so lower political coverage by the duopoly media can be compensated by larger total sales resulting from lower prices. With our parametric assumptions, the share of informed voters is higher under duopoly than under monopoly if $x^d > \sqrt{2} x^m$.

Under both monopoly and duopoly, media coverage and media consumption are increasing in n and T, and falling in d. Proposition 13.2 summarizes the results.

Proposition 13.2
Political coverage and the share of media consumers, and consequently political effort and competence, are greater if: (a) the electorate is larger; (b) the advertising market is larger; or (c) the private value of news is high; and (d) it is inexpensive to distribute news. Political coverage and media consumption may increase or decrease with competition, depending on whether demand elasticity or scale effects dominate.

Proposition 13.2 discusses the determinants of the total amount of political coverage. The political implications are that large countries, and large political jurisdictions within countries, will have higher-quality political reporting, leading to better informed voters and better political selection and incentives. Similarly, a growing advertising market is likely to increase the amount of political coverage and media consumption, and create similar positive effects on political accountability. I will discuss the empirical evidence on competition in the empirical section.

13.2.2.2 Coverage Across Issues and Multitasking

In a world where politicians are charged with a variety of tasks that compete for their attention, information may also create perverse incentives. The tasks about which voters are informed (e.g., by the media) are not necessarily the most important. Because of the externality in news consumption, political information will be a by-product of the demand for entertainment or information used to guide private actions. Thus, electing politicians based on information from the media would risk diverting the attention from the most socially valuable allocation of time and resources. This is the familiar multitasking problem analyzed in Holmström and Milgrom (1991). The link to media is explored by Strömberg (2004b).

To discuss this, we temporarily expand the model to deal with multiple groups, thus making the model more similar to that of Prat and Strömberg (2013). Suppose that there are two groups, with population shares n_i, $i \in \{1, 2\}$. Their utility from the public good is

$$g_i = a_i(\theta_i + e_i). \tag{13.15}$$

The media informs a share s_i of voters of the level of public goods provision, g_i. Their private value is T_i. Suppose that the cost of exerting effort for the incumbent is $(1/2)(n_1 e_1 + n_2 e_2)^2$.

The following three equations (corresponding to equations 2–4 in Prat and Strömberg, 2013) characterize the equilibrium. The expected vote share of the incumbent is

$$\frac{1}{2} + \sum_{i=1}^{2} s_i n_i a_i \left(\theta_i + e_i - e_i^*\right). \tag{13.16}$$

It can be proven that, in a pure-strategy sincere equilibrium, the incumbent selects effort

$$e_i^* = \begin{cases} s_i a_i & \text{if } s_i a_i > s_j a_j \\ 0 & \text{otherwise} \end{cases} \tag{13.17}$$

and the expected competence of re-elected politicians is

$$E[\theta_i | s_i] = \begin{cases} s_i a_i \dfrac{\theta^{-2}}{12} & \text{if } s_i a_i > s_j a_j \\ 0 & \text{otherwise} \end{cases} \tag{13.18}$$

In this model, it is socially efficient for the incumbent to always work on the issue with the highest need (a_i). However, the politician instead works on the issue with the highest news-exposed need ($s_i a_i$). This is the multitasking problem.

We now analyze what issues the media will cover. Suppose that a monopoly media is covering the two issues. This media selects price and political coverage of the two political jurisdictions to maximize its expected profits

$$\max_{p,\rho} \sum_{i=1}^{2} n_i(p - d_i)x_i - \frac{1}{2}(\rho_1 + \rho_2)^2,$$

and the demand for newspapers is again determined by Equation (13.8) for each separate group.

Assuming concavity, its maximum is characterized by the first-order conditions

$$p = d + xg^{-1}(x),$$
(13.19)

$$\rho_i = \begin{cases} n(p - d_i)T_i & \text{if } n_i(p - d_i)T_i \geq n_j(p - d_j)T_j \\ 0 & \text{otherwise} \end{cases}.$$
(13.20)

The media only covers one issue. Media coverage of an issue is increasing in n_i, d_i, and T_i. As discussed, if the monopoly media is a price taker in the advertising market, then $p - d_i$ is replaced by $p_s + p_a - d_i$, where p_s is the subscription price and p_a is the advertising price per media user. We have the following result.

Proposition 13.3

The media coverage of issues that concern group i, and consequently political effort and competence, is greater if: (a) group i is larger; (b) it has a larger advertising potential; or (c) the issue is more journalistically newsworthy; and (d) it is inexpensive to distribute news to that group.

Because the media will only inform voters about one issue, the politician will exclusively work on this. Proposition 13.3 characterizes how the media direct the multitasking problem. It provides predictions for what issues will receive too much attention and resources, relative to the welfare-maximizing benchmark if mass media are the main information providers. Strömberg (1999, 2004b) discusses the welfare losses induced by this type of bias in more detail.

13.2.3 Optimal Regulation and Public Provision of News

We now return to the case with only one group. A social planner maximizes

$$n\int_0^x p(\rho, z)dz - c(\rho, x) + nx\rho W,$$

where the first two terms describe the consumer utility and the producer cost, and the last term is the value of the externality $\theta - T = W$. The first-order conditions are

$$p^{sp} = d - \rho^{sp} W, \qquad (13.21)$$

$$\rho^{sp} = nx^{sp}\theta. \qquad (13.22)$$

Assuming again that G is a uniform distribution on $[-1/2, 1/2]$:

$$x^{sp} = \left(\frac{1}{2} - d\right)\frac{1}{1 - n\theta^2}, \qquad (13.23)$$

$$\rho^{sp} = \left(\frac{1}{2} - d\right)\frac{n\theta}{1 - n\theta^2}. \qquad (13.24)$$

The above can be compared to the market solution; see Equations (13.11) and (13.12).

The social planner sets a price p^{sp} that is below the marginal cost, d; see Equation (13.21). This Pigouvian subsidy compensates for the positive externality of an informed citizenry. Absent the subsidy, consumers have too low a valuation of news and news consumption will be too low. The social planner also supplies more political coverage, ρ^{sp}, than the market solution; see Equations (13.22) and (13.10). This is because the social planner internalizes the positive externality of news on political accountability ($\theta > T$), and because the higher consumption level increases the marginal social benefit of coverage ($x^{sp} > x^m$).

One question is how the social planner solution could be implemented. Disregarding the market power effect, a subsidy to the media firm equaling $nx\rho W$ would correct the market failure. This subsidy is proportional to the size of the audience of the informative content, nx, which will induce the media firm to lower its price to attract audience. This could be achieved by explicitly lowering the subscription or pay-per-view price, or by reducing advertising (lowering the consumers' nuisance cost). The subsidy is also increasing in the informativeness of the content, ρ. This will induce the media firm to increase its political coverage. To reach the social optimum, an additional output subsidy to correct for the market power effect, of size $xg^{-1}(x)$, is needed.

Note that we achieve two goals by a subsidy of size $nx\rho W$. This subsidy increases both the media consumption and political coverage because the subsidy is increasing in both these targets. Just regulating a fixed low subscription price will increase the suboptimally low consumption, but will reduce political coverage (quality) even further. This is because the lower price reduces the incentives to invest in quality (Sheshinski, 1976; Spence, 1975). Similarly, just setting a fixed quality standard, $\rho = \rho^{sp}$, would lead the monopolist to over-price, thus making media consumption too low.

An alternative solution is public service media. A first question is whether voters would like to implement the social planner solution.

People internalize the social value of media coverage as voters, although they do not as consumers. To see this, suppose that public media provision and financing are voted upon in a separate election. Suppose that the public media is financed by a license fee, which is a lump-sum tax on all voters, and a subscription price as before.[2] Let L be the license fee set so that this fee and the subscription revenue cover the cost of running the public service media,

$$nL + npx = C(\rho, x).$$

If there is no heterogeneity among voters at the time of the election over public service media, then voter utility will be perfectly aligned with social welfare. This follows since the voter utility from government policies and media is

$$E\left[g_1 + g_2 + u_{pb} - L | p, \rho\right],$$

where u_{pb} is the utility from watching public media, which is

$$T_i\left(a_j = g_1\right) + \gamma_j - p$$

if the voter watches and zero otherwise. Since the license fee is $L = (1/n)C(\rho, x) - px$, and since the *ex ante* probability of watching public media is x, this simplifies to the social planner's problem.

Proposition 13.4 describes the optimal media policy and how market provision and public media provision relate to this policy.

Proposition 13.4

(a) Because of a positive externality from news consumption, the market solution produces less than optimal levels of news consumption and political coverage.

(b) Optimal media policy can be achieved by public service media or by regulation. Optimal media regulation involves a Pigouvian subsidy equal in size to the positive externality from news consumption, combined with a subsidy to counter markup due to market power. The size of the Pigouvian subsidy is increasing in the amount of political coverage and in the audience of this coverage.

(c) As voters, people internalize the consumption externality. Under a veil of ignorance, they prefer the socially optimal media policies. These policies are hence not paternalistic.

Below, we will present mounting empirical evidence that the media play a key role in enhancing political accountability. Because one voter's consumption of news affects the quality of political selection and incentives, which benefits all voters, this creates an externality to news consumption. Given this, the market under provision of news follows from

---

[2] The license fee is modeled on the BBC's annual television license fee, which is charged to all British households, companies, and organizations using any type of equipment to receive live television broadcasts.

standard economic theory. This has been argued at least since Downs's (1957) model of rational ignorance. The explicit modeling of this externality helps us describe the nature of the problem and the optimal regulation to solve it.

Should this be implemented by regulated private firms or by public service media? The generic arguments from Hart et al. (1997) apply. An argument in favor of public service media is that the amount and informativeness of political coverage are hard to observe and hence in some dimensions non-contractible. Private providers are likely to save costs by reducing quality in these dimensions. There are two main arguments against public service media. One is that these may not be independent of the politicians they are supposed to monitor and hence will not be able to fulfill their role in enhancing political accountability. The public service implementation thus requires a strong *de facto* independence. The second argument is that the media sector is rapidly evolving and that quality innovation is important. Private providers are likely to have stronger economic incentives to innovate.

13.3. EVIDENCE

I now discuss empirical evidence related to the positive implications of the above theory, summarized in Propositions 13.1 and 13.2. Before going into the substantive results, I briefly discuss different strategies used to identify media effects. The share of informed voters is affected by media consumption and the amount of informative media coverage. Studies of media effects typically use variation in one of these factors.

I start with effects of media consumption. These effects are probably most easily measured when new media are introduced. Mass media are not neutral devices, uniformly distributing information to everyone. Rather, each of the large mass media creates its specific distribution of informed and uninformed citizens, partly because of its specific costs and revenue structure. As a result, in the wake of mass-media technology changes, there are dramatic changes in who has access to political information.

Because new media may crowd out consumption of older media, the effects depend on their relative informativeness. Chapter 19 in this volume discuss similar crowding-out effects for other outcomes. Recall from Equation (13.7) that the share of informed voters, s, is the share x that consumes the media, multiplied by the share ρ that finds the news, conditional on consuming, $s = x\rho$. The share that finds the news in turn depends on the amount of news coverage q, but we suppress that notation here and simply refer to ρ as the media's informativeness.

Suppose that media B enters in a market with the pre-existing media A. Let x^B denote consumers of media B that previously did not use any media, x^{AB} consumers who move from A to B, and x^A consumers who stay with A. Let ρ_t^J be the informativeness of media $J = A, B$, before and after entry, $t = 1, 2$. The change in the share of informed voters is

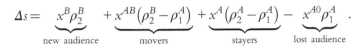

$$\Delta s = \underbrace{x^B \rho_2^B}_{\text{new audience}} + \underbrace{x^{AB}\left(\rho_2^B - \rho_1^A\right)}_{\text{movers}} + \underbrace{x^A\left(\rho_2^A - \rho_1^A\right)}_{\text{stayers}} - \underbrace{x^{A0}\rho_1^A}_{\text{lost audience}} \ .$$

Audiences that did not previously use mass media, x^B, become better informed. This is the obvious case to look for positive media effects. For example, in the 1920s many people in rural America did not have access to a daily newspaper because these were too costly to deliver to remote areas. Radio provided these people with access to a daily mass media. Hence, we would expect the introduction of the radio to have a positive impact on voter information levels in these areas.

For audiences that switch media, x^{AB}, the effect depends on $\rho_2^B - \rho_1^A$, the relative informativeness of the new media post-entry to the old media pre-entry. From Proposition 13.2, we would expect this informativeness to depend on audience shares, advertising revenues, etc. For example, a small share of the audience of the *New York Times* or a TV station is likely to care about any particular congressional district. Hence, they will not cover local politics to any considerable extent and their entry into a market dominated by a local newspaper may lower voter information levels on this topic.

For audiences that stay with the pre-existing media, x^A, the effect depends on the change in informativeness of this media. As discussed, entry and the resulting increase in competition could lead existing media to cover politics more or less. Evidence presented below supports more the latter. Finally, the change in content could cause a share x^{A0} viewers to stop using mass media altogether.

This lost audience becomes less informed. Media consumption is often instrumented because it is related to factors such as income and education that are directly related to political behavior and influence. Strömberg (1999, 2004a) measures the effects of the introduction of radio across US counties from 1920 to 1940, instrumented by factors affecting the quality of reception (ground conductivity and share of woodland). Gentzkow (2006) studies the introduction of television, instrumented by distance to a TV antenna. Olken (2009) improves this instrumentation by taking into account the topography between the antenna and the receiver. Falck et al. (2014) study the introduction of broadband Internet in Germany, instrumented using technical thresholds in the distance to a main distribution frame. The introduction of individual media has also been used. For example, DellaVigna and Kaplan (2007) study the entry of Fox News in cable markets, and Gentzkow et al. (2011) and Cage (2014) study the entry and exit of individual newspapers in markets in the United States and France, respectively.

Other strategies have been developed to identify effects of media coverage, holding media consumption fixed. One cannot credibly identify effects by regressing outcomes on media coverage because this coverage is endogenous. Media tend to cover issues and politicians that are more important, and to cover politics more in areas where consumers are more interested in politics. To identify the effects of the total coverage of politics, Snyder and Strömberg (2010) use exogenous variation in the match between media markets and political jurisdictions, as discussed below. Other studies use randomized controlled trials. Banerjee et al.'s (2011) random sample of slums in a large Indian city received newspapers containing report cards with information on the performance of the incumbent legislator and the qualifications of the incumbent and two main challengers. This randomization affects both media consumption and content.

To identify the effects of particular news stories, Eisensee and Strömberg (2007) use the crowding out of news stories by other news. In particular, they use crowding out of news coverage of natural disasters by coverage of the Olympic Games.

13.3.1 Volume of Coverage

I will first discuss how coverage of politics is affected by two factors: audience size and competition. The above theory predicts that political news coverage will also be increasing in the size of the advertising market, in issue newsworthiness, and falling in delivery costs (Propositions 13.2 and 13.3). These other determinants will be discussed in Section 13.3.5 on multitasking.

Evidence suggests that media competition reduces the volume of political coverage. The most convincing evidence is perhaps that provided by Cage (2014). She studies a county-level panel dataset of local newspapers in France, from 1945 to 2012. She finds that newspaper competition is associated with fewer journalists and news articles in counties with homogeneous populations, with little impact on counties with heterogeneous populations. In a cross-sectional study of coverage of US congressmen, Arnold (2004) finds that newspapers with at least one competing daily paper published fewer articles about its local representative than did a monopoly newspaper, controlling for newspaper circulation and the number of representatives in a newspaper's core circulation area.

As discussed above, standard economic theory does not provide any clear prediction on this issue. The lower political coverage under competition could arise because the greater scale economies for monopolies are more important than the higher demand elasticity under competition. Competition may also affect the amount of political news for other reasons. Cage (2014) argues that competing newspapers may differentiate in quality to avoid price competition. Zaller (1999) argues that it is good for the individual careers of journalists to cover politics; this can help them win awards and recognition among colleagues. Competition forces journalists to instead focus on audience demands.

We next turn to the effect of audience size on political coverage. It may seem obvious that audience size affects coverage. We will still discuss evidence quantifying these effects because they are such central drivers of coverage. Audience size effects are important because they may harm the interest of fragmented audiences, such as minority groups scattered across media markets. Audience size effects are also important to understand the effects of the introduction of new media technologies.

The audience shares of ethnic groups have been related to media coverage and entry (George and Waldfogel, 2003; Oberholzer-Gee and Waldfogel, 2009; Siegelman and

Waldfogel, 2001). Audience effects are also central in the strategy used by Snyder and Strömberg (2010) to identify media effects. They analyze the effects of media coverage on US congressional politics. They note that the match or congruence between media markets and political districts drives the media coverage of congressional politics. Congruence is based on the share of a newspaper m's readership that lives in a certain congressional district d, called the *ReaderShare$_{md}$*. Newspaper coverage of a congressman should be increasing in this readership share. Since more than one newspaper is sold in each district, they define congruence as the market-share weighted average *ReaderShare$_{md}$* for all newspapers sold in a district.

To illustrate the concept, suppose that there are two media, A and B. Media A's market covers district 1 and media B's market covers district 2 (see the left-hand image in Figure 13.1a). In this case, *ReaderShare$_{md}$* is 1 for both papers, and congruence is high (1). Suppose instead that the two monopoly newspapers, A and B, are located in two cities on the border between the political districts. Each media has half of its audience in each political district (see the right-hand image in Figure 13.1a). In this case, *ReaderShare$_{md}$* is one-half for both papers and congruence is low (one-half).

They first document the relationship between congruence and coverage. They study coverage of US House representatives in 161 newspapers covering 385 districts in each congress from 1991 to 2002. Their measure of the amount of coverage of the representative from district i is the number of articles mentioning the representative's name. This was found by searching online editions of the newspapers. On average, the newspapers write 101 articles about each congressman in each 2-year congressional period. They estimate that an increase in congruence from 0 to 1 is associated with 170 more articles written about the congressman.

13.3.2 Voters

13.3.2.1 Information

In the above model, media matter because they provide voters with information relevant for political accountability. I now discuss evidence of this. That the media provide voters with this type of information seems *a priori* likely. Knowing who is responsible for what policy to what effect is quite remote from the experience of most people. Hence, citizens in large societies are dependent on others for most of their political information, such as political campaigns and the mass media. Of these possible sources, survey respondents regularly cite mass media as their main source of political information.

Evidence on learning from news media (Proposition 13.1i) consistently finds significant effects. In their classic study, Berelson et al. (1954) found that voters with high media exposure learned more during the electoral campaigns of 1940 and 1948 than other voters. Naturally, it could be that voters who used media more were more interested in politics and learned more directly from the campaign and from personal interactions. Therefore, the effect of newspapers may be hard to identify. These selection

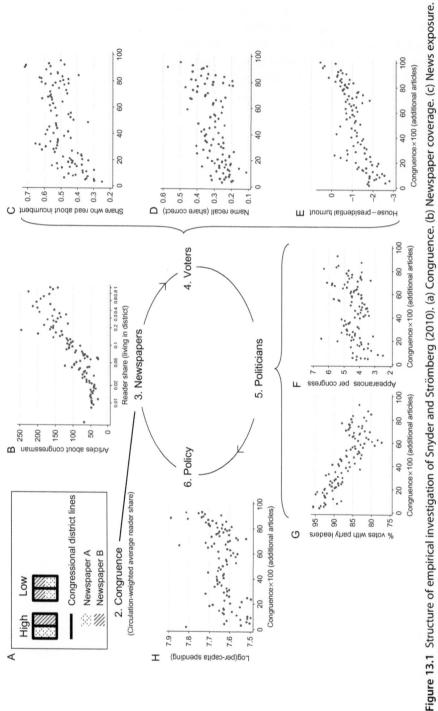

Figure 13.1 Structure of empirical investigation of Snyder and Strömberg (2010). (a) Congruence. (b) Newspaper coverage. (c) News exposure. (d) Information. (e) Turnout. (f) Witness appearances. (g) Party loyalty. (h) Federal spending per capita. *Figure produced with permission from Snyder and Strömberg (2010).*

issues are avoided in laboratory studies (e.g., Neuman et al., 1992; Norris and Sanders, 2003) that find that people learn from watching news in a laboratory. However, it is hard to generalize these results to the effects of years of daily media exposure on voters' knowledge or choices on Election Day.

Snyder and Strömberg (2010) argue that some variation in the congruence discussed above is exogenous and can be used to identify media effects. One specification investigates the consequences of the changing congruence between media markets and congressional districts due to redrawing of the district lines. For example, a newspaper's coverage of a congressman may fall because part of its readers are moved to a different congressional district. Remaining newspaper readers hence get less relevant news about their congressman. Another specification compares differences across counties in the same congressional district and year to identify effects.

Snyder and Strömberg find that local newspapers are key providers of political information. They analyze survey responses from the American National Election Studies 1984–2004, and find that voters are considerably better informed about their representatives in areas where, for the exogenous reasons explained above, the newspapers cover the House representatives more. More precisely, they are better able to correctly name at least one of the candidates in the House election. Figure 13.1d plots the bivariate version of this relationship. They are also more willing to place their representative ideologically, to rate their feelings toward the representative, and mention things that they like or dislike about their representative. The share who can correctly name the House representative increases by 1% for every four exogenous additional newspaper articles about the representative. These estimates suggest that the share who can name their representative would drop from 31% to 15% without newspaper coverage.

Snyder and Strömberg find that people do not learn significantly about their House representative from radio or TV. This could be because local television stations do not cover congressmen to any considerable extent. Prat and Strömberg (2013) study the effects of the entry of commercial TV in Sweden. They find that people who start watching commercial TV increase their level of political knowledge and political participation more than others.

13.3.2.2 Responsiveness

A key role of political information in the above model is to increase voter responsiveness (Proposition 13.1ii): information enables voters to identify and punish politicians that are bad for them, and reward good politicians and policies. This creates good incentives and selection.

Media effects on voter responsiveness have been studied in a couple of papers. Ferraz and Finan (2008) find that radio increased voters' responsiveness to information about corruption among Brazilian mayors. Voters in places with a local radio station punished more mayors who were more corrupt than average and rewarded more mayors who were less corrupt than average.

Larreguy et al. (2014) study the effect of media on Mexican voters' responsiveness to municipal audit reports. Similarly to Ferraz and Finan, they compare mayors who engage in malfeasant behavior that is revealed in audit reports published in the year before an election to similar mayors whose audit reports are not published until after the election. They use within-municipality variation in the electoral precincts that are covered by radio and television stations located within the municipality and that, consequently, cover the relevant audit reports to a larger extent. They find that voters punish the party of malfeasant mayors, but only in electoral precincts covered by local media stations.

Banerjee et al. (2011) find similar results in India. In the run-up to elections, residents in a random sample of slums in a large Indian city received newspapers containing report cards with information on the performance of the incumbent legislator and the qualifications of the incumbent and two main challengers. Relative to the control slums, treatment slums saw a higher turnout, reduced vote buying, and a higher vote share for better performing incumbents and relatively more qualified incumbents.

The media coverage of a particular issue can also increase the voter responsiveness on that issue. This is a prediction of the above model (Proposition 13.1bii) and also a key prediction of the agenda-setting and priming theories of media influence. A very extensive literature tests the agenda-setting and priming hypotheses (see, e.g., Dearing and Rogers, 1996).

13.3.2.3 Political Participation

Although not part of our theoretical framework, I now discuss evidence of media effects on voter turnout. For most people, voting is the main form of political participation. A high voter turnout may be desirable for a number of reasons. Voting is an effective means of holding elected officials accountable for their decisions and behavior in office. A high turnout in fair elections gives legitimacy to public officials and their decisions, while abstention may erode citizens' satisfaction and confidence. It is *a priori* plausible that media influence voter turnout because they provide information and may increase the strength of political preferences and interest in politics.

Strömberg (1999, 2004a) measures the effects of the introduction of radio in the period 1920–1940 on voter turnout. He finds that increased radio consumption led to more people voting in gubernatorial races. Quantitatively, an increase in the share of households with radios from 0 to 1 is estimated to have increased the turnout by 7 percentage points in the 1920–1940 period. The effects are particularly pronounced in rural areas where the prior newspaper readership was low, due to high newspaper delivery costs. In a study of the effects of the introduction of television in the 1940s and 1950s, Gentzkow (2006) finds that television reduced the turnout in congressional races by 2%.[3] He argues that this was because TV was less informative than the newspaper consumption that it crowded out. Looking at the introduction of individual news media, Oberholzer-Gee and Waldfogel (2009) find that a Spanish-language local television station increases the turnout among Hispanics in a metro area by 5–10 percentage points. Gentzkow et al. (2011) study the entry and exit of US newspapers from 1869 to 2004. They find that one extra newspaper is associated with an increase in voter turnout of 0.3%.

A couple of recent papers also study the effects of high-speed Internet on voting. Falck et al. (2014) find negative effects of Internet broadband access on voter turnout, which they relate to a crowding-out of more informative TV consumption and increased entertainment consumption. In a similar study, Campante et al. (2013) find that broadband access initially decreased the turnout in parliamentary elections, but then increased it after 2008, when local online protest groups coalesced into a new electoral list. Broadband access was positively associated with other forms of political participation, both online and offline.

These effects depend on whether the new media are more informative than the old ones that they replace. Snyder and Strömberg (2010) instead look at variation in the amount of informative content. They find that exogenously increased media coverage of politics increases voter turnout. The effects are small, perhaps because when people vote for Congress, they typically also vote for more important offices such as president and this drives people to the polls. See Figure 13.1e for the bivariate relationship between congruence and turnout.

13.3.3 Politicians

We now discuss effects on politicians. Our theory suggests that both media consumption and coverage will improve the political selection as well as the incentives (Proposition 13.1iii).

Snyder and Strömberg (2010) find that media coverage affects politicians' behavior. US congressmen from districts where media coverage is high, for exogenous reasons, are less ideologically extreme, vote more frequently against the party leaders, are more likely to stand witness before congressional hearings, and they are, perhaps, more likely to serve on constituency-oriented committees and also less likely to serve on broad policy-oriented committees. This was found after analyzing data on roll-call voting, committee assignments, and witness appearances for 1982–2004. See Figure 13.1f and g for the bivariate relationship between congruence and these outcomes.[4]

---

[3] This is for years with no simultaneous presidential election.

[4] Congressmen may work for their constituency, for example, by considering constituency (rather than party) interests in voting, and by appearing as witnesses before congressional hearings.

The effects seem to work through both incentives and selection (by studying whether the actions of the same politician change over time with press coverage, they can separately identify the incentive effects). Snyder and Strömberg find that selection effects are entirely responsible for the ideological moderation in roll-call voting, whereas incentive effects are entirely responsible for the increase in witness appearances. Effects on votes against party leadership are a mix of the two. These results make sense, since we would expect selection effects for preferences and constant characteristics (competence in the model and ideology in this example) and incentive effects for variables that capture effort (effort in the model and witness appearances in this example). In terms of magnitudes, their estimates imply that an exogenous increase of about 110 newspaper articles about the House representative is associated with one additional witness appearance, and there is one additional vote against the party leadership per every four exogenous additional newspaper articles about the House representative.

13.3.4 Policy

We have presented evidence that mass media inform voters, and that this information increases both voter turnout and voter responsiveness. This, in turn, improves political incentives and selection. We now finally present evidence that this affects policies. We look at three types of media variation: variation in the access to media; the volume of political coverage; and the coverage of particular events.

13.3.4.1 Who Gets the News?

Are voters with media access better able to hold their representatives accountable, and do they consequently receive better policy outcomes? We will now investigate the hypothesis in Proposition 13.1aiii that public expenditures are increasing in the share of media users in a group.

As mentioned, Strömberg (1999, 2004a) measures the effects of the introduction of radio in the US in the period 1920–1940. Interestingly, this was also an era of rapid changes in economic policymaking. The New Deal was launched in the middle of the radio's expansion period. Strömberg finds that access to radio increased federal spending in the New Deal programs. The effects are economically important. The estimates of this study imply that a one standard deviation increase in the share of households with radios in a certain county would lead the governor to increase per-capita relief spending by 9%. The spread of radio particularly improved the situation of rural voters, accounting for as much as 20% more in social assistance funds to a rural county than an identical urban county. The results are robust to instrumenting radio ownership with exogenous factors that affect the quality of reception: ground conductivity and the share of woodland.

Besley and Burgess (2002) study how the responsiveness of policy to need is affected by media consumption (Proposition 13.1aiv). They study public food distribution and calamity relief in a panel of Indian states (1958–1992). Their main finding is that the interaction term between newspaper circulation and measures of need for relief is positive. This means that spending correlates more with the need in states where many have access to newspapers, in other words that spending is more responsive to need in states with a high newspaper circulation. The results are driven by the circulation of newspapers in local languages (other than Hindi and English). A potential concern is that states with a high circulation of newspapers are different, for example by having a more politically interested and active population. Consequently, the authors instrument newspaper circulation with the share of newspapers that are owned by political parties, societies, and individuals. After instrumentation, the key results remain or become stronger.

13.3.4.2 Volume and Focus of Political Coverage

Our theory suggests that not only media consumption but also media coverage affects government spending (Proposition 13.1biii). We first discuss evidence of the effect of total coverage of politics and the effects of what issues are covered.

As mentioned, Snyder and Strömberg's (2010) study finds that political coverage increases voter information, voter turnout, and the selection and incentives of politicians. The final question is whether the additional effort and better selection of politicians are noticeable in public spending. Snyder and Strömberg find that more federal funds per capita were allocated to areas where the media covered their representative to a larger extent. The estimated effects are substantial. A one standard deviation increase in congruence (which is associated with around 50 additional articles per congress) increases per-capita federal spending by 3%. See Figure 13.1h for the bivariate relationship between congruence and this outcome. Similarly, Lim et al. (2015) study the effect of newspaper coverage of US state-trial-court judges, using the congruence between judicial districts and newspaper markets to identify effects. They find that press coverage significantly increases the sentence length.

13.3.4.2.1 What Issues Are Covered?

Not only the volume but also the distribution of coverage may influence policy. This is important to investigate empirically because excessive coverage of certain topics may distract political attention from more socially important tasks.

Can a news editor, by publishing a particular news story, influence government policy? This is the main hypothesis investigated in the agenda-setting research on policy effects. This research typically performs case studies, or studies the co-movement over time in coverage of an issue in the media, the importance the public attaches to the issue and some policy outcome; see Dearing and Rogers (1996). However, convincing evidence of media effects is hard to establish from these types of correlations. More severe issues are both likely to be in the news and receive policy attention, and it is very hard to convincingly control for severity. In addition, political agendas might drive both media coverage and policy, thus creating a reverse causality problem.

In an attempt to address this problem, Eisensee and Strömberg (2007) analyze the effect of natural disasters being covered because not much other news is around. The idea is that some marginally newsworthy disasters will not be covered in the news because they occur when many competing news stories are available, for example from the Olympic Games. Others are covered because they occur when few alternative stories are available. However, disasters striking during the Olympics will be similar in all other respects to disasters striking at the same time of the year in non-Olympic years.

Eisensee and Strömberg find that the Olympic Games crowd out news coverage of natural disasters and that this decreases the probability of US government relief. They find similar effects using a more general measure of the amount of other available news (the time spent on the top three news stories). The conclusion is that news coverage has a causal effect on relief. Specifically, they study relief from the United States Agency for International Development (USAID) Office of Foreign Disaster Assistance (OFDA) to 5212 natural disasters taking place worldwide between 1968 and 2002. This is combined with data on whether the disaster was covered by the US television network news. They used the Vanderbilt Television News Archives, which has compiled data on the content of the evening news broadcasts of the major US television networks (ABC, CBS, and NBC) since 1968 and CNN since the 1990s.

13.3.5 Multitasking

Proposition 13.2 and Strömberg (2004b) identify policy biases generated by the news-making process, related to group size, newsworthiness, advertiser target group, and media access. I now discuss empirical evidence of these.

13.3.5.1 Audience Share Bias

This is probably the most well-documented type of bias. Media tend to focus their coverage on issues that concern a large share of their audience (which is not perfectly collinear with group size). Politically, this may hurt small groups, such as minorities and special interests, and favor large groups, such as majority ethnic groups and dispersed consumer interests.

A difficulty in empirically identifying the effects of group size is that many factors vary with group size (other than media coverage). An area with many Hispanics is more likely to have a Spanish-language local TV news show. But it is also likely to be different in many other respects, for example having a strong local Hispanic community and connected organizations.

Is it possible to vary the audience size of a group while holding the total population of the group fixed? Consider the setting in Snyder and Strömberg (2010). House districts have approximately the same population, but can differ in size measured by audience size. This is because audience size depends on what papers people buy. Suppose that people in one area of a House district read newspapers that mainly sell outside of their district.

Because they constitute a small share of the audience share of these newspapers, their representative will receive little coverage. We know from Snyder and Strömberg (2010) that people in these types of areas are less well informed, vote less, and receive less public spending. This is direct evidence of an audience size bias in policy.

There is also evidence that where ethnic groups are small, there will be less targeted media and the minority consumption of media will be low and, consequently, the voter turnout will be low (George and Waldfogel, 2003; Oberholzer-Gee and Waldfogel, 2009; Siegelman and Waldfogel, 2001).

Assuming that there is no pre-existing policy bias, the model of Strömberg (2004b) shows that the audience size effect biases policy against the interest of small groups. However, absent mass media, small special interest groups may have an information advantage in relation to dispersed consumer groups. The audience size effect may counter this disadvantage. Therefore, the expanding use of mass media may have reduced the influence of lobby groups. Dyck et al. (2008) investigate this. They find that the more the McClure magazine (one of the most prominent muckraking magazines of that era) sold in a House representative's district, the more pro-consumer was the representative's voting on legislation that was muckraked in the McClure magazine. A potential concern is that the areas where the demand for the McClure magazine is high are different also in other respects.

13.3.5.2 Media Access Bias
There is also relatively strong evidence that people with access to media receive better policies (Besley and Burgess, 2002; Strömberg, 1999, 2004a). The other side of the coin is that voters without access to media risk are being neglected by politicians. This may be of particular concern to poor voters in developing countries, whose lack of access to media could hinder their access to public services (Keefer and Khemani, 2005). The most direct evidence of this is perhaps Reinikka and Svensson (2005), who find that schools to which it was cheaper to deliver newspapers, because they were closer to a newspaper outlet, received more government funds. In this way, newspaper provision of news may produce a political bias disfavoring remote and rural areas.

13.3.5.3 Newsworthiness Bias
There is some evidence that journalistically newsworthy issues receive disproportionate policy attention. Eisensee and Strömberg (2007) estimate that $46 \times$ as many people must be killed in a disaster in Africa to achieve the same probability of being covered by US television network news as an otherwise similar disaster in Eastern Europe. Because they find that news coverage triggers relief, they conclude that this biases US relief against African disaster victims. Similarly, a drought must have $2395 \times$ as many casualties as a volcano to have the same estimated probability of coverage, potentially biasing US relief.

13.3.5.4 Target Group Bias

It seems likely that advertising biases increase the coverage of interest to groups valuable to advertisers and that, consequently, this biases policy in favor of these groups. However, there is less supporting evidence. The literature is still struggling to uncover the first stage of this effect: that media coverage is shaped to target the interest of this group. For example, Hamilton (2005) correlates the number of news stories on 20 issues on each of the networks with the share of different demographic groups that consider that the issue should be the president's top priority. He finds that the news selection correlates most with the interests of young viewers. He notes that this might be because advertisers target marginal consumers, for example the young with less stable purchasing behavior. Although plausible, there is little convincing evidence that groups that are valuable to advertisers benefit politically from media provision of news.

13.4. CONCLUSION

The existing evidence on media effects surveyed in this paper seems to support the following general statements about the political effects of mass media.

There are strong theoretical reasons to believe that the market under-supplies political news. This is because of an empirically documented positive externality from the consumption of political news on political accountability. Socially optimal news provision can be induced by a subsidy that is increasing in both the informativeness of the news media and in the size of the audience attending the news. It can also be achieved by public service media.

Media scrutiny increases the political accountability, which appears to improve policy. A number of surveyed studies find that an increase in media activity is associated with better policy outcomes, some of which use methods that reasonably convincingly identify causal media effects. There is some evidence that these media effects occur because the media transmit information to voters, which improves both the incentives and the selection of politicians.

A caveat to the positive effects is that the media may sometimes induce politicians to work on the wrong issues. Media provision of news systematically benefits groups that are large as audience shares, groups that care about newsworthy issues, and groups to which it is cheap to deliver news. Theory suggests that media also benefit groups that are more valuable to advertisers. However, there is little empirical evidence to this effect.

REFERENCES

Anderson, S.P., McLaren, J., 2012. Media mergers and media bias with rational consumers. J. Eur. Econ. Assoc. 10 (4), 831–859.
Anderson, S.P., De Palma, A., Thisse, J.F., 1992. Discrete Choice Theory of Product Differentiation. MIT Press, Cambridge, MA.

Arnold, R.D., 2004. Congress, the Press, and Political Accountability. Princeton University Press, Princeton, NJ.

Banerjee, A.V., Kumar, S., Pande, R., Su, F., 2011. Do Informed Voters Make Better Choices? Experimental Evidence from Urban India. Harvard University. Unpublished Manuscript.

Berelson, B., Lazarsfeld, P., McPhee, W.N., 1954. Voting: A Study of Opinion Formation in a Presidential Campaign. Chicago University Press, Chicago, IL.

Besley, T., Burgess, R., 2001. Political agency, government responsiveness and the role of the media. Eur. Econ. Rev. 45 (4), 629–640.

Besley, T., Burgess, R.S.L., 2002. The political economy of government responsiveness: theory and evidence from India. Q. J. Econ. 117 (4), 1415–1451.

Besley, T., Prat, A., 2006. Handcuffs for the grabbing hand? The role of the media in political accountability. Am. Econ. Rev. 96 (3), 720–736.

Cage, J., 2014. Media Competition, Information Provision and Political Participation. Harvard University. Unpublished Manuscript.

Campante, F.R., Durante, R., Sobbrio, F., 2013. Politics 2.0: The Multifaceted Effect of Broadband Internet on Political Participation. No. w19029, National Bureau of Economic Research.

Chan, J., Suen, W., 2008. A spatial theory of news consumption and electoral competition. Rev. Econ. Stud. 75 (3), 699–728.

Dearing, J.W., Rogers, E.M., 1996. Agenda Setting. SAGE Publication, Inc., Thousands Oaks, CA.

DellaVigna, S., Kaplan, E., 2007. The fox news effect: media bias and voting. Q. J. Econ. 122, 1187–1234.

Downs, A., 1957. An Economic Theory of Democracy. Harper Collins, New York, NY.

Dyck, A., Moss, D., Zingales, L., 2008. Media versus special interests. J. Law Econ. 56 (3), 521–553.

Eisensee, T., Strömberg, D., 2007. News floods, news droughts, and U.S. disaster relief. Q. J. Econ. 122 (2), 693–728.

Falck, O., Gold, R., Heblich, S., 2014. E-Lections: Voting Behavior and the Internet. CESIFO Working Paper No. 3827.

Ferraz, C., Finan, F., 2008. Exposing corrupt politicians: the effects of Brazil's publicly released audits on electoral outcomes. Q. J. Econ. 123 (2), 703–745.

Gentzkow, M., 2006. Television and voter turnout. Q. J. Econ. 121 (3), 931–972.

Gentzkow, M., Shapiro, J.M., Sinkinson, M., 2011. The effect of newspaper entry and exit on electoral politics. Am. Econ. Rev. 101 (7), 2980–3018.

George, L., Waldfogel, J., 2003. Who affects whom in daily newspaper markets? J. Polit. Econ. 111 (4), 765–784.

Hamilton, J.T., 2005. The Market and the Media. Oxford University Press, New York, NY.

Hart, O., Shleifer, A., Vishny, R.W., 1997. The proper scope of government: theory and an application to prisons. Q. J. Econ. 112 (4), 1127–1161.

Holmström, B., Milgrom, P., 1991. Multitask principal–agent analyses: incentive contracts, asset ownership, and job design. J. Law Econ. Org. 1991 (7), 24–52.

Keefer, P., Khemani, S., 2005. Democracy, public expenditures, and the poor: understanding political incentives for providing public services. World Bank Res. Obs. 20 (1), 1–27.

Larcinese, V., 2007. The instrumental voter goes to the newsagent. J. Theor. Polit. 19 (2007), 249–276.

Larreguy, H.A., Marshall, J., Snyder Jr., J.M., 2014. Revealing Malfeasance: How Local Media Facilitates Electoral Sanctioning of Mayors in Mexico. No. w20697, National Bureau of Economic Research.

Lim, C.S.H., Snyder Jr., J.M., Strömberg, D. The judge, the politician, and the press: newspaper coverage and criminal sentencing across electoral systems. Am. Econ. J. Appl. Econ. (forthcoming).

Merton, R.C., 1987. A simple model of capital market equilibrium with incomplete information. J. Financ. 42, 483–510.

Neuman, W.R., Just, M.R., Crigler, A.N., 1992. Common Knowledge: News and the Construction of Political Meaning. University of Chicago Press, Chicago, IL.

Norris, P., Sanders, D., 2003. Message or medium? Campaign learning during the 2001 British general election. Polit. Commun. 20, 233–262.

Oberholzer-Gee, F., Waldfogel, J., 2009. Media markets and localism: does local news en espanol boost Hispanic voter turnout? Am. Econ. Rev. 99 (5), 2120–2128.

Olken, B.A., 2009. Do television and radio destroy social capital? Evidence from Indonesian villages. Am. Econ. J. Appl. Econ. 1 (4), 1–33.

Prat, A., Strömberg, D., 2013. The political economy of mass media. In: Advances in Economics and Econometrics. Cambridge University Press, Cambridge.

Reddaway, W.B., 1963. The economics of newspapers. Econ. J. 73 (290), 201–218.

Reinikka, R., Svensson, J., 2005. Fighting corruption to improve schooling: evidence from a newspaper campaign in Uganda. J. Eur. Econ. Assoc. 3, 259–267.

Rosse, J., 1967. Daily newspapers, monopolistic competition, and economies of scale. Am. Econ. Rev. 57, 522–533., Retrieved from http://www.jstor.org/stable/1821652.

Shaked, A., Sutton, J., 1987. Product differentiation and industrial structure. J. Ind. Econ. XXXVI, 131–146.

Sheshinski, E., 1976. Price, quality and quantity regulation in monopoly situations. Economica 43, 127–137.

Siegelman, P., Waldfogel, J., 2001. Race and radio: preference externalities, minority ownership, and the provision of programming to minorities. Adv. Appl. Microecon. 10, 73–107.

Sims, C.A., 2003. Implications of rational inattention. J. Monet. Econ. 50 (3), 665–690.

Snyder, J.M., Strömberg, D., 2010. Press coverage and political accountability. J. Polit. Econ. 118 (2), 355–408.

Spence, A.M., 1975. Monopoly, quality, and regulation. Bell J. Econ. 6, 417–429.

Strömberg, D., 1999. The Political Economy of Public Spending. Princeton University. PhD Dissertation.

Strömberg, D., 2001. Mass media and public policy. Eur. Econ. Rev. 45, 652–663.

Strömberg, D., 2004a. Radios impact on public spending. Q. J. Econ. 119 (1), 189–221.

Strömberg, D., 2004b. Mass media competition, political competition, and public policy. Rev. Econ. Stud. 71 (1), 265–284.

Zaller, J., 1999. A Theory of Media Politics. Unpublished Manuscript.

CHAPTER 14

Media Bias in the Marketplace: Theory

Matthew Gentzkow*,†, Jesse M. Shapiro†,‡, Daniel F. Stone§
*Department of Economics, Stanford University, Palo Alto, CA, USA
†NBER, Cambridge, MA, USA
‡Department of Economics, Brown University, Providence, RI, USA
§Department of Economics, Bowdoin College, Brunswick, ME, USA

Contents

14.1. Introduction		624
14.2. What is Bias?		624
14.3. Bias and Welfare		627
14.4. A Model of the Market for News		628
14.5. Supply-Driven Bias		630
14.6. Demand-Driven Bias		633
	14.6.1 Delegation	634
	14.6.2 Psychological Utility	638
	14.6.3 Reputation	641
14.7. Conclusion		643
Acknowledgments		644
References		644

Abstract

We review the theoretical literature on market determinants of media bias. We present a theoretical framework that organizes key themes in the literature and discuss substantive lessons.

Kewords

Media bias, News bias, Media slant, Media competition, Polarization, Information transmission, Hotelling, Confirmation bias, Reputation, Blackwell

JEL Codes

L82, D82, D83, D72

Handbook of Media Economics, Volume 1B
ISSN 2213-6630, http://dx.doi.org/10.1016/B978-0-444-63685-0.00014-0

14.1. INTRODUCTION

In this chapter, we survey the theoretical literature on the market forces that determine equilibrium media bias.[1] We begin by defining bias formally and discussing its normative implications. We then introduce a simple model that we use to organize the literature on the determinants of bias, focusing first on supply-side forces such as political preferences of media owners and then turning to demand-side forces working through consumer beliefs and preferences.

Survey evidence suggests many people are skeptical that media provide voters with accurate, timely information about politics. Trust in media is low and falling (Ladd, 2012). People on each side of the political spectrum believe news reporting is biased in favor of the other (Alterman, 2003; Goldberg, 2001). Pew (2011) reports that 77% of survey respondents in the United States say news stories "tend to favor one side" and 63% of respondents agree news organizations are "politically biased in their reporting."

Empirical evidence discussed in detail in Chapter 15 shows that different media outlets indeed select, discuss, and present facts differently, and that they do so in ways that tend to systematically favor one side of the political spectrum or the other. These differences can have large effects on voter behavior, and thus political outcomes. Concerns about bias have been a central driver of media regulation (Brocas et al., 2011). Understanding the economic forces that determine media content is thus of first-order importance.

14.2. WHAT IS BIAS?

Gentzkow and Shapiro (2006) discuss the following example. On December 2, 2003, American troops fought a battle in the Iraqi city of Samarra. Fox News began its coverage of the event with the following paragraph:

> In one of the deadliest reported firefights in Iraq since the fall of Saddam Hussein's regime, US forces killed at least 54 Iraqis and captured eight others while fending off simultaneous convoy ambushes Sunday in the northern city of Samarra.

The *New York Times* article on the same event began:

> American commanders vowed Monday that the killing of as many as 54 insurgents in this central Iraqi town would serve as a lesson to those fighting the United States, but Iraqis disputed the death toll and said anger against America would only rise.

---

[1] Prat and Strömberg (2011), Andina-díaz (2011), and Sobbrio (2013) provide related surveys. See Zaller (1999), Sutter (2001), and Hamilton (2004) for earlier, less formal contributions that also cover some of the key related work from other fields (communications, sociology, and political science). An important related early work from economics is Steiner (1952).

And the English-language website of the satellite network Al Jazeera began:

> *The US military has vowed to continue aggressive tactics after saying it killed 54 Iraqis following an ambush, but commanders admitted they had no proof to back up their claims. The only corpses at Samarra's hospital were those of civilians, including two elderly Iranian visitors and a child.*

These three news outlets base their stories on the same events but manage to convey strikingly different impressions of what actually transpired. It is such systematic differences in the mapping from facts to news reports—that is, differences which tend to sway naive readers to the right or left on political issues—that we will call bias.[2]

Suppose that there is an unobserved state of the world $\theta \in \{L, R\}$, whose values we associate with outcomes favorable to the left and right sides of a one-dimensional political spectrum, respectively. Define the raw facts gathered by a news outlet to be a (possibly high-dimensional) random variable $s \in S$ whose distribution depends on θ, and define a news report by $n \in N$. A *reporting strategy* σ is a possibly stochastic mapping from S to N.

We define bias as a partial order on reporting strategies. We say a strategy σ is *biased to the right (left)* of σ' if, loosely speaking, a consumer who believed a firm's strategy was σ' would tend to shift her beliefs to the right (left) if the firm deviated to σ.

More precisely, let $\mu(n|\sigma)$ be a Bayesian consumer's posterior probability that the state is R when she observes n from a firm believed to be playing strategy σ. Let $\lambda(\tilde{\sigma}|\sigma)$ be the distribution of μ when a consumer believes a firm is playing σ and it actually plays $\tilde{\sigma}$. Say two reporting strategies σ and σ' are *consistent* if for each of them n has the same support (i.e., the set of n that can be reported is the same), and they preserve the relative meaning of reports (i.e., $\mu(n|\sigma) > \mu(n'|\sigma) \Leftrightarrow \mu(n|\sigma') > \mu(n'|\sigma')$ for any n, $n' \in N$). We say σ is biased to the right (left) of σ' if (i) σ and σ' are consistent and (ii) $\lambda(\sigma|\sigma')$ first-order stochastically dominates (is dominated by) $\lambda(\sigma'|\sigma')$. Note that this definition is symmetric in the sense that σ is biased to the right of σ' if and only if σ' is biased to the left of σ.

This definition nests the leading forms of bias modeled in the literature, which differ in the definitions of S and N, and the constraints placed on the set of allowable σ. We divide these into two categories.[3]

The first category is outright distortion, which we model as a case where $N = S$. In this special case, we can think of reports as objective statements about the value of s, and it is meaningful to talk about a "truthful" strategy (one where $\sigma(s) = s$), and the "amount" of bias (some integral of the distance between $\sigma(s)$ and s). Note that this is a version of cheap talk, as in Crawford and Sobel (1982). Restricting attention to strategies consistent

---

[2] This is equivalent to the definition of "slant" introduced in Gentzkow and Shapiro (2010).

[3] Prat and Strömberg (2011) divide bias into four types: facts bias, issue bias, framing bias, and ideological stand bias. Loosely, facts bias and framing bias are versions of what we call distortion, while issue bias and ideological stand bias are versions of what we call filtering.

with the truthful strategy, our definition implies that σ is biased to the right of σ' if, at every s, it shifts probability toward false reports relatively favorable to R.

This notion of distortion also captures unnecessary omission of information. We model this as a case where one of the elements of S is a null signal that provides no new information about the state. For example, suppose that S consists of either scandal$_R$ (a scandal in the R party), scandal$_L$ (a scandal in the L party), or $\varnothing$ (no information). Suppose further that strategies are constrained so either $n = s$ or $n = \varnothing$ (i.e., firms can hide information about scandals but cannot manufacture it). Note that this is related to disclosure games as in Milgrom and Roberts (1986). Then σ is biased to the right of σ' if it is relatively more likely to hide R scandals and relatively less likely to hide L scandals.

In the example above, if Fox News were to report that there were no civilian corpses at Samarra's hospital, or Al Jazeera were to report definitively that US troops killed no Iraqi insurgents, we could conclude that at least one of the reports must have involved outright distortion. Papers modeling media bias as distortion include Mullainathan and Shleifer (2005), Baron (2006), Besley and Prat (2006), Gentzkow and Shapiro (2006), and Bernhardt et al. (2008).

The second category of bias is filtering of information, which we model as a case where N is coarser or lower-dimensional than S. This can capture selection, where s is a high-dimensional vector and news outlets are constrained to choose one or a subset of the elements of the vector to report in n. It can also take the form of coarse summaries, where s is a continuous variable and reports n take on a finite number of values, such as when the report is an editorial endorsement of one candidate or the other. In the case of selection, our definition implies that σ is biased to the right of σ' if whenever σ selects an element s_i and σ' selects an element $s_j \neq s_i$, s_i is a fact more favorable to R than s_j. In the case of coarse summaries, σ is biased to the right of σ' if σ shifts probability mass from summary reports relatively favorable to L to reports relatively favorable to R. In the example, we can see selection at work, as Fox News is the only outlet to mention that eight Iraqis were captured, the *New York Times* is the only one that reported the angry reaction of Iraqis, and Al Jazeera is the only one that reported on the corpses at the hospital. We can also see coarsening in the reporting of the number of Iraqi insurgents killed, which Fox says was "at least 54" and the *New York Times* says was "as many as 54." Papers modeling bias as selection include Strömberg (2004). Papers modeling bias as endorsements or other coarse summaries include Chan and Suen (2008) and Duggan and Martinelli (2011).

We are not aware of any systematic empirical evidence on the relative prevalence of these forms of bias. But it seems clear that filtering, in the form of both selection and summary, plays a large role in the way media bias occurs in practice. Downs (1957), for one, saw selection as ubiquitous. He writes, "All reporting is biased because the reporter must select only some of the extant facts to pass on to his audience ... Because evaluation begins with emphasis upon—i.e., selection of—certain data in contrast to others, all such selection is evaluative to some extent. In short, there is no such thing as purely objective reporting of any situation or events" (207, 212).

14.3. BIAS AND WELFARE

Under our definition, bias is only defined as a relative concept: one outlet can be to the right of another, but only in special cases, is it meaningful to talk about "unbiased" or "objective" reporting, about "more" or "less" bias, or about whether a given outlet is left or right of "center." There is, in general, no inherent link between bias and welfare.

The benchmark for evaluating information content of signals is the Blackwell (1951) ordering. A reporting strategy σ is Blackwell more informative than σ' if σ' can be produced by combining σ with random noise; in other words, if the distribution of σ' given σ does not depend on s. In this case, any decision-maker who observes σ will have weakly higher expected utility than a decision-maker who observes σ', regardless of preferences. Conversely, if σ is not Blackwell more informative than σ', there exist some preferences such that a decision-maker would strictly prefer σ' to σ.

In the case of distortion bias, a truthful reporting strategy is weakly more informative (in the Blackwell sense) than any biased strategy, and so consumers cannot be better off seeing a biased report. This comparison can be strict, for example, if s is a binary signal and σ sometimes sets $n = s$ and other times sets n to be the opposite of s. Or it may be weak, for example, if $s \in \mathbb{R}$ and $\sigma(s)$ is equal to s plus a constant. In the latter case, a sophisticated consumer can simply invert the mapping σ to recover s. Of course, consumers may not be this sophisticated, and even if they are they may or may not know the correct mapping σ. Even distortion of the "add a constant" form can entail welfare loss if consumers mistakenly interpret reports as if they were accurate.

In the case of filtering bias, on the other hand, two reporting strategies are not typically ordered by Blackwell informativeness. A selection strategy that always reports the facts most favorable to R is optimal for some decision problems and a selection strategy that always reports the facts most favorable to L is optimal for some others. The same applies to endorsement strategies that usually support right-wing candidates and endorsement strategies that usually support left-wing candidates. Bias that is relatively "centrist," such as a selection rule that reports the mean of the facts in s, or an endorsement policy that endorses the right-wing and left-wing candidates with equal frequency, has no special normative status.

Of course, political information may have important externalities beyond the direct effect on consumer welfare. Assessing the effect of bias via these external effects is challenging. Many have argued that, all else being equal, democracy will function better when citizens are better informed. If we accept this premise, distortion bias, which reduces information in the Blackwell sense, will often be bad from both a social and a private perspective. In the case of filtering bias, on the other hand, there is less reason to expect the social and private incentives to be well aligned.

14.4. A MODEL OF THE MARKET FOR NEWS

We now introduce a stylized model of the news market, which we use to capture key points from the discussion above, and to summarize and frame our subsequent discussion of the literature. There is a continuum of consumers indexed by i, and either one or two media firms, each operating at most one outlet. As above, the state is $\theta \in \{L, R\}$, firms observe independent signals s, and firms make reports n. We restrict attention to the case of binary reports, $N = \{l, r\}$. The prior probability of $\theta = R$ is 0.5.

We consider particular forms of both distortion and filtering bias. In both cases, strategies will be represented by a single-dimensional index of bias $b \in [-1, 1]$, where a strategy with bias b is biased to the right of a strategy with bias b' if and only if $b \geq b'$. We assume firms announce and commit to a reporting strategy b before the signal s is observed.[4]

To model distortion bias, we assume that signals are binary, with $S = N = \{l, r\}$, and reports are like cheap talk in that firms can potentially report either l or r following any s. Signals are symmetric, with precision $\pi \equiv Pr(s=l|L) = Pr(s=r|R) > 0.5$. In the cases we consider below, a firm may find it optimal to distort either r signals or l signals (i.e., report $n = l$ when $s = r$ or report $n = r$ when $s = l$) but will never distort both with positive probability. We therefore let $b > 0$ be the probability of reporting $n = r$ following $s = l$, $b = 0$ represent truthful reporting, and $b < 0$ be (minus) the probability of reporting $n = l$ following $s = r$.

To model filtering bias, we assume that signals are continuous, with $S = \mathbb{R}$. We assume that s is normally distributed with standard deviation 1 and mean $m > 0$ in state R and $-m$ in state L. Here, we define precision $\pi \equiv Pr(s \geq 0|R) = Pr(s \leq 0|L)$. We restrict attention to strategies defined by a threshold τ such that $n = r$ if $s \geq \tau$ and $n = l$ otherwise. We let $b = Pr(n=r|s<0)$ when $\tau < 0$, $b = -Pr(n=l|s>0)$ when $\tau > 0$, and $b = 0$ when $\tau = 0$.

In a slight abuse of notation let $\sigma_l = Pr(n=l|L)$ and $\sigma_r = Pr(n=r|R)$, i.e., the probabilities of making a correct report in states L and R, respectively. Under both distortion and filtering, if $b > 0$ then $\sigma_r = \pi + b(1-\pi)$ and $\sigma_l = (1-b)\pi$ (the case of $b < 0$ is analogous). Moreover, for both types of bias and all b, $\sigma_l + \sigma_r$ is continuous in b and maximized at 2π when $b = 0$. Also note that $\partial\sigma_l/\partial b < 0$ and $\partial\sigma_r/\partial b > 0$ for all b. With filtering bias, $\sigma_l + \sigma_r$ is inverted-U-shaped, and thus $[\partial(\sigma_l + \sigma_r)/\partial b]|_{b=0} = 0$. With distortion bias, $\sigma_l + \sigma_r$ is inverted-V-shaped.

Consumers value information about θ, possibly because it has instrumental value for a real decision they must make (e.g., voting, labor supply, what claims to make at a cocktail party), or because they care intrinsically about having accurate beliefs. As a shorthand for

---

[4] The strategy can be thought of as an editorial policy that cannot be easily changed (as explained by, for example, Gehlbach and Sonin, 2013).

these incentives, we assume consumers choose an action $A \in \{A_L, A_R\}$ whose payoff for i is $u_i(A|\theta)$, with $u_i(A_L|L) = \beta_L > 0$, $u_i(A_R|R) = \beta_R > 0$, $u_i(A_L|R) = u_i(A_R|L) = 0$. We let p denote a consumer's prior probability that $\theta = R$, which may be different from the true prior probability 0.5. We take $p = 0.5$ and $\beta_L = \beta_R = 1$ as baseline assumptions. Below, we consider cases in which both the prior p and the payoffs $\{\beta_L, \beta_R\}$ may differ across i, and we introduce the possibility that consumers may receive psychological utility from confirming their prior beliefs. We refer to the average (over i) of $E(u_i(A|\theta))$ as consumer welfare.

Each consumer can choose to consume one report or no report. Consuming news has no monetary cost but entails a time cost c_i which is distributed on $[0, \bar{c})$ with CDF $G(c)$, PDF $g(c)$, and $\bar{c} > 0$. We assume that c_i is independent of preferences and priors. If the consumer is indifferent between the two duopolists' reports, each firm is chosen with probability 0.5.

Each firm earns profit equal to the mass of consumers watching its report times per-consumer advertising revenue ρ. Below, we consider the possibility that firms may also care directly about consumer actions.

The timing of the game is:
1. Nature chooses the state of the world, which is unobserved to all players.
2. The firm or firms choose (and commit to) their biases, which are then known to consumers.
3. The firm or firms observe their signals privately.
4. Firms and consumers simultaneously report and (possibly) consume news, respectively.
5. Consumers update beliefs if they consumed news, choose their actions and receive their payoffs.

Before proceeding, we note that in the baseline case, in which firms only care about profit and consumers are homogeneous with centrist priors and preferences, there will be no media bias. Consumer i consumes news if expected utility from her action given news minus c_i is greater than expected utility without news, which is 0.5. So i will consume news if

$$Pr(n = l|L)Pr(L) + Pr(n = r|R)Pr(R) - c_i > 0.5$$
$$0.5(\sigma_l + \sigma_r - 1) > c_i. \tag{14.1}$$

Thus, the fraction of consumers who get news is $G(0.5(\sigma_l + \sigma_r - 1))$. Since $\sigma_l + \sigma_r$ is maximized when $b = 0$ (for both types of bias), the firm(s) will choose $b^* = 0$. Thus, news is unbiased and consumer welfare is maximized in both monopoly and more competitive markets, and total firm profits are the same in all market structures. Since consumers agree on wanting unbiased news, and the only incentive of firms is to provide consumers with what they want, consumers receive optimal news with or without firm competition, for either signal structure.

14.5. SUPPLY-DRIVEN BIAS

One potential driver of bias is that firms may prefer consumers to take particular actions. Such preferences could arise from many sources. Chapter 16 in this handbook considers incentives arising from pressure by governments, advertisers, or other third parties. Here, we consider incentives internal to the firm. These could include direct political or business-related preferences of media owners, or arise indirectly, from the preferences of reporters or editors.

The literature has reached three main conclusions about the implications of supply-driven bias. First, supply-side incentives can drive both filtering and distortion bias in equilibrium and can lead to manipulation of even rational, sophisticated consumers. If persuasive incentives are strong enough relative to the profit motive, firms will prefer to tilt their reports to affect consumer actions even at the cost of profits. Second, competition generally reduces distortion and moves outcomes back toward what would occur in the absence of persuasive incentives, even if the competing firms have similar biases. Intuitively, competition tends to align outcomes better with the demand of consumers, which in the baseline case is for unbiased news. Third, competition tends to increase consumer welfare although it may increase or decrease total surplus once the ideological payoff of the owners is taken into account.

To illustrate these results in the context of our model, we assume that each firm has a preferred action. In addition to its monetary profit, the firm earns a payoff equal to $\alpha > 0$ times the fraction of consumers taking its desired action. We call firms whose preferred action is A_R right-biased and firms whose preferred action is A_L left-biased.

As shown above, the fraction of (homogeneous, centrist) consumers who get news is $G(0.5(\sigma_l + \sigma_r - 1))$. Consumers who do not get news are indifferent between actions, so suppose they choose A_L with probability 0.5. The probability that a consumer who does get news chooses A_L is $\sigma_l Pr(L) + (1 - \sigma_r)Pr(R) = 0.5(\sigma_l + 1 - \sigma_r)$. Thus, the expected fraction of all consumers choosing A_L is $0.5(\sigma_l + 1 - \sigma_r)G(0.5(\sigma_l + \sigma_r - 1)) + 0.5(1 - G(0.5(\sigma_l + \sigma_r - 1)))$.

Suppose there is just one left-biased firm. Then its objective function is α times the fraction of consumers choosing A_L plus ρ times the fraction of consumers consuming news:

$$\begin{aligned}
\Pi_M &= \alpha[0.5(\sigma_l + 1 - \sigma_r)G(0.5(\sigma_l + \sigma_r - 1)) + 0.5(1 - G(0.5(\sigma_l + \sigma_r - 1)))] \\
&\quad + \rho G(0.5(\sigma_l + \sigma_r - 1)) \\
&= \alpha(0.5(\sigma_l - \sigma_r)G(0.5(\sigma_l + \sigma_r - 1)) + 0.5) + \rho G(0.5(\sigma_l + \sigma_r - 1)).
\end{aligned} \tag{14.2}$$

For distortion bias, the derivative of this expression with respect to b is negative when $b \geq 0$ for sufficiently large α and small ρ, and it is straightforward to show Π_M is not maximized when $b = -1$, so there exists an interior optimum, $b^* \in (-1, 0)$ if $\alpha(\rho)$ is large (small) enough. It can be shown with implicit differentiation that $|b^*|$ is increasing in α and decreasing in ρ. Notice that bias influences the distribution of consumer actions in equilibrium even though consumers are rational. This is an example of rational persuasion as in Kamenica and Gentzkow (2011).

To see the effect of competition, note first that all consumers will choose whichever firm has the lowest $|b|$. If there were a second firm with an opposing preference for consumer actions, then the two firms each offering biased news cannot be an equilibrium since if either firm had an equal or greater bias (than its competitor), then it could be strictly better off in terms of both profits and consumer actions by undercutting its competitor's bias. The only equilibrium is both firms offering unbiased news. More surprisingly, the same result occurs when both firms have the same preference for consumer actions. If one firm offered biased news, the other firm could obtain the entire market by undercutting this bias marginally, while only marginally decreasing the desired consumer actions. Thus, there would always be an incentive to undercut if either firm offered biased news.

Since consumer welfare is decreasing in bias, clearly welfare is higher in duopoly. Results are very similar for filtering bias, except that a monopolist will choose some bias for any $\alpha > 0$. The following proposition summarizes these results.

Proposition 14.1

Suppose firms strategically choose distortion (filtering) biases. Then:

1. If α is sufficiently large and ρ sufficiently small (for all $\alpha, \rho > 0$), then a biased monopolist will choose $|b^*| \in (0, 1)$, with $|b^*|$ increasing in α and decreasing in ρ.
2. In duopoly, both firms will choose $b^* = 0$.
3. Consumer welfare is higher in duopoly than monopoly.

This proposition demonstrates the simple, but important, intuition of the tradeoff a biased firm faces between political influence and direct media profit. As the importance of influence (α) increases, the firm chooses more bias, and as audience size becomes more lucrative (higher ρ), the firm chooses less bias. Anand et al. (2007) and Balan et al. (2004), in addition to the papers noted below, make similar points. Moreover, the addition of just one competitive firm can make consumer demand infinitely bias-elastic, leading to elimination of bias in equilibrium. The proposition also implies that even rational consumers can be influenced by bias, as also shown by Jung (2009) and Adachi and Hizen (2014).

The proposition also implies the more subtle result that even a monopolist with $\rho = 0$ will not choose maximal bias, for any α. Choosing total bias would alienate consumers, causing them to not consume news at all, and hence not be influenced (Gehlbach and Sonin, 2014, stress this point). The literature on supply-driven bias extends these basic intuitions in a variety of ways.

Baron (2006) noted that since many news organizations are part of corporations, it seemed implausible that they would sacrifice profit for political bias. He showed that bias could enhance profit, however, despite the negative effect on readership, if journalists are willing to accept lower pay when allowed to bias the news, which they might want to do to advance their own career concerns or political preferences. In this case, it can be profitable for media owners to allow even distortion bias in exchange for pay cuts. In his model, bias causes news prices to be lower due to lower demand and has an ambiguous effect on welfare as it may increase profits, but the welfare effect is negative if demand for news is high. With competing firms, the relation between bias and profits is ambiguous.

Anderson and McLaren (2012) study a model like ours in that media firms have preferences over consumer actions, and consumers have homogeneous political preferences and are fully rational and sophisticated about equilibrium firm behavior. The media's access to information is exogenous, but the media can strategically withhold information (a version of distortion bias). Consumers can still be manipulated by bias since when political information is bad (from the firm's perspective), and is not reported, the consumers cannot know whether this is due to nondisclosure or the information being unavailable. Their model goes beyond ours in also considering prices, the incentives of firms to merge, media costs, and allowing consumers to get news from more than one source. Consistent with our model, they find that competition is effective in reducing distortion, and preventing mergers can improve welfare. More subtly, they note that when competing media firms have opposing biases, mergers may not occur even when allowed, due to the owners' conflicting political motives. Moreover, joint duopoly profits can be higher than monopoly profit, as a single owner with a political bias cannot credibly commit to offering diverse, differentiated news.

Chan and Suen (2009) also study a model with rational consumers and biased outlets. Their model goes beyond ours by incorporating two-party political competition with endogenous platforms. Voter payoffs depend on the winning party's platform and an unobserved state of the world. The authors compare two cases: one in which the media simply report each party's platform, and another in which the media reports the platforms and also makes a cheap talk report on the state. They find that in the first case (balanced reporting) the parties are undisciplined and choose extreme, polarized platforms, which is socially harmful. Platform convergence, which would be ideal in their model, is not an equilibrium because each party would have an incentive to deviate, and voters could not identify and punish a unilateral deviator. By contrast, in the second case of the model, the media report, even if biased, moderates the policies, since if one party was to deviate and propose a more extreme policy, then this party could be identified by voters given the media report. Greater competition enhances this moderation further. A subtle finding is that bias does not drive policy in its direction but instead polarizes candidate platforms. Since the report is cheap talk, it is a type of distortion bias. The degree of bias is constrained not by the need to keep the audience, as this is exogenous, but by the alignment between the media's and public preferences.

Brocas et al. (2011) consider several variations on a simple model of media competition with biased firms. One novel feature they consider is that in addition to biasing its own news, a firm can signal-jam a rival firm's news, making it uninformative. Consequently, duopoly competition is not sufficient to eliminate bias. However, when there are two firms supporting each of two "viewpoints" (political candidates), i.e., four firms in total, bias is completed eliminated. This is due to what they refer to as "informational Bertrand competition"—if two firms have the same viewpoint and one is slightly more informative, it obtains the entire market for that viewpoint.[5] Hence, there cannot be an equilibrium in which one firm can become marginally more informative and capture the whole market. The authors test their model with experiments, which generally support their theoretical predictions.

The general theme of all these results is that competition will tend to reduce bias that originates on the supply side of the market. Broadly speaking, competition sharpens incentives for firms to give consumers what they want. Since supply-side distortion reduces the quality of media from consumers' perspectives, these incentives push toward reducing distortion.

14.6. DEMAND-DRIVEN BIAS

The other potential driver of bias is demand from consumers themselves. A robust conclusion of the empirical literature discussed in Chapter 15 is that consumers tend to choose media whose biases match their own preferences or prior beliefs—what we will refer to as confirmatory news. In the presence of such tendencies, even profit-maximizing media firms that do not care directly about influencing consumers' beliefs may choose biased reports.

An obvious question is why consumers would demand confirmatory news in the first place. The literature has identified three categories of incentives which could be at play, which we will call delegation, psychological utility, and reputation. We organize our discussion around these three categories.

The broad conclusions of the literature with regard to demand-driven bias differ in important ways from those when bias originates on the supply side. First, demand-side incentives will drive filtering bias but will usually not lead to distortion if consumers are rational and prefer more information (in the Blackwell sense) to less. The exception is when firms have reputational concerns and cannot commit to truthful reporting, as in Gentzkow and Shapiro (2006). Second, the effects of competition on bias are more ambiguous. This largely follows from standard Hotelling logic. For example, duopolists may adopt more extreme biases than a monopolist if they each cater to a single part of the ideological spectrum while the monopolist tries to appeal to both. Third, although it often remains true that competition improves consumer welfare, the broader effects of competition can be less clear-cut if more polarized media outlets generate negative political externalities.

---

[5] A similar effect is found in Ellman and Germano (2009).

Before proceeding, we review the setup and notation of our model for the reader's convenience. There is an uncertain state, L or R, and consumers choose an action, A_L or A_R. If the action matches the state, consumers get a positive payoff of β_L or β_R, and a payoff of 0 otherwise. A news report equal to $n = l$ or $n = r$ can be obtained by consumer i at opportunity cost c_i, with CDF across the continuum of consumers $G(c)$. We consider separate cases of distortion and filtering bias; in each case, σ_n is the probability of correct news report n (conditional on its respective state) and π is the "unbiased" probability of a correct report.

14.6.1 Delegation

The first explanation for why consumers demand confirmatory news is specific to the case where bias takes the form of filtering. Recall that in this case, reporting rules are not typically Blackwell ordered, and so the value of a signal to a rational consumer will be a function of the consumer's priors and preferences. An observation originally due to Calvert (1985) and expanded on by Suen (2004) shows that consumers whose preferences (or priors) favor state R will tend to get higher (subjective) expected utility from right-biased signals. Thus, even rational consumers will exhibit a preference for confirmatory news.

To see the intuition in the context of our model, note first that a signal only has value if it affects consumers' actions; we can thus focus attention on signals such that $A = A_R$ if $n = r$ and $A = A_L$ if $n = l$. Second, observe that basing one's action on such a signal is equivalent to delegating one's decision to the media outlet. The mapping from the underlying signal s to the consumer's action A becomes simply the reporting rule σ. Consumers will then clearly prefer reporting rules that are close to the mapping from s to actions they would have chosen if they could have observed s directly themselves. As either priors or preferences shift to the right, the consumer's optimal mapping chooses A_R for a larger set of s, so their preferred signal reports $n = r$ for a larger set of s as well.

Several results seem intuitive when delegation incentives drive bias. First, firms should never engage in outright distortion, since this strictly reduces the value of firms' products to consumers; the delegation incentive can only explain differences in filtering. Second, the analysis of competition will be similar to the analysis of differentiated product competition in other settings: increasing the number of firms tends to make consumers better off, because it makes it more likely someone will produce a product that caters specifically to their tastes. Third, welfare effects are subtly different when consumers have heterogeneous priors than when they have heterogeneous preferences because in the former case at least some consumers are making systematic mistakes and so catering to their demands need not be optimal.

To show these results in the context of our model, we consider two cases. In the first, consumers have heterogeneous preferences: half are "leftists," with $\beta_L > \beta_R = 1$, and half are "rightists," with $\beta_R > \beta_L = 1$. In the second, consumers have heterogeneous priors: they all have $\beta_R = \beta_L = 1$, but half are "leftists" with prior belief that R is true of $p_i = p_L < 0.5$ and half are "rightists" with prior $p_i = 1 - p_L > 0.5$.

To see that firms never engage in distortion bias, consider the case of a rightist consumer under heterogeneous preferences, with right-distortion biased news. The utility of a consumer who bases her action on the firm's report would be:

$$\sigma_l Pr(L) + \beta_R \sigma_r Pr(R) - c_i = 0.5(\pi(1-b) + (\pi + (1-\pi)b)\beta_R) - c_i. \qquad (14.3)$$

This expression is decreasing in b if $\beta_R < \pi/(1-\pi)$ and increasing in b otherwise. But in the latter case, the consumer values the R action so much that she takes that action no matter what (feasible) news she receives, and so it cannot be utility-maximizing for her to bother to consume news. Thus, for consumers who do choose to consume news in equilibrium, utility is decreasing in distortion bias, and so utility must be maximized with zero distortion bias. Since firms only want to attract as many consumers as possible, and can only do so by offering them greater utility, there will be no distortion bias in any equilibrium. This result holds for consumers with heterogeneous priors by equivalent reasoning. Intuitively, distortion bias makes reporting Blackwell less informative, reducing utility for any consumer.

For filtering bias, given a consumer's action follows the firm's report, the derivative of utility with respect to b is $0.5\partial(\sigma_l + \sigma_r \beta_R)/\partial b$, which must be strictly positive when $b = 0$ if $\beta_R > 1$, since as mentioned above, $[\partial(\sigma_l + \sigma_r)/\partial b]|_{b=0} = 0$, and $\partial\sigma_r/\partial b > 0$ for all b. Thus, for a rightist with $\beta_r > 1$, utility must be maximized for some $b > 0$, and a firm that targets just one consumer segment will offer the segment its optimal bias.

A monopolist that operates one outlet may find it optimal to do this—to cater to just one segment—if the segments are sufficiently polarized. Otherwise, a monopolist would find it optimal to appeal to both segments with $b = 0$. If we assume that $g' \leq 0$, it is then unambiguous that the share of consumers gained on one side of the spectrum from increasing bias is less than the share of consumers lost on the other side. But for any degree of consumer heterogeneity, duopolists would have incentives to differentiate via filtering bias. If both duopolists offered $b = 0$, then they would split the monopoly audience. They would then each face an incentive to at least marginally change b, since by doing so they would continue to attract half the monopoly audience (all the consumers consuming news with $b = 0$ whose preferences are on the side of the firm's new bias), plus they would attract new consumers only willing to consume biased news. Given that one duopolist offers $b \neq 0$, the best response for the other duopolist is to offer the utility-maximizing filtering bias to the other consumer segment. In equilibrium, then, each firm delivers one segment of consumers its optimal bias. The bias cannot be extreme ($|b| \neq 1$) because then news would be uninformative. Let $0.5(\hat{\sigma}_l + \hat{\sigma}_r)$ denote the unconditional probability of a correct signal with these optimal thresholds (this is the same for the optimal threshold of either a leftist or rightist). Note that a monopolist that operates two outlets would behave in the same way as the duopolists.

It is intuitive, and easily verified, that consumer welfare is higher in duopoly than monopoly if consumers have heterogeneous preferences. This is not necessarily the case if consumers have heterogeneous priors. Let $\hat{c}_D$ denote the cost above which a consumer will not consume news even if it is optimally biased. Then, using our assumption that the objective prior is the mean of subjective priors (0.5), welfare in duopoly, W_D, can be written as:

$$W_D = 0.5(\hat{\sigma}_l + \hat{\sigma}_r)G(\hat{c}_D) + 0.5(1 - G(\hat{c}_D)). \tag{14.4}$$

In monopoly with one outlet with $\tau = 0$, letting $\hat{c}_M$ be the analog to $\hat{c}_D$, welfare W_M is

$$W_M = \pi G(\hat{c}_M) + 0.5(1 - G(\hat{c}_M)). \tag{14.5}$$

Duopoly minus monopoly welfare can be written

$$W_D - W_M = \underbrace{(\pi - 0.5)(G(\hat{c}_D) - G(\hat{c}_M))}_{\text{market size effect} > 0} + \underbrace{(0.5(\hat{\sigma}_l + \hat{\sigma}_r) - \pi)G(\hat{c}_D)}_{\text{information effect} < 0}. \tag{14.6}$$

Since $\hat{c}_D > \hat{c}_M$, the "market size effect," the growth in consumers getting news due to differentiation, is strictly positive, while the "information effect," the news being incorrect more often than necessary due to filtering bias, is strictly negative. Which effect is larger simply depends on $G()$ and $\hat{\sigma}_l + \hat{\sigma}_r$. The market size effect is larger when $G()$ is steeper and $g()$ is flatter, and differentiation expands the news audience substantially because getting news is costly for many consumers. The information effect is larger when consumers are more polarized and filtering bias is more costly (m is larger). Since either effect can be shrunk arbitrarily close to zero, either effect could dominate and the difference could take either sign. Chan and Suen (2008) (in their equations 7, 10, 11) and Chan and Stone (2013) (in their equation 4) decompose the effects of competition in a similar way.

We summarize these results as follows.

Proposition 14.2

Suppose consumers have heterogeneous preferences (priors). If β_L and β_R (p_L and p_R) are sufficiently close to 1 (0.5), then:

1. Under distortion bias, $b^* = 0$ for all firms under either monopoly or duopoly.
2. Under filtering bias, a monopolist chooses $b^* = 0$ and duopolists choose $b^* \in (0, 1)$, $b^* \in (-1, 0)$ that maximize (subjective) expected utility for each segment. Consumer welfare is (may or may not be) higher under duopoly.

If β_L and β_R (p_L and p_R) are sufficiently large (far from 0.5), then:

1. Under distortion bias, no consumer will consume news for any level of bias.
2. Under filtering bias, a monopolist will offer one segment its (subjective) optimal bias. Duopolists will offer each segment its (subjective) optimal bias, and welfare is strictly greater than in monopoly.

We now discuss a few papers from the literature that relate to this case and expand on it.

Chan and Suen (2008)'s model is similar to ours, but incorporates political competition. In their model, all consumers are interested in news on one issue, a one-dimensional state of the world, but have different preferences on which party to vote for in a given state. The media can only report a binary signal although the true state is continuous, and so consumers have different preferences over reporting strategies—some want the media to only endorse the leftist party in extreme states (as these are the only states in which those voters prefer to vote leftist), some want the rightist party only endorsed rarely, and some want a more even mix. This leads to endogenous filtering bias, as in our model. Unlike in our model, however, due to the continuum of consumer heterogeneity in their model, competing duopoly outlets take the same position. This is akin to the classic Hotelling result of convergence in duopoly with horizontal differentiation and no price competition, first applied to media markets by Steiner (1952). Like Steiner, Chan and Suen point out that if the two firms have the same owner, this can cause differentiation. However, Chan and Suen's results are more complex as their model incorporates political platform competition. This causes the relationship between media differentiation and welfare to be more ambiguous than in our model. Related papers are Sobbrio (2014) and Fang (2014).

Burke (2008)'s basic model with heterogeneous consumer priors is also very similar to ours, with a binary state and news report, and firms that just want to maximize market size. He considers a type of filtering bias in which firms can choose σ_l and σ_r, but the sum of the two, $\sigma_l + \sigma_r$, is constant (the foundations of this reporting technology are not modeled). He shows this setup implies that if a consumer's prior is at least marginally noncentrist, then the consumer thinks that she gets maximal information value from extremist media, and consequently duopolists maximally differentiate. A monopolist may still take a centrist position, as it does not want to alienate either side of its audience. In this model, given the filtering technology, there is no information loss (or gain) from filtering bias, so welfare unambiguously improves with differentiation due to market expansion. Burke extends the analysis by looking at a dynamic setting, showing results hold even if consumers are initially unbiased—being forward looking and knowing the future value of biased news, they prefer biased news from the start. He also shows results are robust to incorporating price competition.

Strömberg (2004) develops a model in which duopoly newspapers do not care about manipulating consumers and only want to maximize profits. The firms are *ex ante* identical. His model goes beyond ours in incorporating news production costs (assuming an increasing returns to scale technology), multiple dimensions of news on different government programs, and political competition. Filtering bias in his model takes the form of firms focusing coverage on some programs more than others. He finds that (unlike in our model) the two firms behave the same in equilibrium, both focusing coverage on groups that are larger, more valuable to advertisers, and care more about the policy outcome, due to the increasing returns to scale. He also models political behavior and shows that this filtering bias leads these consumers to receive better policy outcomes.

Duggan and Martinelli (2011) assume that media are constrained to make a one-dimensional report on a two-dimensional policy space. In their model, an election winner chooses levels of an income tax and a public good, and consumers choose whether or not to make an investment necessary to obtain a high-paying job. Voters are informed about the incumbent's platform but only know the challenger prefers more of the tax and public good, but not the exact platform. Duggan and Martinelli analyze not only the case of the media having political preferences but also optimal filtering for voters, which is the filtering that would occur if the media just wanted to maximize profits. If the return on jobs is high enough, optimal bias (for consumers) is no information on the tax since consumers will invest in the high-paying job anyway, and full information on the public good, so consumers can vote for the challenger if her public good proposal is optimal. If the return on jobs is low, optimal bias balances information on taxes to induce consumers to invest while providing some information on the public good to improve voting on that dimension. However, "no bias" (equal reporting on both dimensions) is never optimal, consistent with the principle that biased preferences cause demand for biased information.

14.6.2 Psychological Utility

We next consider the case in which consumers get direct utility from news whose bias matches their own prior beliefs. This "psychological" utility is a function only of bias and consumers' priors and is separable from the instrumental value of the information in a news report. The foundations for preferences over bias have been developed in both psychology and economics (Lord et al., 1979; Nickerson, 1998; Rabin and Schrag, 1999; Tirole, 2002). Such a taste could result from a preference for self-image, esteem or consistency (it may "feel good" or be more entertaining to receive news confirming one's beliefs are correct, and others are wrong), a desire to avoid complexity (updating away from the prior may involve cognitive costs), or other reasons.

We denote psychological utility by $\phi(b; p_i)$. Assume $\phi(0; p) = 0$ for all p, and $\phi(b; p = 0.5) = 0$ for all b (that is, this utility is only received if news is biased and the prior is not perfectly centrist). If $p_i > 0.5$, then $\phi()$ is increasing in b at a decreasing rate, and $\phi()$ is symmetrically decreasing in b for $p_i < 0.5$.[6] We maintain the assumption that $g' \leq 0$.

Assume consumers have heterogeneous priors and again consider first the case of a monopoly outlet. Utility without news for a leftist is $1 - p_L$, so the condition for a leftist to get greater utility from news and therefore consume it is:

$$(1 - p_L)Pr(n_l|L) + p_L Pr(n_r|R) + \phi(b; p_L) - c_i > 1 - p_L$$
$$(1 - p_L)(\sigma_l - 1) + p_L \sigma_r + \phi(b; p_L) > c_i. \tag{14.7}$$

---

[6] It is not necessary for our analysis to specify different properties of $\phi()$ for distortion and filtering bias, so we omit this notation for simplicity.

The condition for rightists is symmetric. If these conditions are satisfied for some $c_i > 0$, then the monopolist's payoff is

$$\Pi_M = 0.5(G((1-p_L)(\sigma_l - 1) + p_L\sigma_r + \phi(b; p_L)) + G((1-p_R)\sigma_l + p_R(\sigma_r - 1) + \phi(b; p_R))). \tag{14.8}$$

It can be shown that this expression decreases as b moves away from zero, and so $b^* = 0$ is a local maximum, for either bias type. It may also be optimal to offer one of the two segments its optimal bias (if p_L, p_R are sufficiently far apart).

Thus far, the analysis for this case has been basically the same as that of the delegation case. The situation is different though for distortion bias in duopoly. The effect of a marginal decline in left bias on a leftist consumer's utility from news (stated in (14.7)) is the derivative of this utility when $b < 0$, since larger b then indicates less left bias. This derivative is $(1-p_L)(\partial\sigma_l/\partial b) + p_L(\partial\sigma_r/\partial b) + [\partial\phi(b; p_L)/\partial b] = -(1-p_L)(1-\pi) + p_L\pi + [\partial\phi(b; p_L)/\partial b]$. This expression needs to be negative for a leftist consumer's utility to increase when left distortion bias increases. This occurs when $\pi - (1-p_L) < |\partial\phi(b; p_L)/\partial b|$. The interpretation of this inequality is straightforward: the left-hand side is the marginal cost of lost information due to bias (which increases as π grows larger and decreases as the prior grows more extreme), and the right-hand side is the marginal psychological utility from bias. If the latter is greater than the former, then the consumer prefers more bias on the margin. This means that if $\pi - (1-p_L) < |\partial\phi(b; p_L)/\partial b|_{b=0}$, then in duopoly the firms will differentiate and offer each segment of consumers its optimal bias, whether bias is distortion or filtering bias (the logic for why differentiation is an equilibrium is the same as that discussed above). Henceforth assume this condition holds.

The comparison between monopoly and duopoly welfare is ambiguous, for the same reason as the case without psychological utility—there is a tradeoff between more consumers getting news, and consumers getting less informative news. We summarize these results as follows.

Proposition 14.3
Suppose consumers have heterogeneous priors and get psychological utility from news. If p_L and p_R are sufficiently close to 0.5, then:
1. A monopolist will choose $b^* = 0$ under distortion or filtering bias.
2. In duopoly, under either type of bias, firms will choose $b^* > 0$, $b^* < 0$ that maximize subjective expected utility for each segment. Welfare may be higher or lower in duopoly than monopoly.

If p_L and p_R are sufficiently far from 0.5, then:
1. Under distortion or filtering bias, a monopolist will offer one segment its optimal bias.
2. Under distortion or filtering bias, duopolists will offer each segment its optimal bias, and welfare is strictly greater than in monopoly.

Note that for this case, unlike the delegation case, duopolists might prefer to use distortion bias, rather than filtering bias if distortion bias is less costly. It is also worth noting that this is the only case that we analyze in which total bias, i.e., $|b| = 1$, is possible, and news would become completely uninformative. This would occur if psychological utility were important enough.

Mullainathan and Shleifer (2005) study a model in which the state of the world is a real number, utility is lost when the news is further from the consumer's prior mean, and media firms only want to maximize profits. Their model also incorporates price competition. They show that uninformative distortion bias can exist in many types of equilibria. Propositions 4 and 5 from their paper correspond to our results: with heterogeneous consumers, a monopolist takes a middle ground to attract a wide audience, while duopolists differentiate their slants and segment the market. They also show that when consumers are homogeneous, duopoly reduces price but not bias (if consumers have "biased priors," i.e., a prior mean not equal to zero); when consumers are heterogeneous, duopolist differentiation is even more extreme than the most extreme consumers, as this softens price competition. Mullainathan and Shleifer also examine an extension in which consumers who wish to can cross-check news in duopoly and show these consumers can become more informed this way than they would be in monopoly. See Rüdiger (2013) for a model focusing on cross-checking.

Gabszewicz et al. (2001) analyze a similar Hotelling-style model of politically differentiated duopoly newspaper competition. They assume consumers prefer media content to be closer to their political ideologies. Gabszewicz et al. also consider price as an endogenous variable and confirm that with quadratic transportation costs, in equilibrium the firms maximally differentiate to soften price competition. The authors add to this result by showing that if firms then sell their readership to advertisers, this moderates differentiation and may drive prices to zero. See Chapter 9 for further discussion of Gabszewicz et al (2001).

Bernhardt et al. (2008) study a voting model in which media consumers are rational information processors, but partisan voters get utility from negative news about the opposing party. Although voters draw correct inferences from their news, they choose news to maximize this noninstrumental, psychological utility from news, given that their votes are not pivotal, and so are often not as informed as they could be. Their paper thus highlights the importance of knowledge externalities, which are not incorporated in our model. Again, consumers demand information-destroying distortion bias although in this case it is distortion by omission. Since voters do not become as informed as possible, suboptimal electoral outcomes may occur; these are more likely when the distribution of voter preferences is asymmetric and the median voter is partisan. Even when the median voter is nonpartisan and receives unbiased news, there can be electoral problems though, as partisan voters may vote (*ex post*) incorrectly due to distortions in their news.

Schulz and Weimann (1989) were, as far as we know, the first to study a model of media competition incorporating this type of nonstandard consumer psychology. They assume consumers prefer to avoid cognitive dissonance, and for this reason prefer newspapers with ideologies similar to their own. In their model, two political parties and two newspapers both choose ideological locations and a separate, vertical aspect of information, while newspapers choose prices as well. The newspapers and parties do not directly interact in the model. The authors find that both parties and newspapers differentiate, but newspapers differentiate more, but not maximally, due to the presence of the vertical type of information.

14.6.3 Reputation

The last reason we discuss that consumers may receive confirmatory news is that they trust the firms that provide it more. A rational consumer who is uncertain about an information source's accuracy will tend to judge it to be higher quality when its reports match the consumer's priors. Thus, firms can have incentives to produce confirmatory news to improve their reputations, increasing future demand. This observation was made by Prendergast (1993) and Brandenburger and Polak (1996) in the context of labor and financial markets, respectively, and applied to media markets by Gentzkow and Shapiro (2006).

There are two main takeaways for this case. First, if firms cannot commit to their strategies ahead of time, their incentives to build a reputation for quality can lead them to engage in distortion bias in equilibrium, even though this strictly reduces the value of their reports to consumers, and can make both them and consumers worse off. Second, the relationship between bias and competition involves a new element. As above, Hotelling-type forces may or may not lead duopolists to adopt more biased positions than monopolists. Additionally, however, consumers can use the reports of one outlet to cross-check the other, and this may discipline firms' incentives to bias their reports. We illustrate the first of these implications formally and refer the reader to Gentzkow and Shapiro (2006) for more detail on the second.

To capture reputation in the context of our model, we extend it to include two types of media firms: a high-quality type that observes the state directly and reports it honestly, and a normal type that observes a noisy signal and reports strategically (as above). We focus on the case of distortion bias, where the normal firms observe $s \in \{r, l\}$ and can freely choose $n \in \{r, l\}$, and we drop the assumption that such a firm commits to its strategy *ex ante*. (If we kept this assumption, consumers could infer the firm's type directly from its announced strategy.) We assume there is a monopoly firm and assume the *ex ante* probability it is a high type is λ. We assume consumers are homogeneous with prior belief $p \in (0.5, 1)$.

Firm profits depend on both current advertising revenue and future profits; we capture the latter in reduced form by simply assuming they are increasing in consumers' posterior belief that the firm is high quality. Thus, since the normal-type firm cannot commit to its reporting strategy, it will always choose whichever strategy maximizes consumers' posteriors.

A consumer who observes $n = r$ will have a posterior belief that the firm is a high type of

$$Pr(\text{high}|r) = \frac{Pr(r|\text{high})Pr(\text{high})}{Pr(r)} = \frac{p\lambda}{p\lambda + [\sigma_r p + (1 - \sigma_l)(1 - p)](1 - \lambda)},$$

and a consumer who observes $n = l$ will have posterior belief

$$Pr(\text{high}|l) = \frac{Pr(l|\text{high})Pr(\text{high})}{Pr(l)} = \frac{(1 - p)\lambda}{(1 - p)\lambda + [(1 - \sigma_r)p + \sigma_l(1 - p)](1 - \lambda)},$$

where σ_r and σ_l now denote $Pr(n = r|R)$ and $Pr(n = l|L)$, respectively, from the perspective of the consumer given her beliefs about the firm's strategies. The firm will report r whenever $Pr(\text{high}|r) > Pr(\text{high}|l)$ and will report l whenever $Pr(\text{high}|r) < Pr(\text{high}|l)$.

Suppose, first, that consumers expected the firm to report its signal truthfully. In this case, $\sigma_r = \sigma_l$, and so $Pr(\text{high}|r) > Pr(\text{high}|l)$. The firm would prefer to deviate and always report r. Thus, truthful reporting cannot be an equilibrium.

There also cannot be an equilibrium in which the firm biases its reports left, nor one where it only reports r, because in this case $\sigma_r = 1$, $\sigma_l = 0$, and $Pr(\text{high}|r) < Pr(\text{high}|l)$.

The unique equilibrium must therefore be in mixed strategies, with an interior bias $b \in (0, 1)$ chosen such that $Pr(\text{high}|r) = Pr(\text{high}|l)$. This occurs at the point where

$$\frac{p}{1 - p} = \frac{1 - \sigma_l}{1 - \sigma_r}.$$

Substituting $\sigma_r = \pi + (1 - \pi)b$ and $\sigma_l = \pi(1 - b)$, we can solve for the equilibrium bias:

$$b^* = \frac{(2p - 1)(1 - \pi)}{p(1 - \pi) + \pi(1 - p)}.$$

It is straightforward to show that this expression is increasing in p so that bias is greater the more extreme are consumer beliefs. It also happens that it is decreasing in π so that firms with more accurate signals engage in less bias.

Bias can occur in equilibrium even when it makes all market participants strictly worse off. Bias always reduces consumer welfare. More surprisingly, it can also decrease firm profits. To see this, suppose that low-type firms were required to report their signals truthfully. This would unambiguously increase first-period profits because the value of signals would be higher and so more consumers would read the firm's report. The effect on continuation payoffs is ambiguous. However, Gentzkow and Shapiro (2006) show that if the baseline share λ of high-type firms is sufficiently low, the first-period effect dominates and firm profits fall.

Gentzkow and Shapiro (2006) extend this basic analysis in several ways. First, they allow consumers to receive feedback on the news before firms receive their reputation payoffs. They show that in the case of homogeneous but noncentrist priors, in the unique equilibrium, a monopolist distorts its report towards the prior. The degree of distortion decreases as the chance of feedback increases, disappearing when feedback is certain. This helps explain why empirically bias is lower for news on events where "truth" is revealed relatively quickly and clearly, such as sports, weather, and election outcomes (as opposed to events where it is difficult to immediately evaluate truth, e.g., the effects of fiscal stimulus on GDP or climate change). Second, as already mentioned, they study a specific form of media competition, in which the presence of multiple firms allows consumers to cross-check the firms' reports, and they show that this form of competition reduces bias. The role of competition here is closely related to the observation in other settings that competing advocates may be more effective at eliciting truth than a single nonpartisan (e.g., Dewatripont and Tirole, 1999). Panova (2006) presents a similar model.

Stone (2011) analyzes a related model with distortion bias, and consumers trusting like-minded media to deliver more accurate news. In his model, both consumers and reporters have information processing biases. Consumers think of themselves as unbiased, however, causing them to infer that reporters with similar ideologies are also unbiased. This makes consumers believe (often falsely) that ideologically similar media are less biased and more informative. Consequently, consumers unwittingly demand distortion biased confirmatory news. Increased media differentiation resulting from greater competition can cause media to become more biased and less informative. This can reduce welfare. However, greater differentiation due to competition can also improve welfare due to a positive market size effect.

14.7. CONCLUSION

Bias can persist in commercial media markets for a variety of theoretical reasons. Supply-side bias persists when media management or labor are willing to sacrifice profits for political gain. Demand-side bias persists when consumers perceive biased media to be more informative or more enjoyable. Bias caused by reputation concerns persists when feedback on truth is weak.

Despite its negative connotations, bias as we have defined it need not be socially harmful. In some cases—outright distortion or needless omission—the consequences for consumer information, at least, will be unambiguously negative, and it is meaningful to talk about a benchmark of "unbiased" reporting. In other cases—filtering or selection—an efficient market may supply different varieties of bias, and there is no meaningful notion of unbiasedness.

The effects of competition on bias and consumer welfare are in general ambiguous. Competition tends to sharpen firms' incentives to give consumers what they want. When supply-side incentives lead firms to distort their reports, competition tends to lessen bias and improve welfare. When consumers themselves demand bias, competition may lead to more extreme biases that cater to these tastes. This often improves welfare if consumers are rational and information-seeking, but otherwise may not. When distortions originate in firms' incentives to build a reputation for quality, the availability of information from competing sources may allow consumers to distinguish true quality more accurately and so reduce bias by softening these reputational incentives.

ACKNOWLEDGMENTS

We thank David Strömberg for valuable comments and suggestions.

REFERENCES

Adachi, T., Hizen, Y., 2014. Political accountability, electoral control and media bias. Jpn Econ. Rev. 65 (3), 316–343.

Alterman, E., 2003. What Liberal Media?: The Truth About Bias and the News. Basic Books, New York, NY.

Anand, B., Di Tella, R., Galetovic, A., 2007. Information or opinion? Media bias as product differentiation. J. Econ. Manag. Strategy 16 (3), 635–682.

Anderson, S.P., McLaren, J., 2012. Media mergers and media bias with rational consumers. J. Eur. Econ. Assoc. 10 (4), 831–859.

Andina-díaz, A., 2011. Mass media in economics: origins and subsequent contributions. Cuadernos de Ciencias Económicas y Empresariales 61, 89–101.

Balan, D.J., DeGraba, P., Wickelgren, A.L., 2004. Ideological Persuasion in the Media. Available at SSRN 637304.

Baron, D.P., 2006. Persistent media bias. J. Public Econ. 90 (1–2), 1–36.

Bernhardt, D., Krasa, S., Polborn, M., 2008. Political polarization and the electoral effects of media bias. J. Public Econ. 92 (5–6), 1092–1104.

Besley, T., Prat, A., 2006. Handcuffs for the grabbing hand? Media capture and government accountability. Am. Econ. Rev. 96 (3), 720–736.

Blackwell, D., 1951. Comparison of experiments. In: Proceedings of the Second Berkeley Symposium on Mathematical Statistics and Probability. University of California Press, Berkeley, CA, pp. 93–102.

Brandenburger, A., Polak, B., 1996. When managers cover their posteriors: making the decisions the market wants to see. RAND J. Econ. 27 (3), 523–541.

Brocas, I., Carrillo, J.D., Wilkie, S., 2011. Media Ownership Study No. 9: A Theoretical Analysis of the Impact of Local Market Structure on the Range of Viewpoints Supplied, Federal Communications Commission, Washington, DC.

Burke, J., 2008. Primetime spin: media bias and belief confirming information. J. Econ. Manag. Strategy 17 (3), 633–665.

Calvert, R.L., 1985. The value of biased information: a rational choice model of political advice. J. Politics 47 (2), 530–555.

Chan, J., Stone, D.F., 2013. Media proliferation and partisan selective exposure. Public Choice 156 (3–4), 467–490.

Chan, J., Suen, W., 2008. A spatial theory of news consumption and electoral competition. Rev. Econ. Stud. 75 (3), 699–728.

Chan, J., Suen, W., 2009. Media as watchdogs: the role of news media in electoral competition. Eur. Econ. Rev. 53 (7), 799–814.

Crawford, V.P., Sobel, J., 1982. Strategic information transmission. Econometrica 50 (6), 1431–1451.

Dewatripont, M., Tirole, J., 1999. Advocates. J. Polit. Econ. 107 (1), 1–39.

Downs, A. 1957. An Economic Theory of Democracy. Harper, New York, NY.

Duggan, J., Martinelli, C., 2011. A spatial theory of media slant and voter choice. Rev. Econ. Stud. 78 (2), 640–666.

Ellman, M., Germano, F., 2009. What do the papers sell? A model of advertising and media bias. Econ. J. 119 (537), 680–704.

Fang, R.Y., 2014. Media Bias, Political Polarization, and the Merits of Fairness. Working Paper.

Gabszewicz, J.J., Laussel, D., Sonnac, N., 2001. Press advertising and the ascent of the 'Pensée Unique'. Eur. Econ. Rev. 45 (2), 641–651.

Gehlbach, S., Sonin, K., 2014. Government control of the media. J. Pub. Econ. 118, 163–171.

Gentzkow, M., Shapiro, J.M., 2006. Media bias and reputation. J. Polit. Econ. 115 (2), 280–316.

Gentzkow, M., Shapiro, J.M., 2010. What drives media slant? Evidence from US daily newspapers. Econometrica 78 (1), 35–71.

Goldberg, B., 2001. Bias: A CBS Insider Exposes How the Media Distort the News. Regnery Publishing, Washington, DC.

Hamilton, J.T., 2004. All the News That's Fit to Sell: How the Market Transforms Information into News. Princeton University Press, Princeton, NJ.

Jung, H.M., 2009. Information manipulation through the media. J. Media Econ. 22 (4), 188–210.

Kamenica, E., Gentzkow, M., 2011. Bayesian persuasion. Am. Econ. Rev. 101 (6), 2590–2615.

Ladd, J.M., 2012. Why Americans Hate the Media and How it Matters. Princeton University Press, Princeton, NJ.

Lord, C.G., Lee, R., Lepper, M.R., 1979. Biased assimilation and attitude polarization: the effects of prior theories on subsequently considered evidence. J. Pers. Soc. Psychol. 37 (11), 2098–2109.

Milgrom, P., Roberts, J., 1986. Price and advertising signals of product quality. J. Polit. Econ. 94 (4), 796–821.

Mullainathan, S., Shleifer, A., 2005. The market for news. Am. Econ. Rev. 95 (4), 1031–1053.

Nickerson, R.S., 1998. Confirmation bias: a ubiquitous phenomenon in many guises. Rev. Gen. Psychol. 2 (2), 175–220.

Panova, E., 2006. A Model of Media Pandering. UQAM.

Pew Research Center for the People and the Press, 2011. Views of the News Media: 1985–2011: Press Widely Criticized, But Trusted More Than Other Information Sources. Accessed at http://www.people-press.org/files/legacy-pdf/9-22-2011%20Media%20Attitudes%20Release.pdf. on December 16, 2013.

Prat, A., Strömberg, D., 2011. The Political Economy of Mass Media. CEPR Discussion Paper No. DP8246.

Prendergast, C., 1993. A theory of 'Yes Men'. Am. Econ. Rev. 83 (4), 757–770.

Rabin, M., Schrag, J.L., 1999. First impressions matter: a model of confirmatory bias. Q. J. Econ. 114 (1), 37–82.

Rüdiger, J., 2013. Cross-Checking the Media. Available at SSRN 2234443.

Schulz, N., Weimann, J., 1989. Competition of newspapers and the location of political parties. Public Choice 63 (2), 125–147.

Sobbrio, F., 2013. The political economy of news media: theory, evidence and open issues. In: Handbook of Alternative Theories of Public Economics. Edward Elgar Press, Cheltenham.

Sobbrio, F., 2014. Citizen-editors' endogenous information acquisition and news accuracy. J. Public Econ. 113, 43–53.

Steiner, P., 1952. Program patterns and preferences, and the workability of competition in radio broadcasting. Q. J. Econ. 66 (2), 194–223.

Stone, D.F., 2011. Ideological media bias. J. Econ. Behav. Organ. 78 (3), 256–271.

Strömberg, D., 2004. Mass media competition, political competition, and public policy. Rev. Econ. Stud. 71 (1), 265–284.

Suen, W., 2004. The self-perpetuation of biased beliefs. Econ. J. 114 (495), 377–396.

Sutter, D., 2001. Can the media be so liberal? The economics of media bias. Cato J. 20 (3), 431.

Tirole, J., 2002. Rational irrationality: some economics of self-management. Eur. Econ. Rev. 46 (4–5), 633–655.

Zaller, J., 1999. A Theory of Media Politics. Unpublished manuscript.

CHAPTER 15

Empirical Studies of Media Bias

Riccardo Puglisi*, James M. Snyder, Jr.[†,‡]
*Department of Political and Social Sciences, Università degli Studi di Pavia, Pavia, Italy
[†]Department of Government, Harvard University, Cambridge, MA, USA
[‡]NBER, Cambridge, MA, USA

Contents

15.1. Introduction		648
15.2. Estimating Bias		649
	15.2.1 Measures of Explicit Bias	650
	15.2.2 Measures of Implicit Bias	651
	15.2.2.1 The Comparison Approach	*652*
	15.2.2.2 The Issue Intensity Approach	*654*
	15.2.2.3 The Third Approach—Measuring Tone	*656*
	15.2.3 Is There One Dimension?	658
15.3. Factors Correlated with Bias		659
	15.3.1 Demand-Side Factors	659
	15.3.2 Supply-Side Factors	659
	15.3.3 The Role of Competition	661
15.4. Bias and Voter Behavior		662
15.5. Conclusions		664
References		664

Abstract

In this chapter we survey the empirical literature on media bias, with a focus on partisan and ideological biases. First, we discuss the methods used to measure the relative positions of media outlets. We divide bias into two categories, explicit and implicit bias. We group existing measures of implicit bias into three categories: measures based on comparing media outlets with other actors, measures based on the intensity of media coverage, and measures based on tone. In the second part of the chapter we discuss the main factors that are found to be correlated with media bias, dividing these into demand-side and supply-side factors. We also discuss the role of competition across media outlets. In the third part of the chapter we discuss some of the attempts to measure the persuasive impact of media bias on citizens' attitudes and behavior.

Keywords

Agenda setting, Competition, Mass media, Media bias, Ideological bias, Newspapers, Press, Persuasion

JEL Codes

D22, D72, D78, D83, K23, L00, L82

Handbook of Media Economics, Volume 1B
ISSN 2213-6630, http://dx.doi.org/10.1016/B978-0-444-63685-0.00015-2

15.1. INTRODUCTION

A clear majority of Americans believe that mass media outlets are biased.[1] Media biases can take a variety of forms: in favor of the incumbent government, in favor of a particular political party, ideologically liberal or conservative, in favor of industries or companies that advertise heavily in the outlet or that own the outlet, or in favor of audiences that are more valuable to advertisers.

Although the belief in some sort of bias is widespread, measuring bias in a relatively objective, replicable, and affordable manner is a difficult task. Even defining bias requires considerable care. Perhaps the most difficult question is: Bias relative to what? Relative to what a "neutral" or "fair" or "balanced" outlet would do? Relative to the average or median preference that citizens have—or would have, if fully informed? Relative to the average preference of voters (sometimes a small and unrepresentative subset of citizens), or the outlet's audience (an even smaller and probably more unrepresentative subset of citizens)? In many cases, the most straightforward quantity to measure—and therefore the quantity most commonly measured—is bias relative to other media outlets.

Measuring media outlets relative to one another, it seems clear that there is variation in bias across media outlets. For example, in many countries some outlets are relatively liberal or supportive of left-leaning parties, while others are relatively conservative or supportive of right-leaning parties. This is true not only in the United States, but also in other countries where bias has been measured, such as the United Kingdom, Australia, and Italy. It is less clear whether there is any overall bias relative to citizens, voters, or consumers.

It is also not clear what factors produce the observed biases. Are the biases mainly due to supply-side factors—owners, editors, or journalists expressing their views, or trying to influence political opinions and behavior? Or are they due to demand-side factors—media outlets catering to the tastes of their readers or viewers? If the demand side dominates, what does the audience want? Do viewers and readers want "neutral" information, or confirmation of their prior beliefs and attitudes? How does competition affect the amount and direction of bias? Finally, it is not clear whether media bias has a large influence on citizens' beliefs, or on citizens' behavior, such as turnout and vote choice, although several studies have found modest effects.

In this survey, we focus on partisan and ideological biases. We begin by discussing the methods used to measure the relative positions of media outlets. We divide bias into two categories, explicit and implicit bias. Researchers define and measure implicit bias in a

---

[1] For example, in a 2011 Pew Research Center poll, 66% of respondents said that news stories are "often inaccurate" and 77% said that news organizations "tend to favor one side" (http://www.people-press.org/2011/09/22/press-widely-criticized-but-trusted-more-than-other-institutions/). Similarly, in a 2011 Gallup poll, 60% said either that the media are "too liberal" or "too conservative," while only 36% said they are "about right" (http://www.gallup.com/poll/149624/Majority-Continue-Distrust-Media-Perceive-Bias.aspx).

variety of ways, and we group these into three categories: measures that compare media outlets with other actors, measures based on the intensity of media coverage, and measures of tone. In the second part of the chapter, we discuss the main factors found to be correlated with media bias, dividing these into demand-side and supply-side factors. We also discuss the role of competition across media outlets. In the third part of the chapter, we discuss some of the attempts to measure the persuasive impact of media bias on citizens' attitudes and behavior.[2]

15.2. ESTIMATING BIAS

A substantial and growing empirical literature seeks to identify replicable and intuitive measures of the partisan or ideological position of media outlets. Underlying most of this research is a simple left–right, liberal–conservative view of politics, in which political actors have preferences over a one-dimensional ideological space. It seems natural to use this framework for two reasons. First, it is how journalists, pundits, politicians, and many voters talk about politics much of the time. Second, at least since Downs (1957), it has served as the foundation for most theoretical models of politics, as illustrated by the discussion in Chapter 14 in this volume.

Regarding the informational content of bias, Gentzkow et al. (2015) distinguish between two categories of bias, "distortion" and "filtering." Distortion arises when news reports are direct statements about raw facts, and the statements have the same "dimensionality" as the facts. Omission of facts is also included within this notion of bias as a special case. In these cases, the notion of "objective reporting" is relatively easy to define—a media outlet that ignores the event or reports a number other than the official figure (as if it was the official figure) engages in distortion.[3] On the other hand, filtering arises when news reports are necessarily of a lower dimensionality *vis a vis* the raw facts so that media outlets can offer only a summary of events. The notion of objective reporting does not apply to filtering. However, one can still slant news to the left or the right through a proper filtering strategy. Here, we discuss such partisan filtering. Chapter 13 discusses filtering across policy issues and in total.

---

[2] We do not have space for detailed treatment of other types of bias. See, e.g., Qian and Yanagizawa-Drott (2015) for evidence of a pro government bias, especially in coverage of foreign policy. See, e.g., Larcinese (2007) for evidence that some outlets in the UK "over-provide" news that is of interest to audiences that are more valuable to advertisers. See, e.g., Reuter and Zitzewitz (2006) and Gambaro and Puglisi (2015) for evidence that media outlets exhibit bias in favor of firms that buy advertising space on them.

[3] That is, distortion takes place when there are measurable facts, figures, or events that are so salient that they "must" be reported. Examples might be the number of troops killed in action in a war in which the country under consideration participates, a corruption scandal involving a prominent politician, or newly released figures on the official unemployment rate.

As Gentzkow et al. (2015) discuss in their chapter, filtering is more pervasive than distortion. This follows almost directly from the definition of what media outlets do. Since readers and viewers have limited time and attention, the business of the media is to select from the mass of raw facts produced by the events of each day, distill those selected into useful summaries, and then disseminate the resulting distillations. As a result, the various measures of media bias we discuss below fall mainly into the filtering bias category. To paraphrase Coase (1937), distortions are islands of conscious misreporting of salient facts in an ocean of more or less salient facts that go through filtering and selection.

15.2.1 Measures of Explicit Bias

Journalistic norms allow the free and open display of opinions in the editorial section, but not in news sections. As a result, it is typically easier to estimate the *explicit* ideological and partisan bias of newspapers, as it appears in their editorial sections. One straightforward way to do this is to investigate their endorsements in races for political offices or ballot propositions.[4]

Ansolabehere et al. (2006) analyze the political orientation of endorsements by US newspapers in statewide and congressional races, using a panel data design. They find a clear change in the average partisan slant of endorsements. In the 1940s and 1950s, Republican candidates enjoyed a strong advantage in newspaper endorsements—after controlling for incumbency status, Republican candidates were more than twice as likely to be endorsed as Democratic candidates. This advantage gradually eroded in subsequent decades so that by the 1990s there was a slight tendency for newspapers to endorse Democrats (even controlling for incumbency).[5]

Ho and Quinn (2008) code the editorials in 25 newspapers on about 495 Supreme Court cases during the period 1994–2004 to determine whether the newspaper favored the majority or minority position in each case.[6] Combining this information with the actual votes cast by the Supreme Court justices in those same cases, they estimate the relative positions of newspapers and justices. They find that the majority of newspapers in their sample are centrist relative to the distribution of positions estimated for justices—e.g., 50% are between Justice Kennedy and Justice Breyer (justices 4 and 6 on the estimated ideological scale).

Puglisi and Snyder (2015) study ballot propositions to measure bias. They exploit the fact that newspapers, parties, and interest groups take positions on propositions, and the fact that citizens ultimately vote on them. This allows them to place newspapers, parties,

---

[4] This is, of course, feasible only in a context where media outlets routinely endorse candidates in electoral races.

[5] They also find an upward trend in the average propensity to endorse one or the other major-party candidate, and a particularly large increase in the propensity to endorse incumbents.

[6] The period of study is the last natural Rehnquist Court.

interest groups, and voters within each state on the same scale. They study 305 newspapers over the period 1996–2012. They find that newspapers are distributed evenly around the median voter in their states and on average are located almost exactly at the median. Newspapers also tend to be centrist relative to interest groups. In California, for example, 16% of the newspapers in their sample (of 57) take a position to the right of the median more than twice as often as they take a position to the left of the median—exhibiting a substantial conservative bias—and 19% do the opposite. They also find differences across issue areas. In particular, newspapers appear to be more liberal than voters on many social and cultural issues such as gay marriage, but more conservative on many economic issues such as the minimum wage and environmental regulation.

Other aspects of explicit media bias include the choice of which syndicated columnists to publish, which letters to the editor to print, and, for television or radio, how much airtime to give to politicians from different parties. In the interest of space, we discuss only two examples of these. Butler and Schofield (2010) conduct a field experiment in which they randomly sent pro-Obama or pro-McCain letters to the editor to 116 newspapers around the United States in October 2008 of the presidential election campaign.[7] After controlling for newspaper circulation, they find that newspapers were significantly more likely to publish the letter or contact the authors for verification purposes if the letter supported McCain rather than Obama, suggesting an overall pro-Republican (or at least pro-McCain) bias.[8] Durante and Knight (2012) consider the last type of bias, for the case of Italian television news during the period 2001–2007. They find that the stations owned by Berlusconi (Mediaset) exhibit a bias in favor of the right—these stations allocate more speaking time to right-wing politicians than left-wing politicians, even when the left is in power. One of the public stations, Rai 2, also exhibits a clear bias in favor of the right, while Rai 3 exhibits a relatively pro-left bias.

15.2.2 Measures of Implicit Bias

Many observers are more concerned about the *implicit* political behavior of media outlets. One reason for the concern is that implicit bias can be more insidious, since readers and viewers might be less aware of it.

There are three broad approaches used to estimate the implicit ideological stances of media outlets. The first is the comparison approach. Media outlets are classified by comparing the text of news stories or broadcasts to the text (usually in speeches) of politicians of known ideological or partisan positions. Outlets that "talk like" Republican or conservative politicians are classified as Republican or conservative, and those that "talk like" Democratic or liberal politicians are classified as Democratic or liberal. The second is the issue emphasis approach. Media outlets are classified according to the amount of coverage

---

[7] Other than the name of the candidate supported, the text of the letters was the same.
[8] See Grey and Brown (1970), Renfro (1979), and Sigelman and Walkosz (1992) for other studies.

they give to different politically relevant topics. Outlets that emphasize topics that favor Republicans—e.g., dwelling on the economy when the president is a Democrat and the economy is performing poorly, or dwelling on issues that are "owned" by Republicans—are classified as Republicans, while outlets that emphasize topics that favor Democrats are classified as Democratic. In the third approach, media outlets are classified according to the "tone" of their coverage. Outlets that praise Republicans and criticize Democrats are classified as Republican, while outlets that do the opposite are classified as Democratic.

15.2.2.1 The Comparison Approach

The comparison approach adopts the basic idea of one of the pioneering subfields of automated text analysis, "author identification" (also known as "stylometry"). In stylometry, the goal is to identify who actually wrote an anonymous or disputed text, by comparing the frequency of various words or phrases in the target text with the corresponding frequencies in texts of known authorship. The first well-known example of this is Mosteller and Wallace (1963), who attribute to Madison, rather than Hamilton, the authorship of 12 disputed *Federalist Papers*.[9]

The most prominent papers that use the comparison approach to estimate media biases are Groseclose and Milyo (2005) and Gentzkow and Shapiro (2010).

Gentzkow and Shapiro (2010) measure media bias based on similarities between the language used by media outlets and congressmen. They first identify "partisan" words and phrases in the *Congressional Record*—those words and phrases that exhibit the largest difference in the frequency of use between Democratic and Republican representatives. They then measure how frequently these expressions appear in a sample of 433 newspapers in 2005. They find that the partisan bias of newspapers depends mainly on consumers' ideological leaning and far less on the identity of owners. Newspapers that adopt a more liberal (conservative) language tend to sell more copies in Zip codes that are more liberal (conservative), as proxied by the propensity of their inhabitants to donate to Republican or Democratic candidates. Overall, variation in consumer preferences accounts for about 20% of the variation in their measure of slant. On the other hand, after controlling for geographical factors, the ideological slant of a given newspaper is not significantly correlated with the average ideological slant of those belonging to the same chain. They conclude that, "Our data do not show evidence of an economically significant bias relative to the benchmark of profit maximization" (p. 60).

Groseclose and Milyo (2005) measure media bias based on similarities between the think-tanks cited by media outlets and the think-tanks cited by congressmen. They study

---

[9] According to Holmes (1998), the first published work in stylometry is Mendenhall (1887), who attempts to determine the authorship of certain plays to Bacon, Marlowe, or Shakespeare on the basis of average word length. Holmes argues that the work of Mosteller and Wallace (1963) is the most important early breakthrough. More recent examples applying this approach to the study of politics include Laver and Garry (2000) and Laver et al. (2003).

17 media outlets during the years 1990–2003.[10] They first estimate the political leaning of each think-tank by computing the average ideological position (ADA score) of the representatives who quote the think-tank in a non-negative way. They then measure the bias in media outlets based on how frequently these outlets cite the different think-tanks. They find that all the outlets in their sample—except *Fox News Special Report* and the *Washington Times*—are located to the left of the average Congress member. At the same time, media outlets are relatively centrist. All but one (the *Wall Street Journal*) are located between the average Democrat and the average Republican Congressmen. The exception is the *Wall Street Journal*—it is the most liberal outlet and also the most extreme, with an estimated "ADA score" of 85.1.[11]

Groseclose and Milyo (2005) make strong and provocative claims, so their study has been the subject of several critiques. For example, Gasper (2011) explores the robustness of their findings. He argues that their conclusions are robust to different measures of the ideological positions of senators and congressmen, but not to the time period studied. In particular, the average estimated position of the media shifts to the right if one uses more recent time periods. Nyhan (2012) discusses other potential weaknesses of their method.

One other paper that uses the comparison approach deserves mention. Gans and Leigh (2012) focus on Australia and measure media bias based on similarities between the public intellectuals mentioned by media outlets and the public intellectuals mentioned by federal members of parliament. They study 27 media outlets—newspapers, and radio and television stations—over the period 1999–2007. They first estimate the partisan leaning of each public intellectual in their sample by computing the degree to which members of the Coalition (conservative party), rather than the Labor Party, mention the intellectual (in a non-negative way), as recorded in the parliamentary record. They then measure the bias in media outlets based on how frequently these outlets mention the different public intellectuals. They find that in all but one of their media outlets, the pattern of mentions is statistically indistinguishable from the average pattern of mentions by members of parliament.[12]

---

[10] The total sample size is 20 since they include both the morning and evening news programs on the three major television networks. The time period covered varies for each outlet. For example, the period is 10 months long, 7/1/2001 to 5/1/2002, for the *New York Times*; only 4 months long, 1/2/2002 to 5/1/2002, for the *Wall Street Journal*, the *Washington Post*, and the *Washington Times*; almost 2 years long, 8/6/2001 to 6/26/2003 for *Time Magazine*; and 15 and a half years long, 1/1/1990 to 6/26/2003, for the *CBS Evening News*.

[11] The scores run from 0 to 100, 0 being the most conservative score and 100 being the most liberal.

[12] With respect to mentions of public intellectuals, for example, the authors find that all media outlets except one are located within two standard errors of the average pattern of mentions by members of parliament. See Adkins Covert and Wasburn (2007) for another study using the comparison approach.

15.2.2.2 *The Issue Intensity Approach*

Like the comparison approach, the issue intensity approach draws heavily on earlier ideas, especially the literature on agenda-setting. The theory of agenda-setting effects posits that the amount of coverage devoted to an issue by the media can influence the importance readers and viewers attach to that issue. Media effects in the model of Strömberg (2004) are similarly driven by intensity of issue coverage. It suggests that rational voters evaluate politicians more on issues covered in the media, simply because they are better informed about these, and that this causes politicians to work more on those issues. Chapter 13 discusses evidence of this.

As Cohen (1963, p. 13) famously wrote, the press "may not be successful much of the time in telling people what to think, but it is stunningly successful in telling its readers what to think about." The theory of agenda-setting effects was pioneered by Lippmann (1922) and explored empirically by McCombs and Shaw (1972) in a study of Chapel Hill voters during the 1968 presidential campaign. As noted by McCombs (2002), not only can mass media coverage highlight some topic as an object of attention, but the coverage can also emphasize particular attributes of the topic, making these attributes more salient.[13]

Puglisi (2011) provides an account of the agenda-setting behavior of the *New York Times* over the period 1946–1997. According to the issue ownership hypothesis, introduced by Petrocik (1996), an issue is said to be Democratic (or "owned" by the Democratic party) if the majority of citizens stably believe that Democratic politicians are better at handling the main problems related to that issue than Republican politicians. To measure the bias of the *New York Times*, Puglisi (2011) computes the relative frequency of stories on various issues as a function of which party controls the presidency and time period. He finds that the *Times* displays pro-Democratic bias, with some anti-incumbent aspects. More specifically, during presidential campaigns the *Times* systematically gives more coverage to Democratic issues (e.g., civil rights, health care, labor issues) when the incumbent president is a Republican.[14]

Larcinese et al. (2011) analyze the coverage of economic issues in a sample of 102 US newspapers over the period 1996–2005. The idea is straightforward. Suppose that the incumbent president is a Democrat. When the news on some economic issue is bad (e.g., unemployment is high or rising), then newspapers with a pro-Republican bias that

---

[13] This is closely related to "issue priming"—how readers and viewers, when assessing a given situation or individual, are pushed towards giving a higher weight to the aspect emphasized by the mass media. See Krosnick and Miller (1996) for a review of this literature. See, e.g., Iyengar et al. (1982) for experimental evidence regarding these hypotheses.

[14] The magnitude of the estimated effect is substantial. Under a Republican president, there are on average 26% more stories about Democratic topics during the presidential campaign than outside of it. On the other hand, under a Democratic president there is no significant difference in the amount of coverage of Democratic topics during and outside presidential campaigns.

wish to decrease the popularity of the president should devote more coverage to that issue, while newspapers with a pro-Democratic bias should devote less coverage to that issue. The opposite should occur when the economic news is good, and the patterns should be reversed if the incumbent president is a Republican.[15] The authors first estimate the bias in economic news coverage exhibited by each newspaper in their sample of newspapers and find considerable variation.[16] They then study whether there is a significant correlation between the explicit bias of newspapers—as exhibited by their endorsement policies—and the implicit partisan bias in their coverage of bad/good economic news as a function of the political affiliation of the incumbent president. They find a significant and robust correlation for unemployment. Newspapers with a pro-Democratic endorsement pattern systematically give more coverage to high unemployment when the incumbent president is a Republican than when the president is Democratic, compared to newspapers with a pro-Republican endorsement pattern. This result is robust to controlling for the partisanship of readers. They also find some evidence that newspapers cater to the partisan tastes of readers in the coverage of the budget deficit. Regarding the coverage of inflation or trade deficits, they find no robust evidence of a partisan bias that is correlated with either the endorsement or reader partisanship.[17]

Puglisi and Snyder (2011) focus on political scandals, which are inherently "bad news" for the politicians and parties implicated. They study the coverage of 32 scandals involving members of congress or statewide officers over the period 1997–2007 in a sample of 213 newspapers. They find that newspapers with an explicit pro-Democratic bias—again, measured as a higher propensity to endorse Democratic candidates in elections—give relatively more coverage to scandals involving Republican politicians than scandals involving Democratic politicians, while newspapers with an explicit pro-Republican bias tend to do the opposite.[18] This is true even after controlling for the average partisan leanings of readers. In contrast, newspapers appear to cater to the partisan tastes of readers only for local scandals.

---

[15] The extreme case in which a newspaper does not report at all about a highly salient economic news item would be a case of distortion (via omission) in the Gentzkow et al. (2015) sense.

[16] Consider news about unemployment. The *Fresno Bee* is at the liberal end of the spectrum. Given a one-percentage-point increase in the unemployment rate, it would publish almost 1% fewer stories on the topic under Clinton than under Bush. In relative terms, this difference is large, since on average there are just 1.35% stories on unemployment in the newspaper. The *Bismarck Tribune* is at the conservative end of the spectrum. Given a one-percentage-point increase in the unemployment rate, it would print 0.5% more unemployment stories under Clinton than under Bush. The distribution is unimodal, so most newspapers are, in relative terms, centrist. This includes the largest ones, such as the *New York Times* and the *Los Angeles Times*.

[17] They also conduct a case study of the *Los Angeles Times* over the post-war period, documenting a sharp change in its coverage before and after Otis Chandler took over as editor of the newspaper.

[18] Again, the extreme case in which a newspaper does not report at all about a highly salient scandal would be a case of distortion (via omission) in the Gentzkow et al. (2015) sense.

Fonseca-Galvis et al. (2013) conduct an analysis similar to Puglisi and Snyder (2011), but they study US newspapers from 1870 to 1910, an era when the press was much more explicitly partisan than today and many newspapers were closely affiliated with a political party. They study the coverage of 122 scandals in a sample of 166 newspapers. They find that Democratic (Republican) newspapers publish significantly more articles about scandals involving Republican (Democratic) politicians, and significantly fewer articles about scandals involving Democratic (Republican) politicians, relative to independent newspapers. For example, after controlling for geography (newspapers are much more likely to cover local scandals), on average partisan newspapers published about 30% more stories about a scandal if it involved a politician from the opposite party. They also find that as the level of competition faced by a newspaper increases, the bias exhibited—both against the opposition party and in favor of the newspaper's own party—decreases.

Finally, Brandenburg (2005) is interesting because it combines the issue emphasis approach with the comparison approach. He studies seven British newspapers during the 2005 election campaign. In one analysis, he compares the issue agenda of newspapers as measured by the percentage of coverage devoted to different policy issues with the issue agendas of the political parties as measured by the percentage of attention devoted to these issues in press releases. This type of analysis could be applied relatively easily to other countries and time periods.

15.2.2.3 The Third Approach—Measuring Tone

The third approach—measuring bias in the "tone" or "sentiment" of coverage—also has a long history. The idea is simple: a media outlet is biased in favor of a political party or position if it systematically portrays this party or position in a favorable manner, and/or it portrays the opposing party or position in a negative manner. Pioneering studies include Berelson and Salter (1946) on the portrayal of minority groups in US magazine fiction, and Lasswell et al. (1952) on the portrayal of political symbols in "prestige" newspapers in several countries. Relative to the first two approaches, this approach has traditionally been much more labor intensive, since researchers in this area have tended to emphasize the need for careful, human-based coding of content. Innovations using semantic dictionaries (e.g., the General Inquirer dictionary) or supervised machine learning promise to sharply reduce the costs, and this is likely a fruitful area for research.[19] The decision to use human- or machine-based coding always involves a tradeoff. Compared to human-based coding, automated coding is less accurate in detecting the tone of each specific text analyzed but allows the researcher to quickly code large numbers of texts.[20]

---

[19] See, e.g., Young and Soroka (2012) for an overview.

[20] As Antweiler and Frank (2005) note, other factors to consider in assessing the relative merits of human-based and automated coding include the researcher "degrees of freedom" bias and publication bias.

Lott and Hassett (2014) analyze newspaper coverage when official data about various economic indicators are released. They focus on how newspapers cover the release of official economic data, coding the tone—positive or negative—of newspaper headlines, and relate this to the partisanship of the sitting president and congressional majority. They study a panel of 389 US newspapers from 1991 to 2004.[21] A newspaper exhibits a pro-Democratic bias if it provides a more positive account of the same economic news (e.g., the same unemployment rate) when the sitting president is Democrat. Controlling for underlying economic variables, they find that, on average, the newspapers in their sample publish significantly fewer positive stories when the incumbent president is a Republican. They argue that this indicates an overall liberal bias in the US press.[22] Since their main goal is to measure the "absolute" degree of bias exhibited by US newspapers, they do not present estimates of different positions for different newspapers.

Gentzkow et al. (2006) study how US newspapers covered the Crédit Mobilier scandal during the early 1870s and the Teapot Dome scandal in the 1920s. They measure newspaper bias by counting the relative occurrence of words such as "honest" and "slander" in articles covering the scandals. They find that the coverage of the Crédit Mobilier scandal (which occurred in a period dominated by partisan newspapers) was more biased than the coverage of Teapot Dome (which occurred at a time when fewer dailies were directly linked to political parties). They also find some evidence that the coverage of the Crédit Mobilier scandal was less biased for newspapers with higher circulation.[23] They argue that during the years between these scandals, technological progress in the printing industry, together with increases in population and income in US cities, greatly expanded the potential size of newspapers' markets. In the competition for market shares and advertising revenues, newspapers faced strong incentives to cut the ties with political parties and become more independent and less biased.

A number of other studies measure bias in terms of tone, including Lowry and Shidler (1995), Kahn and Kenney (2002), Niven (2003), Schiffer (2006), Entman (2010), Eshbaugh-Soha (2010), Gans and Leigh (2012), and Soroka (2012). Soroka (2012) studies the tone of news stories on unemployment and inflation in the the *New York Times* over the period 1980–2008. This is the only paper that employs automated content analysis methods to code tone; the rest all rely on human coding.[24]

---

[21] They also study a smaller panel of 31 newspapers from 1985 to 2004.

[22] Since their main analysis only involves a comparison of one Democratic president (Clinton) to two Republican presidents (George Bush and George W. Bush), and since there were many differences in the economic and political situations facing these presidents, it is difficult to make strong claims about a generic, absolute, ideological or partisan bias.

[23] The relationship is not statistically significant except when they exclude the *New York Herald*.

[24] D'Alessio and Allen (2000) conduct a meta-analysis of 59 quantitative studies containing data concerned with partisan media bias in presidential election campaigns since 1948. They find no significant biases for newspapers or news magazines, but a small degree of "coverage" and "statement" bias in television network news.

Finally, a number of studies measure bias in the tone of visual images—whether candidates are portrayed favorably or unfavorably in photographs and television news clips. For example, Barrett and Barrington (2005) study 435 newspaper photographs of candidates in 22 races in seven newspapers during the 1998 and 2002 general election campaign seasons. They find that if a newspaper endorsed a candidate, or exhibited a prior pattern of endorsements and editorials favoring the party of the candidate, then that newspaper also tended to publish more favorable photographs of the candidate than his or her opponent. Other studies of this type of bias include Kepplinger (1982), Moriarty and Garramone (1986), Moriarty and Popvich (1991), Waldman and Devitt (1998), Banning and Coleman (2009), Grabe and Bucy (2009), and Hehman et al. (2012).

15.2.3 Is There One Dimension?

As noted above, almost all of the work on media bias assumes a one-dimensional issue space. This simplification might be realistic enough in the "polarized" political environment of the US today. Partisanship affiliations and ideology are more highly correlated than in the past, and roll-call voting and political debate appear quite partisan and one-dimensional.[25] In previous decades, however, this was not the case. For example, during the period 1940–1970, racial issues cut across the main dimension of partisan conflict. This produced a configuration in which many southern Democrats were moderately liberal on the "economic dimension" but extremely conservative on the "race dimension." In addition, a large literature on party politics outside the US finds that the political landscape is multidimensional—i.e., a multidimensional space is required to adequately describe the relative positions of parties and voters.[26]

This leads naturally to the question: When political conflict is multidimensional, are the political biases exhibited by media outlets multidimensional as well? There is no work yet focusing on this question, but some existing studies provide suggestive evidence. For example, Gans and Leigh (2012) and Puglisi and Snyder (2015) show that, although the correlations between different measures of media bias are positive, they are not huge. The correlations between the three main measures in Gans and Leigh are 0.41, 0.50, and 0.72. The correlation between the proposition-based measure in Puglisi and Snyder and a replication of Gentzkow and Shapiro's measure based on politically slanted language is just 0.43. Of course, these low correlations might be due to measurement error. But, since it is also likely that the measures weigh different issues differently, the low correlations might indicate that the underlying space is truly multidimensional.

---

[25] See, e.g., Abramowitz and Saunders (1998), Fiorina et al. (2005), Carsey and Layman (2006), and Poole and Rosenthal (1997, 2012).

[26] See, e.g., Benoit and Laver (2006), Hix et al. (2006), De La O and Rodden (2008), and Bakker et al. (2012).

15.3. FACTORS CORRELATED WITH BIAS

Having constructed an intuitive and replicable measure of media bias, it is natural to explore the determinants of this bias, or at least to identify variables that are significantly correlated with bias. The ideological stances of media outlets should be viewed as equilibrium phenomena, i.e., as outcomes of the interaction of demand-side and supply-side factors. Thus, our discussion is closely connected with Chapter 14, which focuses on the theoretical aspects of media bias.

15.3.1 Demand-Side Factors

Gentzkow and Shapiro (2010) show that their index of politically slanted language is positively and significantly correlated with the partisan leanings of the Zip codes where each newspaper is sold. To measure the partisan disposition of each Zip code, they use the relative amount of campaign donations given to Democratic and Republican candidates by the area's residents. They also find that the ideological positions of newspaper owners—measured using newspaper chains and political donations—matter much less than the ideological positions of readers. In particular, they show that after controlling for geographic factors and the Republican vote share in each newspaper's market area, there is "no evidence that two jointly owned newspapers have a more similar slant than two randomly chosen newspapers."[27]

Puglisi and Snyder (2011) show that newspapers circulating in Democratic areas give significantly more coverage to scandals involving local politicians that are Republican, relative to newspapers circulating in Republican areas. This result holds even after controlling for the ideological position of the supply side, as proxied by the average propensity to endorse Democratic or Republican politicians on the editorial page. In a similar vein, Larcinese et al. (2011) find that partisan coverage of the budget deficit is significantly correlated with the ideology of readers, with the expected sign: newspapers read by Democratic readers give more coverage to the deficit when it is high and the incumbent President is George W. Bush, than when the president is Bill Clinton, and vice versa in the case of low deficit.

15.3.2 Supply-Side Factors

The ideological positions of owners, editors, and journalists might also affect media bias. For example, Demsetz and Lehn (1985) argue that firms in the media sector offer an "amenity potential" to owners—owners might accept lower profits because they obtain personal gratification from owning the firms and can also impose their personal

---

[27] Gentzkow and Shapiro (2010, p. 58).

ideological views on the outlet's content.[28] Another argument is that media bias can emerge even in the case of profit-maximizing owners if politically biased journalists are willing to be paid less in exchange for the possibility of slanting content accordingly (Baron, 2006).

Larcinese et al. (2011) show that the partisan coverage of unemployment by US newspapers is significantly correlated with the average propensity to endorse Democratic vs. Republican candidates on editorial pages, even after controlling for the Democratic vote share in newspapers' market areas. They also provide an interesting case study of the *Los Angeles Times* and show that at least for this newspaper a change in the ideology of the publisher led to a rapid change in newspaper content. Until the early 1960s, the *LA Times* exhibited a strongly conservative and Republican stance that reflected the ideology of the owners (the Chandler family). In 1960, Otis Chandler became the publisher. He was much more liberal than his predecessors and this quickly affected the editorial pages—e.g., the distribution of endorsements in the newspaper shifted sharply away from Republicans and towards Democrats. Perhaps more surprisingly, Larcinese et al. (2011) also find an effect on news coverage. More specifically, they find that the prior pro-Republican agenda bias in the coverage of unemployment and inflation disappeared after Otis Chandler became publisher.[29]

Additional evidence in Ansolabehere et al. (2006) and Stanley and Niemi (2013) suggests that the *Los Angeles Times* is not a unique case. As noted above, Ansolabehere et al. (2006) find a large pro-Republican bias in the political endorsements made by many big-city newspapers during the 1940s and 1950s. On average, the newspapers in their sample were about twice as likely to endorse Republican candidates than Democratic candidates during this period, even though the voters living in these newspapers' market areas tended to favor Democratic candidates by about 56% to 44%.[30] In a similar vein; Stanley and Niemi (2013) report that in presidential elections over the period 1940–1988 the number of newspapers endorsing the Republican candidate was about five times the number that endorsed the Democratic candidate.[31] Voters, on the other hand, cast 53% of their votes for the Democratic candidates during this period, on

---

[28] The evidence they provide for this is indirect—they find that ownership concentration is significantly higher in media firms. They provide similar evidence for firms in the sports sector.

[29] To rule out demand-side shifts, the authors show that there was no significant increase in the Democratic vote in California during the period, i.e., the 1960s.

[30] The figure on Democratic voting is computed by taking the average of the two-party vote share in all races for president, governor, US Senate, and US House of Representatives in the counties where the newspapers in the Ansolabehere et al. (2006) study are located. It is possible that the newspapers studied were targeting the Republican consumers in these cities, but data from the *American National Election Studies* suggest otherwise. Pooling the 1956 and 1960 surveys, 154 respondents claimed to read one of the newspapers in the Ansolabehere et al. (2006) sample and also self-identified either as Democrats or Republicans. Just over 56% of these respondents identified as Democrats.

[31] Weighting the endorsements by circulation increases the pro-Republican bias.

average. These patterns suggest that many newspapers do not pander to their audience, at least on their editorial pages.[32]

15.3.3 The Role of Competition

The type and amount of competition in the relevant media markets might be systematically related to the size and direction of media bias.

If media bias is driven mainly by the ideological leaning of journalists and editors, then a more competitive media market is likely to mitigate the degree of media bias. A partisan newspaper enjoying a local monopoly (disregarding imperfect substitutes like TV news, radio news, and the Internet) can unabashedly disregard negative news involving politicians from its preferred party, e.g., political scandals. On the other hand, in the presence of competitors, each newspaper might decide to cover news that is bad to both sides. One reason is simply profits—if a newspaper does not cover attention-grabbing bad news then it risks losing readers, and revenue, to other newspapers that do. A newspaper may also cover bad news involving its preferred party for ideological motives. If it does not cover a potentially bad story, then it leaves the field wide open for newspapers with opposing political views to cover the story and frame it in the most negative way possible. So, the newspaper may prefer to cover the story, with a less negative frame, as part of a defensive strategy.[33]

In the model of confirmation-seeking readers by Mullainathan and Shleifer (2005), a monopolistic newspaper will position itself in the middle of the ideological spectrum of its market area.[34] On the other hand, in a duopoly situation the newspapers would locate on opposite sides of the middle, each carving out a part of the readership for itself. So, this model predicts that competition may increase the amount of "bias" (ideological differentiation) in media coverage.

The model of Bayesian news consumers by Gentzkow and Shapiro (2006) predicts the opposite.[35] In their model, increased competition tends to reduce the bias (increase the accuracy) of each newspaper. The reason is that with a larger number of media outlets

---

[32] Durante and Knight (2012) provide another case study that shows a "supply-side" effect of publicly owned media. They show that when the television news director of the largest government-owned station (TG1) was replaced with a director more ideologically close to the newly elected conservative prime minister (Silvio Berlusconi), the station's news content shifted significantly to the right. More specifically, compared to other private and public TV news programs, TG1 gave significantly more time to conservative politicians than it had before.

[33] See Gentzkow et al. (2006). Anderson and McLaren (2012) note how those mitigating effects might disappear if mergers dilute the effective amount of competition on the market.

[34] Gentzkow et al. (2015) classify this model of demand-driven bias within the category of "psychological utility" models.

[35] This is a "reputation" model of demand-driven bias, again according to the Gentzkow et al. (2015) classification.

readers will typically have access to follow-up stories that investigate the accuracy of prior stories (scoops). So newspapers *ex ante* face stronger incentives to report in an unbiased fashion.

To summarize, the simple supply-side model of Gentzkow et al. (2006) and the model of Gentzkow and Shapiro (2006) predict a negative relationship between competition and the degree of media bias, while Mullainathan and Shleifer (2005) predict a positive relationship.

Compared to the empirical literature on demand-driven and supply-led media bias, there are few econometric contributions about the effects of competition on equilibrium media bias. Puglisi and Snyder (2011) find a negative but statistically insignificant effect of competition on biased coverage of scandals. On the other hand (as noted above), in their historical analysis of scandal coverage Fonseca-Galvis et al. (2013) find that bias is significantly decreasing in the level of competition a newspaper faces. Finally, Gentzkow et al. (2011) deal with a different but related topic, i.e., the effects of competition in US local newspaper markets on electoral turnout, and provide robust evidence of positive but decreasing effects.[36]

15.4. BIAS AND VOTER BEHAVIOR

Does media bias affect voter behavior?[37] A number of studies attempt to determine whether media bias affects the political attitudes and decisions of the mass public. Since DellaVigna and Gentzkow (2010) provide a recent and thorough survey of this topic, we will be brief here.

Gerber et al. (2009) use an experimental approach to examine not whether media outlets are biased, but whether they influence political decisions and attitudes. They conduct a randomized controlled trial just prior to the November 2005 gubernatorial election in Virginia and randomly assign individuals in Northern Virginia to (a) a treatment group that receives a free subscription to the *Washington Post* (a relatively liberal newspaper), (b) a treatment group that receives a free subscription to the *Washington Times* (a relatively conservative newspaper), or (c) a control group. They find that individuals who were assigned to the *Washington Post* treatment group were 8 percentage

---

[36] The analysis of the effects of competition among information providers on "bias" is not confined to the study of mass media. For example, Hong and Kacperczyk (2010) test whether competition reduces reporting bias in the market for security analyst earnings forecasts. They show mergers of brokerage houses are positively correlated with optimism bias in reporting, which is consistent with the hypothesis that competition reduces bias.

[37] Media bias might also affect the behavior of politicians and other actors such as interest groups. We do not discuss this here.

points more likely to vote for the Democrat in the 2005 election, while those who were assigned the *Washington Times* were only 4 percentage points more likely to vote for the Democrat.[38]

DellaVigna and Kaplan (2007) use a natural experiment, exploiting the gradual introduction of Fox News in cable markets in order to estimate its impact on the vote share in presidential elections, between 1996 and 2000. They find that Republicans gained 0.4–0.7 percentage points in the towns which started to broadcast Fox News before 2000.

Knight and Chiang (2011) investigate the relationship between media bias and the influence of the media on voting in the context of newspaper endorsements. They study the largest 20 newspapers during the 2000 US presidential elections. They find that "surprising" endorsements—i.e., endorsements of the Republican candidate by Democratic-leaning newspapers and endorsements of the Democratic candidate by Republican-leaning newspapers—influence voters, but "predictable" endorsements do not. Other studies of endorsements include Robinson (1972, 1974), Erikson (1976), St. Dizier (1985), Kahn and Kenney (2002), and Ladd and Lenz (2009). To take one example, Ladd and Lenz (2009) study the effects of newspaper endorsements on voting in the United Kingdom, exploiting the fact that four newspapers changed their editorial stance between 1992 and 1997. The switch by the Murdoch-owned *Sun*, from strongly supporting the Conservative party in 1992 to explicitly endorsing Labour in 1997, was an especially big "surprise." They find evidence of media persuasion.

Of course, these papers do not isolate the effect of newspaper endorsements *per se*, because endorsements may be accompanied by other changes in behavior. For example, Kahn and Kenney (2002) find that the newspapers tend to give significantly more favorable coverage (in terms of tone) to the incumbents they endorse. Ladd and Lenz (2009) note that, in addition to endorsing Labour, the *Sun*'s overall coverage was critical of the incumbent Conservative prime minister (John Major) and favorable toward the Labour leader (Tony Blair). They state the identification issue clearly: "In exploiting changes by these papers, we capture both the effects of the editorial endorsement and changed slant in news coverage" (p. 396).

A final group consists of laboratory experiments. One seminal contribution (Iyengar et al., 1982) provides the first experimental evidence of a significant agenda-setting effect of TV news broadcasts on viewers' issue salience. A host of subsequent experimental studies, mainly in the communications and political science literatures, has yielded empirical support for various media effects, from agenda-setting to priming and framing effects. Iyengar and Simon (2000) provide a review of this literature. See also Jerit et al. (2013) for a comparison between a laboratory and a field experiment on media effects that were administered to the same subjects.

---

[38] The latter effect is not statistically significant at the 5% level. In addition, one cannot reject at the 5% level the null hypothesis that the two treatments have the same effect on the probability of voting Democrat.

15.5. CONCLUSIONS

In this chapter, we have surveyed and classified the empirical methods to measure the ideological/partisan position of media outlets. We have also looked at the determinants of those positions, and at the persuasive effects on readers and viewers.

Regarding the link between theoretical models of media bias and their empirical counterpart, we share with Gentzkow et al. (2015) the view that bias due to filtering is more pervasive than bias due to distortion. Interestingly, this is consistent with the idea—and the common wisdom—that media owners, editors, and journalists have "power" because they enjoy considerable discretion in the choice of what stories to cover.[39] This agenda-setting power would be much narrower if we lived in a world where distortion bias is the norm rather than filtering and selection.[40]

We conclude by noting some potential avenues for future research. First, the third strategy for estimating bias, measuring the tone of articles and editorials, is relatively underutilized in economics. The explosion in "big data" in the form of text—including the text of media outlets—may change this, by providing greater incentives for researchers to design techniques to measure tone in a robust and replicable manner. Second, almost all empirical studies of media bias are about one specific country during one specific and relatively short time period (Ansolabehere et al., 2006; Gentzkow et al., 2006, are exceptions). Cross-country comparisons, or within-country studies over long periods, are necessary to put the various estimates of media bias in a comparative perspective. Among other things, this could lead to comparative measures of the "pluralism" of media systems based on actual media content rather than subjective expert opinions. Third, more work on the determinants of bias is clearly needed, particularly regarding the role of competition among media outlets. The structure of media markets has changed rapidly in recent years as more and more people get news online. Finally, exploiting the network aspects of social media such as Twitter and Facebook may yield new approaches to measuring the ideological positions of media outlets relative to politicians and various groups of citizens.

REFERENCES

Abramowitz, A.I., Saunders, K.L., 1998. Ideological realignment in the U.S. electorate? J. Polit. 60 (3), 634–652.
Adkins Covert, T.J., Wasburn, P.C., 2007. Measuring media bias: a content analysis of time and Newsweek coverage of domestic social issues, 1975–2000. Soc. Sci. Q. 88, 690–706.
Anderson, S.P., McLaren, J., 2012. Media mergers and media bias with rational consumers. J. Eur. Econ. Assoc. 10 (4), 831–859.

[39] There is some sound empirical evidence on the effects of this agenda-setting power: Eisensee and Strömberg (2007) find that the choice of news stories affects government policy.
[40] See McCombs and Shaw (1972) for more discussion of agenda-setting.

Ansolabehere, S., Lessem, R.R., Snyder Jr., J.M., 2006. The orientation of newspaper endorsements in U.S. elections, 1940–2002. Q. J. Polit. Sci. 1 (4), 393–404.

Antweiler, W., Frank, M.Z., 2005. Do US Stock Markets Typically Overreact to Corporate News Stories? Sauder School of Business, University of British Columbia, Canada.

Bakker, R., Jolly, S., Polk, J., 2012. Complexity in the European party space: exploring dimensionality with experts. Eur. Union Polit. 13 (2), 219–245.

Banning, S., Coleman, R., 2009. Louder than words: a content analysis of presidential candidates' televised nonverbal communication. Vis. Commun. Q. 16, 4–17.

Baron, D.P., 2006. Persistent media bias. J. Public Econ. 90 (1), 1–36.

Barrett, A.W., Barrington, L.W., 2005. Bias in newspaper photograph selection. Polit. Res. Q. 58, 609–618.

Benoit, K., Laver, M., 2006. Party Policy in Modern Democracies. Routledge, London.

Berelson, B., Salter, P.J., 1946. Majority and minority Americans: an analysis of magazine fiction. Public Opin. Q. 10 (2), 168–190.

Brandenburg, H., 2005. Political bias in the Irish media: a quantitative study of campaign coverage during the 2002 general election. Irish Polit. Stud. 20, 297–322.

Butler, D.M., Schofield, E., 2010. Were newspapers more interested in pro-Obama letters to the editor in 2008? Evidence from a field experiment. Am. Polit. Res. 38, 356–371.

Carsey, T.M., Layman, G.C., 2006. Changing sides or changing minds? Party identification and policy preferences in the American electorate. Am. J. Polit. Sci. 50 (2), 464–477.

Coase, R.H., 1937. The nature of the firm. Economica 4 (16), 386–405.

Cohen, B.C., 1963. The Press and Foreign Policy. Princeton University Press, Princeton, NJ.

D'Alessio, D., Allen, M., 2000. Media bias in presidential elections: a meta-analysis. J. Commun. 50, 133–156.

De La O, A.L., Rodden, J.A., 2008. Does religion distract the poor? Comp. Polit. Stud. 41 (4–5), 437–476.

DellaVigna, S., Gentzkow, M., 2010. Persuasion: empirical evidence. Annu. Rev. Econ. 2, 643–669.

DellaVigna, S., Kaplan, E., 2007. The fox news effect: media bias and voting. Q. J. Econ. 122, 1187–1234.

Demsetz, H., Lehn, K., 1985. The structure of corporate ownership: causes and consequences. J. Polit. Econ. 93 (6), 1155–1177.

Downs, A., 1957. An Economic Theory of Democracy. Harper, New York, NY.

Durante, R., Knight, B.G., 2012. Partisan control, media bias, and viewers' responses: evidence from Berlusconi's Italy. J. Eur. Econ. Assoc. 10 (3), 451–481.

Eisensee, T., Strömberg, D., 2007. News floods, news droughts, and U.S. disaster relief. Q. J. Econ. 122 (2), 693–728.

Entman, R.M., 2010. Media framing biases and political power: explaining slant of news in campaign 2008. J. Cancer Educ. 11 (4), 389–408.

Erikson, R.S., 1976. The influence of newspaper endorsements in presidential elections: the case of 1964. Am. J. Polit. Sci. 20 (2), 207–233.

Eshbaugh-Soha, M., 2010. The tone of local presidential news coverage. Polit. Commun. 27 (2), 121–140.

Fiorina, M.P., Abrams, S.J., Pope, J.C., 2005. Culture War? The Myth of a Polarized America. Longman, New York, NY.

Fonseca-Galvis, A., Snyder Jr., J.M., Song, B.K., 2013. Newspaper Market Structure and Behavior: Partisan Coverage of Political Scandals in the U.S. from 1870 to 1910. Harvard University, Cambridge, MA.

Gambaro, M., Puglisi, R., 2015. What do ads buy? Daily coverage of listed companies on the Italian press. Eur. J. Polit. Econ. 39, 41–57.

Gans, J.S., Leigh, A., 2012. How partisan is the press? Multiple measures of media slant. Econ. Rec. 88, 127–147.

Gasper, J.T., 2011. Shifting ideologies? Re-examining media bias. Q. J. Polit. Sci. 6, 85–102.

Gentzkow, M., Shapiro, J.M., 2006. Media bias and reputation. J. Polit. Econ. 114, 280–316.

Gentzkow, M., Shapiro, J.M., 2010. What drives media slant? Evidence from U.S. daily newspapers. Econometrica 78 (1), 35–71.

Gentzkow, M., Glaeser, E.L., Goldin, C., 2006. The rise of the fourth estate: how newspapers became informative and why it mattered. In: Glaeser, E.L., Goldin, C. (Eds.), Corruption and Reform: Lessons from America's History. National Bureau of Economic Research, Cambridge, MA.

Gentzkow, M., Shapiro, J.M., Sinkinson, M., 2011. The effect of newspaper entry and exit on electoral politics. Am. Econ. Rev. 101 (7), 2980–3018.

Gentzkow, M., Shapiro, J.M., Stone, D.F., 2015. Media bias in the marketplace: theory. Chapter 14. In: Anderson, S., Waldfogel, J., Stromberg, D. (Eds.), Handbook of Media Economics, vol. 1B, Elsevier, Amsterdam.

Gerber, A., Karlan, D.S., Bergen, D., 2009. Does the media matter? A field experiment measuring the effect of newspapers on voting behavior and political opinions. Am. Econ. J. Appl. Econ. 1 (2), 35–52.

Grabe, M.E., Bucy, E.P., 2009. Image Bite Politics: News and the Visual Framing of Elections. Oxford University Press, Oxford, UK.

Grey, D.L., Brown, T.R., 1970. Letters to the editor: hazy reflections of public opinion. Journal. Q. 47, 450–456.

Groseclose, T., Milyo, J., 2005. A measure of media bias. Q. J. Econ. 120, 1191–1237.

Hehman, E., Graber, E.C., Hoffman, L.H., Gaertner, S.L., 2012. Warmth and competence: a content analysis of photographs depicting American presidents. Psychol. Pop. Media Cult. 1, 46–52.

Hix, S., Noury, A., Roland, G., 2006. Dimensions of politics in the European parliament. Am. J. Polit. Sci. 50 (2), 494–511.

Ho, D.E., Quinn, K.M., 2008. Assessing political posititions of the media. Q. J. Polit. Sci. 3 (4), 353–377.

Holmes, D.I., 1998. The evolution of stylometry in humanities scholarship. Lit. Linguist. Comput. 13 (3), 111–117.

Hong, H., Kacperczyk, M., 2010. Competition and bias. Q. J. Econ. 125 (4), 1683–1725.

Iyengar, S., Simon, A.F., 2000. New perspectives and evidence on political communication and campaign effects. Annu. Rev. Psychol. 51, 149–169.

Iyengar, S., Peters, M.D., Kinder, D.R., 1982. Experimental demonstrations of the "Not-So-Minimal" consequences of television news programs. Am. Polit. Sci. Rev. 76 (4), 848–858.

Jerit, J., Barabas, J., Clifford, S., 2013. Comparing contemporaneous laboratory and field experiments on media effects. Public Opin. Q. 77 (1), 256–282.

Kahn, K.F., Kenney, P.J., 2002. The slant of the news. Am. Polit. Sci. Rev. 96 (2), 381–394.

Kepplinger, H.M., 1982. Visual biases in television campaign coverage. Commun. Res. 9, 432–446.

Knight, B.G., Chiang, C.-F., 2011. Media bias and influence: evidence from newspaper endorsements. Rev. Econ. Stud. 78 (3), 795–820.

Krosnick, J.A., Miller, J.M., 1996. The anatomy of news media priming. In: Iyengar, S., Reeves, R. (Eds.), Do the Media Govern? Politicians, Voters, and Reporters in America. Sage, Thousand Oaks, CA.

Ladd, J.M., Lenz, G.S., 2009. Exploiting a rare communication shift to document the persuasive power of the news media. Am. J. Polit. Sci. 53 (2), 394–410.

Larcinese, V., 2007. The instrumental voter goes to the newsagent: demand for information, marginality and the media. J. Theor. Polit. 19 (3), 249–276.

Larcinese, V., Puglisi, R., Snyder Jr., J.M., 2011. Partisan bias in economic news: evidence on the agenda-setting behavior of U.S. newspapers. J. Public Econ. 95 (9–10), 1178–1189.

Lasswell, H.D., Lerner, D., de Sola Pool, I., 1952. The Comparative Study of Symbols. Stanford University Press, Stanford, CA.

Laver, M., Garry, J., 2000. Estimating policy positions from political texts. Am. J. Polit. Sci. 44, 619–634.

Laver, M., Benoit, K., Garry, J., 2003. Extracting policy positions from political texts using words as data. Am. Polit. Sci. Rev. 97 (2), 311–331.

Lippmann, W., 1922. Public Opinion. Macmillan, New York, NY.

Lott Jr., J.R., Hassett, K.A., 2014. Is newspaper coverage of economic events politically biased? Public Choice 160 (1–2), 65–108.

Lowry, D.T., Shidler, J.A., 1995. The sound bites, the biters, and the bitten: an analysis of network TV news bias in campaign. J. Mass Commun. Q. 72, 3–43.

McCombs, M.E., 2002. The agenda-setting role of the mass media in the shaping of public opinion. In: Paper Presented at Mass Media Economics 2002 Conference, London School of Economics.

McCombs, M.E., Shaw, D.L., 1972. The agenda-setting function of mass media. Public Opin. Q. 36 (2), 176–187.

Mendenhall, T.C., 1887. The characteristic curves of composition. Science IX, 237–249.

Moriarty, S.E., Garramone, G.M., 1986. A study of newsmagazine photographs of the 1984 presidential campaign. Journal. Q. 63, 728–734.

Moriarty, S.E., Popvich, M.N., 1991. Newsmagazine visuals and the 1988 presidential election. Journal. Q. 68, 371–380.

Mosteller, F., Wallace, D.L., 1963. Inference in an authorship problem. J. Am. Stat. Assoc. 58 (302), 275–309.

Mullainathan, S., Shleifer, A., 2005. The market for news. Am. Econ. Rev. 95 (4), 1005–1030.

Niven, D., 2003. Objective evidence on media bias: newspaper coverage of congressional party switchers. J. Mass Commun. Q. 80 (2), 311–326.

Nyhan, B., 2012. Does the U.S. media have a liberal bias? Perspect. Polit. 10 (3), 767–771.

Petrocik, J.R., 1996. Issue ownership in presidential elections, with a 1980 case study. Am. J. Polit. Sci. 40 (3), 825–850.

Poole, K.T., Rosenthal, H., 1997. Congress: A Political-Economic History of Roll Call Voting. Oxford University Press, New York, NY.

Poole, K.T., Rosenthal, H., 2012. Ideology and Congress. Transactions Publishers, New Brunswick, NJ.

Puglisi, R., 2011. Being the New York Times: the political behaviour of a newspaper. B. E. J. Econom. Anal. Policy. 11 (1)(contributions): Article 20.

Puglisi, R., Snyder Jr., J.M., 2011. Newspaper coverage of political scandals. J. Polit. 73 (3), 1–20.

Puglisi, R., Snyder Jr., J.M., 2015. The balanced U.S. press. J. Eur. Econ. Assoc. 13 (2), 240–264.

Qian, N., Yanagizawa-Drott, D., 2015. Government Distortion in Independently Owned Media: Evidence from U.S. Cold War News Coverage of Human Rights. Yale University. Unpublished manuscript.

Renfro, P.C., 1979. Bias in selection of letters to the editor. Journal. Q. 56, 822–826.

Reuter, J., Zitzewitz, E., 2006. Do ads influence editors? Advertising and bias in the financial media. Q. J. Econ. 121 (1), 197–227.

Robinson, J.P., 1972. Perceived media bias and the 1968 vote: can the media affect behavior after all? Journal. Q. 49, 239–246.

Robinson, J.P., 1974. The press as king maker. Journal. Q. 51, 587–594.

Schiffer, A.J., 2006. Assessing partisan bias in political news: the case(s) of local Senate election coverage. Polit. Commun. 23 (1), 23–39.

Sigelman, L., Walkosz, B.J., 1992. Letters to the editor as a public opinion thermometer. Soc. Sci. Q. 73, 938–946.

Soroka, S.N., 2012. The gatekeeping function: distributions of information in media and the real world. J. Polit. 74 (2), 514–528.

Stanley, H.W., Niemi, R.G., 2013. Vital Statistics on American Politics 2013–2014. CQ Press, Washington DC.

St. Dizier, B., 1985. The effect of newspaper endorsements and party identification on voting choice. Journal. Q. 62, 589–594.

Strömberg, D., 2004. Mass Media Competition, Political Competition, and Public Policy. Rev. Econ. Stud. 71 (1), 265–284.

Waldman, P., Devitt, J., 1998. Newspaper photographs and the 1996 presidential election: the question of bias. J. Mass Commun. Q. 75, 302–311.

Young, L., Soroka, S., 2012. Affective news: the automated coding of sentiment in political texts. Polit. Commun. 29, 205–231.

CHAPTER 16

Media Capture and Media Power

Andrea Prat
Columbia University, New York, NY, USA

Contents

16.1.	Introduction	669
16.2.	Media Capture	672
16.3.	Media Power	676
16.4.	Implications for Media Regulation	682
16.5.	Conclusions	685
	References	685

Abstract

This chapter studies situations where media sources deliberately deviate from truthful reporting in order to manipulate electoral outcomes. Media capture occurs when the government actively attempts to influence the media industry. We instead speak of media power when news organizations engage in biased reporting for political reasons. Existing theories identify factors that make these phenomena more likely to occur, suggest ways of measuring them, and study their welfare effect and policy implications.

Keywords

Media capture, Media power, Media concentration, Biased news, Political economy

JEL Codes

D03, D72, H5, L82

16.1. INTRODUCTION

This chapter surveys models of media capture and media power. In both cases, media sources deliberately deviate from truthful reporting in order to affect electoral outcomes. We will speak of media capture when the government has an active role: it uses threats and promises to suppress unfavorable information. We will instead speak of media power when the government has a passive role, while politically driven media organizations use reporting strategically to manipulate electoral outcomes. Theories of media power and media capture identify circumstances when news manipulation is more likely to succeed and electoral outcomes are more likely to be distorted. Both phenomena are facilitated by the presence of a concentrated media industry and we will review ways to quantify. As

Handbook of Media Economics, Volume 1B
ISSN 2213-6630, http://dx.doi.org/10.1016/B978-0-444-63685-0.00016-4

both media capture and media power can reduce citizens' welfare, the chapter also discusses how media regulation can reduce the extent of these two phenomena.

In modern democracies, citizens receive information about the behavior of their government through the media. Very few of us get a chance to observe government in action directly. Mostly, we rely on the press, television, radio, the Internet, and other forms of mass communication to learn about the behavior of our policy-makers. This information is crucial to the functioning of democracy because citizens use it to keep elected officials accountable.[1] Without it, we do not know how our current rulers have behaved and it is more difficult for us to discipline them. Canonical agency theory predicts that the principal's welfare increases when she has more information about her agent because the agent behaves better (Holmström, 1979; Prat, 2006).

In an ideal world, the government and the media act independently. The former exercises its constitutionally defined powers, the latter engages in truthful and vigorous reporting. As Jefferson (1792) put it: "No government ought to be without censors, and where the press is free, no one ever will. If virtuous, it need not fear the fair operation of attack and defence. Nature has given to man no other means of sifting out the truth whether in religion, law or politics. I think it as honorable to the government neither to know nor notice its sycophants or censors, as it would be undignified and criminal to pamper the former and persecute the latter." This chapter studies situations when this ideal independence is violated, and the media industry and the government interact in ways that undermine democratic accountability.

News manipulation can take many forms (see Chapter 17 for a survey of the empirical literature on media capture). In particular, the government may play an active role or a passive role. A stark example of active capture—which we refer to as media capture—is the one documented by McMillan and Zoido (2004) through a forensic approach. In the 1990s the government of Peru made monetary transfers to most mainstream media sources on the understanding that they would provide positive coverage and suppress damaging news. Freedom House (2014) documents its presence in a large number of countries. Capture can occur through bribery or threats. For instance, Freedom House (2014, p. 10) concludes: "The media environment in Russia [...] is characterized by the use of a pliant judiciary to prosecute independent journalists, impunity for the physical harassment and murder of journalists, and continued state control or influence over almost all traditional media outlets."

To engage in media capture, the government must be able to single out individual organizations for reward or punishment. This becomes more difficult in political systems with strong checks and balances and an independent judiciary system. In such a system, news manipulation takes a different form. The government is unable to influence the

---

[1] See Persson and Tabellini (2002) for an in-depth analysis of the role of information in political accountability models.

media through bribes and threats, but powerful media organizations can choose to bias reporting in order to influence government policy or even affect electoral outcomes. We refer to this situation as media power.

The canonical example of media power goes back to then end of the nineteenth century. William Randolph Hearst, the source of inspiration for Orson Welles' *Citizen Kane*, inflamed American public opinion against Spain through highly biased coverage of the Cuban Rebellion. Hearst's propaganda is cited as a key cause of the Spanish–American War of 1898. In more recent times, Silvio Berlusconi, after developing the largest commercial television network in Italy in the 1980s, went on to exert a major influence on Italy's democratic process, becoming Prime Minister three times over two decades. Durante and Knight (2012) document the reporting bias in Berlusconi's television channels.[2]

Obviously, media capture and media power are two stylized extremes. Often the interaction between government and news takes the form of a complex, mutually beneficial agreement between politicians and the media, where the bargaining power is shared between the two parties. However, for the purpose of building a theoretical framework to analyze capture, it is useful to focus on the two extreme formulations.

Methodologically, the analysis of the interaction between media, government, and electorate requires concepts from both industrial organization and political economy. The media industry is modeled as an oligopoly where firms may be pursuing both standard commercial revenues, which can be based on pay-per-view, subscriptions, or advertising, and "non-standard" benefits coming from politics, which take the form of bribes or other policy benefits in media capture, or the form of direct political payoffs in media power. Voters are modeled as Bayesian but with limited information.

Media capture and media power imply manipulation of news. This can happen in a direct way through suppression of news, or even fabrication of false news, and in a more indirect manner through biased reporting. This chapter focuses mainly on the effect of news manipulation rather than the mechanisms through which it can be achieved. See Chapter 13 for a survey of the influence of media coverage on government, Chapter 14 for a survey of the theoretical work on media bias, and Chapter 15 for a survey of the theoretical work on media bias.

Section 16.2 will discuss media capture models like that of Besley and Prat (2006), where the government has the bargaining power and has instruments to affect the payoff of individual news sources. The government attempts to induce media outlets to suppress

---

[2] While media capture requires somewhat weak democratic institutions, media power can be present in countries with a tradition of checks and balances and journalistic independence. The Leveson Inquiry concluded: "Taken as a whole, the evidence clearly demonstrates that, over the last 30–35 years and probably much longer, the political parties of UK national Government and of UK official Opposition, have had or developed too close a relationship with the press in a way which has not been in the public interest" (Leveson 2012).

potentially damaging news. Capture arises when this attempt is successful. Two factors make capture harder: media plurality and transaction costs between the government and the media. Media plurality—namely the existence of a large number of independently owned outlets—raises the incentive for an individual outlet to publish information that voters find interesting and hence makes it more difficult for the politician to suppress a scandal. Transaction costs—akin to the checks and balances mentioned above—reduce the government's ability to reward favorable media sources and punish critical ones.

Section 16.3 assumes that transaction costs are so high that the government cannot bribe and threaten the media. The focus of the analysis shifts to media power: media sources may want to bias reporting in order to affect policy (Anderson and McLaren, 2010; Chan and Suen, 2008; Duggan and Martinelli, 2011). Following Prat (2014), we discuss robust bounds to the ability of media organizations to affect electoral outcomes. Here again, media concentration plays a crucial role. A media organization operating in a pluralistic news landscape struggles to influence policy both because it reaches a lower number of citizens and because those citizens are more likely to receive information from other sources as well. The main goal of the section is to provide a relatively simple way of quantifying power as a function of media concentration that can be quantified with existing media consumption data.

Section 16.4 discusses possible regulatory responses to the risk of capture. As media capture and media power require a concentrated industry, mature democracies have put in place a number of provisions against excessive concentration, which fall into two categories: *ad hoc* platform-specific rules and general competition policy principles. We argue that both sets of provisions are insufficient both conceptually and practically, especially in a world characterized by the proliferation of new media platforms. We discuss the recent evolution of the regulatory framework in this area. Section 16.5 concludes.

16.2. MEDIA CAPTURE

Capture is a complex phenomenon that straddles political economy and industrial organization. However, we can identify some of the key determinants of capture with a relatively simple model (Besley and Prat, 2006). The setup combines a simple model of electoral politics with assumptions on the objectives of media companies and their possible dealings with political incumbents.

On the political side, consider a basic retrospective voting model where the quality of politicians is unknown. An incumbent is exogenously in power in the first period. The quality of the incumbent can be high, $\theta = g$, or low, $\theta = b$. The probability that quality is high is $\gamma = \Pr(\theta = g)$. A high-quality incumbent delivers a payoff of 1 to voters; a low-quality incumbent delivers a zero payoff. However, voters do not observe payoffs directly: they rely on media reporting. For example, voters may not know whether a certain public project was useful or whether it was developed in a cost-effective way.

At the end of the first period, the incumbent faces re-election against a challenger of unknown quality (for the challenger $\gamma = \Pr(\theta = g)$ as well).

There are n *ex ante* identical media outlets. As an incumbent would never have a reason to suppress positive news, we simplify the analysis by restricting attention to negative signals. If the incumbent is good ($\theta = g$), outlets receive no signals. If she is bad ($\theta = b$), they receive a negative signal with probability q. Again, for simplicity assume that either they all receive the signal or none of them does. The signal is verifiable: for instance, it is hard information that the project was useless or too expensive.

If there is no media capture, outlets will report a signal whenever they receive one. It is easy to see that voters prefer re-electing the incumbent rather than electing the challenger if and only if there is no negative signal. Hence, a bad incumbent is re-elected with probability $1 - q$ and the challenger wins with probability γq.

The possibility of capture comes by adding a stage, after the media observe their signal and before they report it, where the incumbent can attempt to silence them. The incumbent offers a vector of non-negative monetary transfers $(t_i)_{i=1,\ldots,n}$ to every outlet. Transfer t_i costs t_i dollars to the incumbent but yields t_i/τ to the outlet that receives it.

The parameter τ can take any value between zero and infinity and represents the ease with which the government can make transfers that benefit the media. If τ is very low, the government can condition media decisions at a very low cost. This may represent a situation where the media is government-owned and the governance structure is so weak that the government can replace the director at any time. The incumbent can promise a large payoff to the media (the director is not removed) at a minimal cost. In the case of McMillan and Zoido (2004), the value of τ was arguably 1, as benefits took the form of cash. Other, more indirect benefits, may be more or less expensive. Djankov et al. (2003) report that a majority of private media organizations around the world are owned by families (rather than diffuse shareholders). Often those are powerful local families with other economic interests in the country. The incumbent can favor them with government contracts or beneficial legislation. We therefore view τ as the lack of transaction costs between the government and the media.

Media outlets have two sources of revenues. Besides government transfers, they enjoy commercial revenue in proportion to their audience (or readership). Such revenues may come from subscription, sales or advertising. As there is a mass 1 of voters and the commercial revenue per individual is a, if outlet i receives a share s_i of the total audience, its revenue is as_i. Every media outlet maximizes $as_i + t_i/\tau$. The parameter a measures the relative strength of the commercial motive with respect to government-related revenues. The audience is attracted by informative outlets, namely those that are reporting a signal. If m of the n outlets report a signal, then each of them will receive a share $s = 1/m$ of the audience and the remaining outlets will have no audience.

To understand what happens in equilibrium, consider an outlet that has observed a negative signal and receives an offer of t_i to suppress the signal. The outlet will be willing to accept if benefit of the transfer t_i/τ is at least as large as the foregone commercial revenue a/m, implying $t_i \geq a\tau/m$.

The incumbent is willing to pay an outlet to suppress its signal only if all the other outlets are quiet too. If the incumbent pays transfers in equilibrium, then an outlet who deviates and rejects her transfers will be the only one reporting the negative signal and will thus make a monopoly commercial profit. If in equilibrium all outlets are silenced, it must be that each of them receives a transfer $t_i \geq a\tau$. This implies that the minimal amount the incumbent spends to suppress the negative signal is $na\tau$. If we assume that the incumbent derives a benefit r from being re-elected, we get:

Proposition 16.1

The media is captured if and only if media plurality, the commercial motive, and transaction costs are sufficiently low, namely if $na\tau \leq r$.

Note that plurality here has a literal meaning of "quantity" of media outlets. Without capture, all outlets are reporting the same information. The only benefit of these otherwise redundant outlets is that they make capture harder for the incumbent because commercial revenue is higher if other outlets are captured. In this simple setup, the incumbent must compensate each outlet as if it were a media monopolist, because that is what it would be if it deviated. In a more general setting, the result may not be so stark but it will still be true that buying out multiple independent media with a certain total audience is more expensive than buying out one media outlet with the same total audience.

Capture is bad for voters because it makes them unable to distinguish between a good incumbent and a bad incumbent.[3] As a result, incumbents are less likely to lose their job and the average quality of politicians decreases:

Proposition 16.2

Turnover of politicians and voter welfare are increasing in media plurality, the commercial motive, and transaction costs.

The last proposition is consistent with cross-country patterns observed by Brunetti and Weder (2003), Djankov et al. (2003), and Besley and Prat (2006). The political longevity of the country's most important elected official (prime minister or president, depending on the constitutional system) is increasing in media owned by the government (which presumably decreases τ) and decreasing in media concentration (as measured by the share of audience controlled by the top five outlets). The effect is large: for example, the average political longevity in countries with "low" concentration (the top five

---

[3] *Ex post*, voters are indifferent between re-electing the incumbent or not re-electing, yet they vote for her. It is easy to see that there is no (undominated) equilibrium where voters would vote for the challenger if there is no signal. In such an equilibrium, the incumbent would have no incentive to capture the media and hence the lack of a signal would be good news about the incumbent.

newspapers control less than 75% of the audience) is around 5 years; longevity in countries with "high" concentration is over 10 years.

The baseline model considers a homogeneous electorate and assumes that capture comes only from the government. Corneo (2006) allows voters to have heterogeneous preferences, reflected in the presence of different interest groups. The media can collude with the various interest groups. The media (a monopolist) can make a secret agreement with a particular interest group. This model highlights the role of ownership concentration. Media capture is more likely when there are a few large shareholders than when ownership is diffuse.

Petrova (2008) considers the effect of income distribution. The government uses taxes to provide a public good that is relatively more useful to the poor than to the rich. There is uncertainty about the usefulness of the public good and the media can provide voters with information. However, the rich may offer bribes to the media to understate the value of the public project. Media capture arises in equilibrium, and its extent is greater when society is more unequal. Media capture accomplishes its goal: a country whose media is captured has on average lower public good investment. As this effect is due to electoral incentives, one of the predictions is that the relation between media capture and public good provision is stronger in countries with stronger democratic institutions.

The baseline model can be extended to allow for media differentiation. Suppose individual outlets decide how much effort to put into government monitoring. Outlet i chooses investment level $q_i \in [0, 1]$ at cost $c(q_i)$, under the assumption that c is increasing and convex. The idea is that some negative signals are easy to uncover while others require extensive investigative journalism. Every bad incumbent produces a negative signal, characterized by a difficulty of detection $\nu \in [0, 1]$. A signal with value ν is observed only by outlets with an investment above that level: $q_i \geq \nu$.

Let us first see what happens in the media differentiation case when there is no capture. Higher levels of journalistic investment must be rewarded with higher marginal commercial revenues. In equilibrium, *ex-ante* identical media will choose different levels of journalistic investment. One outlet—let's say $i = 1$—will make the highest investment, and will equalize the marginal cost of investment, $q'(\nu)$, with the marginal revenue of investment under the assumption that it will be the only one to report a marginal signal, a. Another outlet—$i = 2$—will make the second-highest investment, equalizing the marginal cost of investment with the marginal revenue of duopoly reporting: $q'(\nu) = a/2$. The kth outlet will choose ν to solve

$$q'(\nu) = \frac{a}{k}.$$

Thus, a non-captured media industry will exhibit vertical differentiation.

If we consider the possibility of capture, we must ask under what conditions the incumbent would be willing to put up the resources to silence the media. If the signal is easy to detect, the incumbent would have to pay off a large number of outlets, while if ν becomes higher the number of media is smaller. In equilibrium there is a threshold $\bar{\nu}$ such that the media is captured if and only if $\nu \geq \bar{\nu}$. Obviously, if ν is very high, no outlet observes the signal and capture is not necessary.

With capture, vertical differentiation is reduced. The marginal revenue of the outlet with the highest investment does not come from commercial sources but from government transfers. As we saw in Proposition 16.1, such revenue equals monopoly profit. But now there can be more than one top outlet. In fact, in equilibrium there will typically be multiple outlets with the highest level of investment. There is also a fringe of lower-investment media (with $q < \bar{\nu}$) who pursue commercial revenues in the case of easy-to-detect signals. The high-level outlets will report their signal if $\nu < \bar{\nu}$ and will conceal it in exchange for a transfer from the government if $\nu \geq \bar{\nu}$. From the point of view of the audience, which does not observe the unreported signals, the media landscape is composed of a number of equally mediocre media outlets. Thus, realized vertical differentiation is lower in a captured market than in a non-captured one.

So far, the only action that citizens could take was voting. Gehlbach and Sonin (2014) model a more general mobilizing role of the media. For instance, government may want citizens to support war efforts. Citizens make individual investment decisions based on the information they have. By manipulating news provision, the government can affect aggregate investments levels. Media bias is stronger in the presence of a mobilizing motive. The authors explore the difference between state-owned media and privately owned media. The bias difference between the two increases when a country becomes more democratic.

16.3. MEDIA POWER

The previous section offered a one-sided view of capture, where all the bargaining power is on the government's side. However, there are important examples of powerful media owners who have exerted influence on the political system of their countries.

To analyze phenomena like Hearst and Berlusconi, we must move beyond the assumption—made for analytical convenience in the first part of the chapter—that all media outlets are *ex ante* identical. On the contrary, we now begin from a situation where citizens are following specific media sources and we ask how much sway those sources have on the political process.

As Polo (2005) argued, market power notions do not fully capture the specificity of the media industry. Market power measures, like the Hirschmann–Herfindahl Index (HHI), define the relevant market in terms of cross-elasticity of demand. This leads to identifying markets in terms of technological platforms: newspapers, radio, television, social media, etc. This definition is both too broad because it includes a lot of activity that does not relate to political information (e.g., most television programs are not news) and too narrow because it segments political information by platform. In an attemt to bridge this gap, in 2003 the US Federal Communications Commission proposed a cross-platform measure: the Media Diversity Index. The index assigned a weight to every platform: broadcast TV (33.8%), newspapers (20.2%), weekly periodicals (8.6%), radio (24.9%), cable Internet (2.3%), and all other Internet (10.2%). Within each platform, every outlet was given equal weight. The index was eventually struck down by the courts in *Prometheus Radio Project v. FCC* because of "irrational assumptions and inconsistencies." In an attempt to overcome these issues, Prat (2014) develops a micro-founded model of media power.

Let us begin by describing the electoral part of the model. There are two candidates or parties, A and B. The relative quality of candidate B over candidate A is a random variable σ, uniformly distributed on $[0,1]$. In expectation, the two candidates are equally attractive, but a given σ voters prefer candidate B if and only if $\sigma \geq 1/2$. Specifically, voters' payoff is $1/2$ if they elect A and σ if they elect B.

As in the first part of the chapter, voters rely on the media for information on σ. There is a set of media outlets that receive a number of binary signals drawn from a binomial distribution with parameter σ. As the goal of this analysis is to measure distortions due to bias rather than lack of information, we assume that the number of signals each outlet receives tends to infinity. Let $\mathbb{M}$ denote the finite set of media outlets, with typical individual outlets denoted $1 \leq m \leq |\mathbb{M}|$. Let $x_m = (x_{m1}, ..., x_{mN})$ denote a vector of N binary signals—*news items*—observed by outlet m, with $\Pr(x_{mi} = 1|\sigma) = 1$. News items are, conditional on σ, independent within and across media outlets.

There is a unitary mass of voters. Each voter follows one or more media sources according to the following media consumption matrix. Let $M \subset \mathbb{M}$ denote some subset of outlets. Then voters are partitioned into *segments*, indexed by the subset M of outlets they consume, and for each $M \subset \mathbb{M}$ let q_M be the fraction of voters who consume (exactly) the subset M. Clearly

$$\sum_{M \subset \mathbb{M}} q_M = 1.$$

(If some voters follow zero sources, we can disregard them under the assumption that their vote is random.) Table 16.1 is an example of a media consumption matrix.

If a cell of the matrix contains a full square, it indicates that the voters in the segment of that row follow the media source in the column. For instance, voters in segment a follow Media 1 and Media 2. The reach is the percentage of the population that follows a particular media source: in this case all media outlets reach half of the population.

The example is designed so that all sources have the same reach. Does it mean they have the same power? Intuitively the answer is no. Compare for instance Media 3 and Media 4. They are both present in Segment d, and it is reasonable to expect that—barring other unmodeled factors—they should have the same influence on voters in d. However, Media 4 is the monopolist in Segment c, while Media 3 competes with three other sources for the attention of voters in Segment b. It is reasonable to expect that Media

Table 16.1 Media consumption matrix

Segment	Share	Media 1	Media 2	Media 3	Media 4	Media 5
a	25%	■	■			
b	25%	■	■	■		■
c	25%				■	
d	25%			■	■	■
Reach		50%	50%	50%	50%	50%

4 will have more influence on voters in c than Media 3 on voters in b. As we will see in what follows, this intuition is correct and can be quantified.

Voters have a potentially limited bandwidth. They only process or remember a certain number of news items. For now, assume they only remember an (odd) number K of news items for every source they follow. The items are chosen randomly among those published.

As in the first part of the chapter, let us first look at what happens when all media are unbiased. Each outlet reports all the signals it receives. Each voter remembers K signals and uses them to make decisions. If the majority of the binary signals are in favor of A, he votes for A. If the majority is in favor of B, he votes for B. The total share of votes for B is therefore σ, and B is elected if and only if her quality is greater than A. Thus, with unbiased media, elections produce an efficient outcome.

Now consider the possibility that media can be biased. Assume that a subset G of the set M of media sources is controlled by an owner whose only objective is to get A elected. He has no financial constraints or motive. The effect of the owner's bias depends on the response of voters. One approach is to estimate these factors carefully and find the exact effect of the bias given the estimates. However, if it is difficult to obtain reliable estimates, an alternative approach consists of considering a large set of possible parameter values and identifying an upper bound to the potential influence of biased media on the election. The latter approach is inspired by a recent literature on robust bounds in agency problems, which includes Chassang (2013), Madarasz and Prat (2010), and Chassang and Padro i Miquel (2013).

The biased media owner can report news selectively. While the set of signals his media outlets receive contains a share σ of items favorable to B, the owner reports only a share $s \in [0, 1]$ of signals favorable to B (while he reports all signals favorable to A). As the media consumers have limited bandwidth, they cannot count the number of items reported (which tends to infinity for both biased and unbiased media). Hence, in the spirit of analyzing the worst-case scenario, citizens have no direct way of ascertaining the presence of bias.

The difficult question is: how will voters process biased news? This depends on whether they understand the motives of the biased owner. Let $\beta \in (0, 1)$ be the prior probability that voters assign to the presence of an evil media owner. This is a subjective parameter that captures the voters' views on the possibility that G is under the effective control of a unitary owner and that such an owner is biased in favor of candidate A. The value of β is hard to predict in practice, especially if we are considering a country that has hitherto had unbiased media.

As both the sophistication parameter β and the bandwidth parameter K are difficult to estimate, we will compute the maximal value of the power index over the whole parameter set. This will give us an upper bound on the ability of a media owner to influence the electoral system.

We begin by holding bandwidth K constant and by computing an upper bound to the power index over β. Consider a voter i in group M, who observes a particular realization of the K_M-sized signal vector y^i he receives from media outlets in M. The vector includes news items randomly drawn from outlets in M. Let y^i_k denote the kth realization of the vector and let $m(k)$ denote the media outlet it is drawn from. Suppose the voter believes that the evil owner would use reporting strategy $\hat{s}$. Then, the probability of realization $y^i = Y$ would be given by:

$$\Pr\left(y^i = Y|\sigma,\hat{s}\right)$$
$$= \sigma^{N_1(M/G)}(1-\sigma)^{N_0(M/G)}\left((1-\beta)\sigma^{N_1(G)}(1-\sigma)^{N_0(G)} + \beta(\hat{s}\sigma)^{N_1(G)}(1-\hat{s}\sigma)^{N_0(G)}\right),$$

where $N_y(M/G)$ is the number of signals with value y coming from unbiased outlets, while $N_y(G)$ is the same variable for potentially biased outlets.

The voter computes the posterior on candidate quality as follows:

$$E[\sigma|Y,\hat{s}] = \frac{\displaystyle\int_0^1 \Pr(y^i = Y|\sigma,\hat{s})\sigma\,d\sigma}{\displaystyle\int_0^1 \Pr(y^i = Y|\sigma,\hat{s})\,d\sigma}$$

and votes for A if and only if $E[\sigma|Y,\hat{s}] \leq 1/2$.

If we wanted to compute the equilibrium for a particular value of β we would now have to find a fixed point where the reporting strategy of the biased media does coincide with the voters' conjecture $\hat{s}$. This is in general an untractable problem. Instead, we look for a lower bound to this expression and we show that this lower bound is indeed attained (see Prat, 2014, for details of the derivation). Given the lower bound in posteriors, one can move to deriving an upper bound to the vote share of the candidate favored by the biased owner.

It can be shown that the upper bound to A's vote share in a segment where G controls a share g_M of outlets and voters have bandwidth K_M is given by:

$$p_A(g_M, K_M, \sigma) = \sum_{k=0}^{\lceil K_M/2\rceil-1} \binom{K_M}{k}((1-g_M)\sigma)^k(1-(1-g_M)\sigma)^{K_M-k}. \qquad (16.1)$$

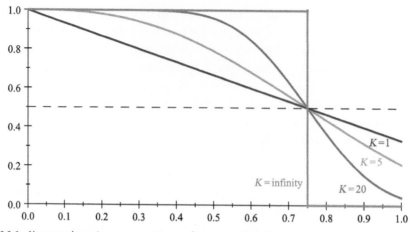

Figure 16.1 A's vote share in segment M as a function of quality σ.

Figure 16.1 depicts a segment where 33.3% of the outlets are biased. This would correspond to Segment b in the example above under the assumption that exactly one of three outlets is biased. The x-axis represents σ, while the y-axis represents the share of voters who choose A. The figure depicts $p_A(1/4, K_M, \sigma)$ for various values of K_M.

In the plot, A's vote share is a decreasing function of σ and it is more s-shaped as bandwidth increases. All curves intersect the 1/2 horizontal line at $\sigma > 3/4$.

As one can see from the figure, the role of K on media power is ambiguous. If B is slightly better than A ($\sigma \in (0.5, 0.75)$), the biased owner has more power in a segment where K_M is high, because he manages to get an absolute majority of signals favorable to A. If instead the difference is large ($\sigma > 0.75$), the power is greater when bandwidth is minimal. We shall return to this point shortly when we analyze bandwidth.

The two extreme cases are particularly easy to characterize. When bandwidth is minimal, A's vote share is a linear function of σ:

$$p_A(g_M, 1, \sigma) = (1 - g_M)(1 - \sigma) + g_M;$$

when bandwidth is maximal, the vote share is a step function

$$\lim_{K_M \to \infty} p_A(g_M, k_M, \sigma) = \begin{cases} 1 & \text{if } \sigma < \dfrac{1}{2(1 - g_M)} \\ 1/2 & \text{if } \sigma = \dfrac{1}{2(1 - g_M)} \\ 0 & \text{if } \sigma > \dfrac{1}{2(1 - g_M)} \end{cases}.$$

We are now ready to define the media power index. Let $\bar{\sigma}$ be the highest value of σ such that the A-vote share is at lease 1/2, namely the solution to

$$\sum_{M \subset \mathbf{M}} q_M p_A(g_M, k_M, \overline{\sigma}) = \frac{1}{2}.$$

Let the power index be defined as

$$\pi = \min(2\overline{\sigma} - 1, 1).$$

The minimal value, zero, occurs when $\overline{\sigma} = 1/2$, meaning that A gets elected only when she would get elected if reporting were unbiased, in which case the media owner has no influence on elections. The maximal value occurs when $\overline{\sigma}(K) \geq 1$, meaning that A is always elected, regardless of how bad she is in comparison to B.

The power index π corresponds to the maximal welfare loss that voters can experience as a result of biased reporting: instead of having B elected and receiving σ, they receive $1 - \sigma$, generating a difference $2\sigma - 1$. This can be computed by summing the vote shares over all segments, as described by (16.1), and finding the maximal value of $\overline{\sigma}$ that still allows G to get A elected. This step yields the main result of this section:

Proposition 16.3

For a given bandwidth vector K, the power index of media group G is $\pi = (2\overline{\sigma} - 1, 1)$, where $\overline{\sigma}$ is the largest solution between $1/2$ and 1 of the following polynomial equation:

$$\sum_{M \subset \mathbf{M}} q_M \sum_{k=0}^{\lceil K_M/2 \rceil - 1} \binom{K_M}{k} ((1 - g_M)\overline{\sigma})^k (1 - (1 - g_M)\overline{\sigma})^{K_M - k} = \frac{1}{2}.$$

As one would expect, the index is monotonic in g_M. An increase in the attention share of biased media leads to more power.

The power index takes a particularly simple value when bandwidth is either minimal or maximal. When $K_M = 1$ in all segments the power index is simply

$$\overline{\sigma}(1) = \min\left(1, \frac{a_G}{1 - a_G}\right),$$

where $a_G = \sum_M q_M g_M$ is the average attention share of the biased owner.

For the maximal case, instead we have:

$$\lim_{K_M \to \infty, \text{ all } M} \overline{\sigma}(K) = \min\left(1, \frac{\text{median}(g_M)}{1 - \text{median}(g_M)}\right),$$

where median(g_M) is defined as the g_M for the median voter.

One can go one step further and compute the maximal value of the power index over all possible values of the bandwidth vector K. This case is characterized in Prat (2014). In practice, the relative values of the index in the worst-case scenario are similar to the relative values in the minimal-bandwidth case. So from now on, we focus on the minimal-bandwidth case.

Table 16.2 Power indices

	Media 1	Media 2	Media 3	Media 4	Media 5
Attention share	18.75%	18.75%	14.58%	33.33%	14.58%
Minimal-bandwidth index	0.231	0.231	0.171	0.500	0.171

As an illustration, we can compute the minimal-bandwidth index of some outlets in Table 16.1. All we need to know is the attention share of each outlet. For instance, Media 1 has 50% of the attention in Segment a, 25% of the attention in Segment b, and no attention share in the other two segments. The total attention share is therefore 18.75%. This yields a power index of

$$\overline{\sigma}(1) = \min\left(1, \frac{0.1875}{1 - 0.1875}\right) = 0.231.$$

The value $\overline{\sigma}(1) = 0.231$ can be interpreted as the maximal damage that Media 1 can inflict on the electorate if bandwidth is minimal in all segments. Table 16.2 reports the minimal-bandwidth value of the index for all five media outlets. One could also compute the value of the maximal-bandwidth index, which in this case is zero for all media because no single media outlet is followed by a strict majority of voters. The values of the index for the five media outlets are reported in Table 16.2.

Given any media consumption matrix, one can use Proposition 16.1 to compute the power index of any media organization. Prat (2014) obtains power indices for major media organizations in the United States from 2000 to 2012. The relative rankings are quite stable across different specifications of the index. While a discussion of media power in the United States is outside the scope of this brief survey, the results highlight the continued importance of broadcasting. Three media conglomerates stand out in terms of power and all of them are mainly involved in television. New media and the press are ranked much lower because their attention share is much smaller than broadcasters, both because they have fewer followers and those followers tend to follow a larger number of sources. The media power index makes this relative ranking transparent.

16.4. IMPLICATIONS FOR MEDIA REGULATION

As we saw in the two previous sections, media manipulation is detrimental to citizens.[4] Both media capture and media power lead to worse outcomes for the electorate. In this section, we explore regulatory approaches to reducing this type of effect. As we saw that plurality is an effective defense against capture and power, we will pay particular attention to regulation aimed at controlling media concentration levels.

[4] For discussions of the welfare effects of media, see Prat and Strömberg (2013) and Stromberg (2015).

Existing media regulation falls under three broad categories: platform-specific regulation, general competition policy provisions, and direct provision. We examine them one by one, in light of the analysis of Sections 16.2 and 16.3.

The first category comprises a large set of provisions that apply only to media and usually only to one particular platform, like newspapers or broadcast television. They can be limits on ownership of a single company (in France and Spain, no single entity can own more than 49% of the shares of a media company), cross-ownership (e.g., newspapers and TV stations), and foreign ownership. They can also be limits on individual media organizations, in terms of number of licenses, market shares, and advertising. Platform-specific rules appear increasingly outdated in a world where platforms are proliferating and the same content is often delivered through different platforms. At a normative level, why should the same news item be subject to a certain set of rules if it is delivered over aerial television as opposed to the Internet? At a positive level, how can governments effectively control a large set of news sources operating with a continuously evolving set of technologies? As Section 16.3 argued, the relevant unit of analysis is not a particular media market but rather how individual voters aggregate political information coming from different sources. Two media sources may compete for the attention of voters even though they are in entirely different markets.

The second category of regulatory instruments comprises the standard set of competition rules that govern all industries. Those rules have the objective to protect consumer welfare measured in terms of price, quantity, and quality of products and services offered by firms. A highly debated question is whether such a set of rules is adequate for the media industry. Noam (2009) finds that most US media markets—including radio, newspapers, and television—have low levels of concentration, as measured by the HHI, lower than the threshold for regulatory scrutiny. Noam, however, argues that HHI misses an important element of plurality that is specific to the media industry: "As a citizen, I am better off if an alternative paper exists that keeps the city council and the big paper on their toes."

Polo (2005) too concludes that competition policy cannot be used as a substitute for policies aimed at fostering media plurality. While both types of regulation focus heavily on market shares, they do so for different reasons. This becomes apparent when one considers standard competition policy efficiency arguments in favor of merger: "Regulation for pluralism, on the other hand, having as objective to preserve independent operators and access for political views, has no reason to consider these efficiencies in its evaluation: from the point of view of pluralism, the only relevant effect of such concentration would be that of extending the control of a company on more media, something dangerous if partisans or lobbying motivations condition the editorial choices of the company in political information."

The analysis so far supports the view that competition policy is not sufficient to avoid media capture. In Besley and Prat (2006), the parameters that determine capture are $na\tau$ (number of media sources, commercial revenue, transaction costs), and they cannot be reduced to HHI. In Prat (2014), influence is determined by attention shares. These are different from the market shares used to compute HHI because they are not determined on the basis of markets but voter attention. This means that a given media landscape may generate no concerns from a competition policy viewpoint and still be dangerous from a capture viewpoint.

Capture models predict that concentration leads to a lower amount of political information and a higher level of bias. Both predictions are due to the desire of the media and the government to censor information that puts the government in a bad light, while still letting through favorable information. This leads to a reduction in the number of signals available to voters as well as a systematic distortion in favor of the incumbent.

Anderson and McLaren (2010) analyze the welfare effect of media mergers in the world with supply-driven media bias. Firms combine a profit motive and a commercial motive. Voters are rational. Media firms can withhold but not fabricate information. The authors show that citizen welfare is higher under duopoly than under monopoly, but that firms have an incentive to merge. There is therefore a role for regulation to prevent media mergers, beyond standard competition analysis.

The third category of regulatory instruments consists of direct news provision. Many countries, with the notable exception of the United States, have a large public service broadcasting (PSB) organization. In fact, in most countries the largest television network is publicly owned (Djankov et al., 2003). Can PSBs be a response to the risk of capture? The answer hinges on whether we think that a PSB has more or less incentives than private broadcasting organizations to engage in misreporting with the goal to affect the democratic process. One part of the literature, which begins with Coase (1950), and includes Hargreaves Heap (2005), Armstrong (2005), and Armstrong and Weeds (2007), abstracts from the risk of capture and focuses on different issues, such as the underprovision of socially desirable content and the interaction between public and private content provision. Other authors emphasize that PSB organizations can be biased too. Durante and Knight (2012) document stark changes in the bias of the Italian PSB when Silvio Berlusconi came to power. Djankov et al. (2003) find that high levels of public ownership of television networks are associated with negative political outcomes, such as less press freedom, fewer political and economic rights, and inferior governance.

Whether the presence of a PSB increases or decreases news manipulation depends on whether we face media capture or media power. In a country with low transaction cost (the τ parameter of Section 16.2), the presence of a large PSB is likely to make things worse because it makes it even easier for the government to control the media, both because it increases concentration and because, presumably, transaction cost is even lower in the interaction between the government and a government-controlled PSB organization. Indeed, in most early-stage democracies the PSB is simply a propaganda channel for the government. In a country with a high transaction cost, media power becomes the main issue. An independent PSB may give more guarantees of impartiality and unbiasedness than a private broadcaster. The BBC may be the most successful example in this sense, where editorial independence is secured by a governance structure designed to make transaction costs extremely high. It is unclear whether the BBC example can be replicated in democracies with fewer checks and balances.

16.5. CONCLUSIONS

This chapter surveyed the burgeoning literature on media capture (situations where the government controls the media) and media power (situations where the government is controlled by the media). The former is more likely in countries with low transaction costs between the government and the media, while the latter can be found in highly established democracies. Models of media capture highlight the role of media plurality, transaction costs, and commercial revenues. Models of media power also uncover an important role for media plurality, which can be quantified by a media power index (Prat, 2014), which can be computed on the basis of existing media consumption data. Media capture and media power should be viewed as two extremes on a spectrum where the government and the media industry collude to manipulate electoral outcomes.

Can the risk of media capture be reduced by regulation? We reviewed three sets of existing regulatory instruments: platform-specific regulation, competition policy provisions, and PSB. In all three cases, we highlighted important limitations in their effectiveness. Platform-specific regulation is increasingly arbitrary and ineffective in a world where news platforms are proliferating. Competition policy targets the right phenomenon, concentration, but focuses on markets rather than the political arena: a media power measure would be more appropriate. Finally, public service broadcasting is an effective defense against capture only if transaction costs between government and media are high. If instead media capture is a possibility, it may actually be facilitated by the presence of a larger publicly owned media organization.

REFERENCES

Anderson, S.P., McLaren, J., 2010. Media mergers and media bias with rational consumers. J. Eur. Econ. Assoc. 10, 831–859.

Armstrong, M., 2005. Public service broadcasting. Fisc. Stud. 26 (3), 281–299.

Armstrong, M., Weeds, H., 2007. Public service broadcasting in the digital world. In: Seabright, P., von Hagen, J. (Eds.), The Economic Regulation of Broadcasting Markets: Evolving Technology and Challenges for Policy. Cambridge University Press, Cambridge.

Besley, T., Prat, A., 2006. Handcuffs for the grabbing hand? the role of the media in political accountability. Am. Econ. Rev. 96 (3), 720–736.

Brunetti, A., Weder, B., 2003. A free press is bad news for corruption. J. Public Econ. 87 (7–8), 1801–1824.

Chan, J., Suen, W., 2008. A spatial theory of news consumption and electoral competition. Rev. Econ. Stud. 75 (3), 699–728.

Chassang, S., 2013. Calibrated incentive contracts. Econometrica 81 (5), 1935–1971.

Chassang, S., Padro i Miquel, G., 2013. Corruption, Intimidation and Whistle-Blowing: A Theory of Inference from Unverifiable Reports. Working Paper, Princeton University.

Coase, R.H., 1950. British Broadcasting: A Study in Monopoly. Longmans, London.

Corneo, G., 2006. Media capture in a democracy: the role of wealth concentration. J. Public Econ. 90, 37–58.

Djankov, S., McLeish, C., Nenova, T., Shleifer, A., 2003. Who owns the media? J. Law Econ. 46 (2), 341–381.

Duggan, J., Martinelli, C., 2011. A spatial theory of media slant and voter choice. Rev. Econ. Stud. 78, 667–692.

Durante, R., Knight, B., 2012. Partisan control, media bias, and viewer responses: evidence from Berlusconi's Italy. J. Eur. Econ. Assoc. 10, 451–481.

Freedom House, 2014. Freedom of the Press: 2014. Available from, www.freedomhouse.org.

Gehlbach, S., Sonin, K., 2014. Government control of the media. J. Public Econ. 118, 163–171.

Hargreaves Heap, S.P., 2005. Television in a digital age: what role for public service broadcasting? Econ. Policy 20, 112–157.

Holmström, B., 1979. Moral hazard and observability. Bell J. Econ. 10, 74–91 (Spring).

Jefferson, 1792. Letter to the President of the United States. Sep. 9.

Madarasz, K., Prat, A., 2010. Screening with an Approximate Type Space. CEPR Discussion Paper No. DP7900.

McMillan, J., Zoido, P., 2004. How to subvert democracy: montesinos in Peru. J. Econ. Perspect. 18 (4), 69–92.

Noam, E.M., 2009. Media Ownership and Concentration in America. Oxford University Press, Oxford.

Persson, T., Tabellini, G., 2002. Political Economy: Explaining Economic Policy. MIT Press, Cambridge, MA.

Petrova, M., 2008. Inequality and media capture. J. Public Econ. 92 (1–2), 183–212.

Polo, M., 2005. Regulation for pluralism in the media markets. In: Seabright, P., von Hagen, J. (Eds.), Regulation of Media Markets. Cambridge University Press, Cambridge.

Prat, A., 2006. The more closely we are watched, the better we behave? In: Hood, C., Heald, D. (Eds.), Transparency: The Key to Better Governance? Oxford University Press, Oxford.

Prat, A., 2014. Media Power. CEPR Discussion Paper 10094.

Prat, A., Strömberg, D., 2013. The political economy of mass media, in advances in economics and econometrics: theory and applications. In: Proceedings of the Tenth World Congress of the Econometric Society. Cambridge University Press, Cambridge.

Stromberg, D., 2015. Media and politics. Ann. Rev. Econ. 7, 173–205.

The Leveson Inquiry, 2012. An Inquiry into the Culture, Practices, and Ethics of the Press: Executive Summary, London. Available from, nationalarchives.gov.uk.

CHAPTER 17

Media Capture: Empirical Evidence

Ruben Enikolopov, Maria Petrova
Icrea-Barcelona Institute of Political Economy and Governance, Barcelona, Spain
Universitat Pompeu Fabra, Barcelona, Spain
Barcelona Graduate School of Economics, Barcelona, Spain
The New Economic School, Moscow, Russia

Contents

17.1. Introduction	688
17.2. Evidence on Media Capture	689
17.2.1 Capture and Media Content	689
17.2.2 Capture by Other Interest Groups	691
17.2.3 Related Evidence	692
17.3. Determinants of Media Capture	693
17.4. Media Effects in the Presence of Media Capture	694
17.4.1 Impact of Captured Media	694
17.4.2 Impact of Independent Media in Captured Environments	695
17.4.3 Adverse Effects of Media Transparency in Captured Environments	696
17.5. Limits of Media Capture	697
17.6. Conclusion	698
References	699

Abstract

This chapter overviews the empirical literature on the determinants and the consequences of media capture, i.e., the situation in which governments or other interest groups try to control the content of media outlets. We start by examining the evidence on the effect of media capture on the content of media outlets. Then we discuss the methods governments and other special interests use to control media. We review the literature on the determinants of media capture and the factors that affect the likelihood of media capture. Next, we present evidence on the effects of captured media on the behavior of people, as well as the effects of independent media in a captured environment. We conclude by discussing the factors that limit the effect of propaganda.

Keywords

Media capture, Propaganda, Media effects, Censorship, Independent media

JEL Codes

D72, L82, P26

Handbook of Media Economics, Volume 1B
ISSN 2213-6630, http://dx.doi.org/10.1016/B978-0-444-63685-0.00017-6

17.1. INTRODUCTION

Mass media are an important source of information about politics in most countries. Media reports have a potential to affect public opinion and to generate public support of particular politicians and policies. As a result, politicians have incentives to control the media whenever they see the opportunity to do so. The goal of this chapter is to see whether media capture indeed occurs, and, if it does, how it changes the way media and politics interact with each other.

One of the most detailed forensic examples of media capture is described in McMillan and Zoido (2004). Their paper studies Fujimori's Peru, where the head of secret police, Vladimir Montesinos, kept records of bribes paid by the government to different actors. The paper shows that directors of TV channels were offered much higher bribes, as compared with politicians or judges, so that in the end he paid 100 times more in bribes to media outlets than to all judges and politicians combined.[1] In other words, mass media turned out to be the most expensive among checks and balances in the Peruvian political system. The heads of TV channels, in exchange, allowed Montesinos to review daily news programs before broadcasting, and to broadcast information about political candidates only with his written approval. Mass media also contributed to the fall of Fujimori's regime. When one of the videos showing bribe taking was leaked, one small unbribed TV channel started to show the video around the clock. Even controlled channels soon started to show the video, as they were losing their audience otherwise. To increase dissemination, people placed large TV sets in windows and in the streets, and the number of the regime's opponents quickly increased.

According to a Freedom House 2014 study, 44% of the world's population lives in countries with media environments that are not "free," i.e., in which mass media are almost fully captured, while only one in seven people in the world live in countries where media is considered as "free." In recent years, researchers have started to look into issues of media capture and its economic implications. Chapter 16 in this volume outlines the theoretical foundations of this literature.

The aim of this chapter is to overview empirical contributions to the study of the process of media capture. What evidence do we have for media capture around the world? When are media more likely to be captured, and what type of information is more likely to be censored? Do media have any real impact on people's behavior if some media outlets on the market are captured? What are the dark sides of transparency? Below we overview recent empirical papers focussed on these questions.

The outline of this chapter is as follows: Section 17.2 summarizes empirical evidence of media capture; Section 17.3 discusses the determinants of media capture and

---

[1] $3 million per month were paid in bribes to TV channel directors, while total bribes paid to politicians were $300,000 per month, and total bribes to judges were $250,000 per month.

media freedom; Section 17.4 describes media effects in a captured environment; Section 17.5 discusses the limits of media capture, and Section 17.6 concludes.

17.2. EVIDENCE ON MEDIA CAPTURE

Is there any evidence that media capture indeed happens? Do media outlets behave differently if governments or interest groups have some means of controlling them? Do consumers of mass media take into account media capture? This section summarizes empirical evidence of media capture by governments and incumbent politicians and the way it affects media content.

17.2.1 Capture and Media Content

When media is free, it can play an important role in ensuring government accountability by monitoring public officials and publishing stories about government misbehavior (see section on media and accountability in Chapter 13). Governments can exhibit control over mass media through different channels, such as direct ownership, provision of financial resources, media regulation, etc. Whether mass media can promote accountability even if they are controlled by the government is an open question. Theoretically, competition between media outlets can force captured media to reveal relevant information, although not to the same extent as independent media (Besley and Prat, 2006). Thus, it is important to understand to what extent media capture leads to media bias.

Documenting the effect of media capture is not a trivial task. First of all, it is not enough to show the presence of media bias, since it can be driven by demand–side factors, i.e., by outlets catering to the tastes of their audience (see Chapter 15 on media). Thus, it is necessary to show that the bias occurs as a consequence of media capture. In addition, the bias can take many different forms. It can not only affect the information content through "distortion" and "filtering" (see Chapter 14 on media bias), but also the way media outlets try to influence their readers and viewers through agenda setting, priming, and framing (Strömberg, 2015). Chapter 15 provides more details on the ways to measure media bias in different circumstances.

Newspapers in the United States in the second half of the nineteenth century and the beginning of twentieth century provide an appropriate setting for studying media capture, since at that time the newspapers explicitly reported their partisan affiliation. Gentzkow et al. (2015) provide a systematic examination of the influence of government on US newspapers between 1869 and 1928. They find no evidence that incumbent governments influence the press. In particular, they find no systematic effect of the party in power on the political affiliation of newspapers, their circulation, or their content. A notable exception, however, is the South during and after Reconstruction, which was characterized by a low level of political competition. In this setting, they find a strong effect of the party in power on the circulation of newspapers. In particular, the transition from Republican to Democratic control in state government was associated with an increase in the daily circulation share of Democratic newspapers of approximately 10 percentage points. These results suggest that although in democratic countries media capture is usually limited by market forces, it can still take place when the market is particularly weak and the political incentives are strong enough.

Gentzkow et al. (2006) provide content analysis of the media coverage of political scandals in the 1870s and 1920s in the United States. Specifically, they show that during the Credit Mobilier scandal partisan newspapers had different spins when covering the news, but all newspapers wrote about the scandal. In contrast, in the 1920s during the Teapot Dome scandal spin was replaced with bias by omission, with Republican newspapers reporting about the scandal less often and later than Democratic or independent newspapers. In both cases, co-partisan newspapers were less likely to publish articles about the scandals, as compared with newspapers affiliated with a different party or independent newspapers.

Direct provision of money from government, e.g., through government-sponsored advertising, is one of the methods used to ensure that media coverage is favorable to incumbent politicians. For example, Di Tella and Franceschelli (2011) study how often corruption stories are reported in newspapers that receive money from government advertising. They code the content of the front pages and the types of advertising for the four main newspapers in Argentina in 1998–2007. They find that newspapers with government advertising are less likely to talk about government corruption, with a 1 standard deviation increase in government advertising being associated with a decrease in coverage of corruption scandals of 0.23 of a front page per month. The results are robust when controlling for newspaper—president and corruption scandal fixed effects. In sum, the results suggest that indeed newspapers in special relationships with a government are less likely to report corruption.

Media regulation is another method used by governments to affect media coverage. For example, Stanig (2015) shows that defamation laws are important determinants of media coverage of corruption in Mexico. Specifically, local newspapers reported less corruption in Mexico in 2001 in states in which defamation laws were stricter. That is consistent with the notion that government regulation of media markets, and especially defamation laws, is one of the ways to control mass media. Similar conclusions can be drawn from Starr's (2004) historical overview of media development, media regulation, and media capture in different countries. Overall, the evidence indicates that incumbent politicians in places with harsher media regulation face less critical coverage.

In addition to reporting facts, media also give a platform to different politicians. Media capture can lead to a situation in which some politicians have abundant access to broadcast time, while others rarely have the same opportunity. For example, Enikolopov et al. (2011) summarize evidence on the appearances of politicians in Russia in 1999 on different national TV channels, and show that the amount of time devoted to pro-government politicians was disproportionately high on the state-controlled channels. Similarly, Durante and Knight (2012) demonstrate that in Italy politicians from the Berlusconi party had a higher probability of appearing on public TV when Berlusconi was in power. Adena et al. (forthcoming) show that politicians from the NSDAP had almost no access to German radio before 1933, but were given disproportionate access to radio in February 1933, after Hitler became Chancellor. Overall, there is sufficient evidence that captured media disproportionately provide access to the connected politicians.

It is important to note that there is some heterogeneity in media content even in the countries in which governments exhibit almost full control over media. For example, Qin et al. (2014) show that in China the set of topics discussed in newspapers depends on how tightly the newspapers are controlled by the Communist party. Interestingly, they find that the most controlled media outlets were more likely to write about low-level corruption, as compared with more commercial media. This finding is consistent with the idea that mass media can be used by autocratic governments for monitoring lower level public officials (Egorov et al., 2009).

Similarly, even in countries with very high media freedom, media can still be influenced by government through regulatory authority or privileged access to information (Gentzkow and Shapiro, 2008). For example, Qian and Yanagizawa-Drott (2015) present evidence that foreign policy interests shaped human rights reporting in US newspapers during the Cold War. For identification, they use random assignment of non-permanent members of the UN Security Council. They find that coverage of human rights violations in the countries that were not allied with the United States increased with the membership of the UN Security Council, while for countries that were strong allies of the United States, such coverage decreased with membership of the UN Security Council.

17.2.2 Capture by Other Interest Groups

Governments are not the only groups interested in particular media bias. Various interest groups including media owners, advertisers, journalists, politicians, or private companies also have incentives to distort media coverage.[2] For instance, when in 1979 Mother Jones published a critical article written by G. Blair, "Why Dick Can't Stop Smoking?," which described the addictive effects of tobacco smoking, tobacco companies (Phillip Morris, Brown and Williamson, and others) responded by canceling their long-term advertising contracts with the magazine. In addition, "in a show of corporate solidarity," many liquor companies followed their example.[3]

---

[2] Chapter 16 on the theoretical analysis of media capture refers to media capture by non-governmental interest groups as "passive capture."
[3] Bates, E. "Smoked Out," Mother Jones, March/April 1996 issue.

There are theoretical arguments why media might be biased in favor of different interest groups, such as advertisers. Some recent theoretical papers suggest that media can be biased in favor of advertisers, and more so if effectiveness of advertising depends on media reporting or advertisers can commit to punishment strategies (Ellman and Germano, 2009), if the match between advertisers' appeal and the preferences of the audience is better (Gal-Or et al., 2012), or if the marginal returns to bias are increasing in the size of the media audience (Petrova, 2012).[4]

Reuter and Zitzewitz (2006) provide evidence that recommendations of financial magazines and newspapers about investment in mutual funds are biased in the direction of advertisers, with the exception of the *Wall Street Journal*, for which the bias seems to be insignificant. Reuter (2009) shows that wine ratings in specialized magazines are biased in favor of advertisers. Gambaro and Puglisi (2012) show that newspaper coverage is biased in favor of advertisers in modern Italy, by employing a detailed analysis with a rich set of fixed effects.

There is also evidence that media might be biased in favor of different special interest groups, such as landless peasants (Alston et al., 2010) or environmental groups (Shapiro, 2014).

There are theoretical arguments that media can be biased because of journalist preferences (Baron, 2006). Practically, Dougal et al. (2012) show that the identity of a journalist was important for market reaction to news in the *New York Times*.[5] Journalist movie reviews could also be biased, but in practice this bias is very small (DellaVigna and Hermle, 2014).

Overall, empirical evidence suggests that media capture is not limited to capture by governments. However, government control of media received more attention from researchers, since governments have more means to capture media and because the implications of such control for the welfare of society are larger. How different types of media capture interact with each other is so far not clear from the literature, and we expect to see more papers about it in the future.

17.2.3 Related Evidence

In recent years, with the advancement of the new information technologies, media capture also takes new forms. When government cannot perfectly control all pieces of information in the public sphere, such as blogs or online news aggregators, it can engage in

---

[4] Germano and Meier (2013) analyze the setting in which the media internalize how news coverage affects advertisers' sales to the case with more than two firms, suggesting that independent media ownership is important. Ellman (2010) derive how the government can use optimal subsidies to overcome advertising-driven bias. There are also theoretical arguments that advertising leads to search distortions and bias in search engines' content (Burguet et al., 2015).

[5] See Chapter 18 for more evidence of the role of media in financial markets.

selective deletion of information. For example, in China selective deletion of online content is widespread. King et al. (2013) try to understand what types of online content is likely to be censored in modern China by making snapshots of the Chinese blogosphere every 20 min and identifying the content that gets deleted *ex post*. They find that Chinese censors were more likely to delete appeals for coordination and any form of collective action than the criticism of the Communist Party and the incumbent regime. In a related study, King et al. (2014) performed a field experiment to confirm this finding. Using randomized blog postings in Chinese online social media, they find that coordination messages indeed had a higher probability of being censored, as compared with information messages which only contained critical information about the regime.

To assess costs and benefits of media capture, Bignon and Flandreau (2014) estimate the monetary value of media capture based on the control premium paid for publicly traded media companies, i.e., the amount that was paid in excess of the market price in order to acquire a controlling stake. Exploiting the fact that in interwar France many newspapers were publicly traded, they show the evolution of the value of media capture over time and demonstrate that the value of media capture in interwar France was significantly higher than in the United Kingdom during the same period.

17.3. DETERMINANTS OF MEDIA CAPTURE

The extent of media capture depends on both the "demand for capture," i.e., the incentives of government and other special interests to control media, and "supply of capture," i.e., the willingness of the media outlets to change their content. Lack of political competition and direct government ownership of the media are likely to be important factors that make it easier for the government to control media (as summarized in Djankov et al., 2003), but that is not the only driving force. The ability of media to raise independent revenues can become an important safeguard against the ability of politicians to capture the media. For example, Baldasty (1992) summarizes case study evidence suggesting that the growth of advertising indeed was one of the drivers of the development of an independent press in the United States, referring to the process as commercialization of the news.

Gentzkow et al. (2006) summarize key trends in the newspaper market at the end of the nineteenth and the beginning of the twentieth century. They also provide a model that predicts media to be more independent if the marginal cost of production is smaller or marginal advertising revenue is higher. Petrova (2011) empirically tests the claim that an increase in advertising in the nineteenth century helped newspapers in the United States to become independent. Specifically, the paper shows that newspapers were more likely to enter the market as independents or more likely to switch their political affiliation to independent in places with higher advertising revenues. The effect holds if advertising revenues are instrumented using restrictions for outdoor advertising and handbill distribution. The results of this analysis are consistent with the idea that growth of advertising in the late nineteenth century was an important driving force in the development of an independent press in the United States.

Qin et al. (2014) suggest that commercialization of the news is an important factor that affects newspaper content in China. Their results imply that newspapers which depend more on commercial revenues and are less directly controlled by the Communist Party are less likely to report low-level corruption. At the same time, more commercial newspapers are more likely to produce entertaining content like sports or celebrity stories.

A number of studies look at the determinants of media capture and media freedom from an international perspective. Egorov et al. (2009) show that higher oil rents lead to less media freedom and the effect is especially pronounced in non-democratic countries. They argue that free media can improve the quality of bureaucracy, which is the reason it is tolerated even in dictatorships, but only if the quality of bureaucracy is important for economic growth. Higher rents from natural resources make the quality of bureaucracy less valuable, which increases incentives to capture media. Petrova (2008) shows that increased income inequality is associated with lower media freedom and argues that this effect is driven by the incentives of rich elites to manipulate public opinion and prevent redistribution. VonDoepp and Young (2013) show that media capture depends on regime stability, since governments that face threats to maintaining their power have stronger incentives to control the media.

17.4. MEDIA EFFECTS IN THE PRESENCE OF MEDIA CAPTURE

Studying the causal impact of media is not straightforward, since the decision of media consumers which media product they would like to consume, if any, is endogenous. To convincingly identify media effects, one needs to find some source of exogenous variation in either media exposure or media content. Chapter 13 focuses on the study of media influence in competitive, non-captured environments, outlining the basic approaches to the identification of media effects. The goal of this section is to overview the existing approaches to studying media effects in environments in which some or all media outlets are captured.

17.4.1 Impact of Captured Media

The goal of any media control or media censorship is to ensure that media consumers can be influenced by captured content (or not influenced by content that would naturally emerge in a competitive media market otherwise). In a purely Bayesian framework, captured media should have no effect, since the audience should understand that the messages are biased in a particular direction and discount information coming from the captured media. However, there are reasons to doubt that this full discounting actually takes place. For example, countries with state censorship of media do not necessarily have lower levels of trust in media. Global Trust Barometer suggests that the country in which people are most likely to trust their media is China, while the United States and United Kingdom are in the bottom third of the ratings.[6] Thus, whether captured media have any impact remains an empirical question.

A number of empirical works demonstrate that captured media can have a significant effect on people's behavior. Yanagizawa-Drott (2014) provides an important example of the influence of captured media in promoting violence. Exploiting geographical variation in accessibility of the RTLM radio in Rwandan that encouraged violence against the Tutsi minority population, he finds that the radio was responsible for 10% of anti-Tutsi violence during 1994 genocide events. The paper also shows that the impact of radio is multiplied by social interactions, and there were important geographic spillovers in violence.

Using a similar identification strategy, Adena et al. (forthcoming) look at the impact of radio in the Weimar Republic and in Nazi Germany. They show that radio had an important effect on the voting results. In particular, before 1933, when radio was biased against the Nazis, radio exposure decreased the vote share of the NSDAP, while after Hitler was appointed Chancellor in January 1933, exposure to radio had a positive effect on various indicators of Nazi support, such as voting for NSDAP and joining the party in spring 1933, as well as denunciations of Jews and open expressions of anti-Semitism in the late 1930s.

Empirical evidence also indicates that media can have an effect even if it is aimed at a foreign audience. DellaVigna et al. (2014) examine the effect of government-controlled Serbian public radio in Croatia in the 2000s. The paper documents several facts: first, according to surveys, many ethnic Croatians listen to Serbian radio despite it being hostile to them; second, exposure to Serbian radio increased voting for extreme Croatian-nationalist parties and open expression of nationalism; finally, subjects in a lab experiment in the field exhibited more anti-Serbian sentiment after listening to just 10 min of Serbian radio. The lab experiment also sheds some light on the mechanism, as listening to neutral (not nationalistic) Serbian radio also increased anti-Serbian attitudes, although to a smaller extent than listening to nationalistic radio. Overall, the paper demonstrates that hostile foreign radio can lead to increased nationalism.

17.4.2 Impact of Independent Media in Captured Environments

A separate but related question is whether independent media make a difference in a captured environment. Theoretically, media impact is likely to be larger in this case, compared to the case of competitive media markets (Besley and Prat, 2006). Enikolopov et al. (2011) examine the effect of an independent TV channel on the voting for the pro-government *Unity* party that helped Vladimir Putin to come to power. Specifically, they use the fact that during the 1999 Russian Parliamentary elections there was only one independent TV channel available for approximately two-thirds of the population, whereas all the population had access to government-controlled TV channels that

[6] http://www.edelman.com/post/freedom-of-the-press-and-trust-in-media/.

supported *Unity*. Using idiosyncratic geographical variation in access to the independent TV channel, they show that it increased the combined vote share of the opposition parties by 6.3 percentage points, while decreasing the vote share of the pro-Putin's party by 8.9 percentage points. Similarly, in the context of Italy, Barone et al. (2014) show that the introduction of digital TV diminished local support for Berlusconi's party by 5.5–7.5 percentage points. The effect was stronger in places with older and less educated voters. These estimates suggest that at least 20% of digital users were not able to filter out the bias of the Berlusconi-owned channels during the 1994–2010 period. The magnitude of the effects in both above-mentioned papers are higher than the ones found in the United States (DellaVigna and Gentzkow, 2010), which suggests that media effects are stronger in captured environments.

Another example is the influence of cross-border exposure to independent television from Western Germany on the behavior of people in Eastern Germany, where the government tightly controlled all the media inside the country (Hainmueller and Kern, 2009). They find that Eastern Germans with exposure to Western TV were more likely to support communism and less likely to apply for asylum. These results are also consistent with a hypothesis that independent media can have an important effect in an environment in which most other media outlets are controlled by the government or other groups of influence.

Finally, in environments in which traditional media are captured, social media can play a role of unavailable independent media. For example, Enikolopov et al. (2015b) provide evidence that publications in a Russian blog about corruption in state-controlled companies had a significant effect on stock market performance of the targeted companies and their corporate practices. Enikolopov et al. (2015a) show that higher penetration of the leading online social network in Russia had a positive effect on the incidence and the size of political protests in 2011–2012. Acemoglu et al. (2015), however, suggest that in the aftermath of the Arab Spring in Egypt the content of social media did not have an independent impact on the stock market, even though it could predict the size of political protests. The literature on the role of social media in a captured environment, however, is in its infancy, and we expect to see more papers about that in the near future.

17.4.3 Adverse Effects of Media Transparency in Captured Environments

Even though there is evidence that independent media matter in captured environments and that independent media are important for accountability, this does not necessarily imply that independent media can improve accountability in a captured environment. In some cases, increased transparency can lead to adverse outcomes, as politicians in power can use other means to counteract an increase in transparency.

Malesky et al. (2012) study the effect of providing more information about the performance of the members of the National Assembly in Vietnam, a single-party authoritarian regime. In particular, they conducted a field experiment which provided information about the legislative performance of randomly chosen members of parliament in an online newspaper. Their results indicate that, on average, provision of such information did not affect the performance of the delegates, but representatives of the regions with higher Internet penetration decreased their participation in legislative activities that could embarrass regime leaders. Moreover, an increase in the amount of information available about politicians made these politicians less likely to be nominated by the party in the future.

In Colombia, media scandals made targeted politicians more likely to engage in coercion during the elections to offset negative popularity shocks (Fergusson et al., 2013). In particular, the authors use a regression discontinuity design to study the impact of newspaper scandals on electoral coercion in paramilitary-controlled areas in Colombia. They find that candidates sympathetic to paramilitary groups reacted to corruption scandals which threatened their re-election prospects by increasing electoral coercion. Although their results do not speak directly to media effects, they also suggest that in a captured environment increased transparency might have unintended consequences.

17.5. LIMITS OF MEDIA CAPTURE

Although the existing research suggests that media capture can have an important effect, the efficiency of propaganda is limited by several mechanisms. First of all, if readers or viewers know that media are captured they can discount information coming from the biased sources. Bai et al. (2014) test this directly by looking at how people update their beliefs about air pollution in China after receiving information from either government-controlled or independent sources. They document that the results cannot be explained in the Bayesian framework. In particular, people do not fully discount repeated information coming from government sources and they have problems interpreting conflicting information coming from government and independent sources.

If the message in the captured media is too different from the prior beliefs of the audience, propaganda may even backfire. For example, Adena et al. (forthcoming) show that the impact of radio in Nazi Germany depended on citizens' predispositions. Although on average radio exposure increased denunciation of Jews and anti-Semitic violence, in places in which the population was historically tolerant to Jews or in places with low land inequality, exposure to radio actually had a negative effect on denunciation of Jews and anti-Semitic violence.

Newspaper competition can provide an additional protection against media capture, consistent with some theoretical models (see Chapter 16). For example, even though partisan newspapers were biased in the United States in the nineteenth century, their entries and exits had no noticeable effect on voting for particular parties, although they did affect political participation (Gentzkow et al., 2010). Galvis et al. (2013) find that although newspapers in the United States in the nineteenth century were indeed more likely to cover political scandals of their political opponents and less likely to cover political scandals of the politicians from their preferred parties, this effect was mitigated by media competition. In particular, if during the scandal a co-partisan newspaper was the only one in the local media market, it was likely to devote significantly less space (if any) to the scandal. However, in media markets with competing newspapers that were affiliated with other parties, even co-partisan newspapers felt obliged to report on political scandals. Overall, both papers suggest that newspaper competition is an important force in reducing media capture.

In addition to filtering out the bias of captured media, the audience might also react to capture by switching to different news sources. For example, Durante and Knight (2012) show that viewers in Italy responded to changes in the content of TV channels by switching to alternative channels. In particular, when Berlusconi came to power, the news content of public television shifted to the right. In response, some right-wing viewers switched to public television, whereas left-wing viewers, by contrast, switched from the more centrist public channel to the left-leaning public channel. In addition, left-leaning viewers reduced their trust in public television, while right-leaning viewers increased their trust.

Overall, the results suggest that viewers respond to an increase in media bias both by changing the sources of information and by discounting information from the biased source, thus at least partially offsetting the effect of media capture.

17.6. CONCLUSION

The empirical evidence overviewed in this chapter shows that media outlets can be captured, i.e., that the content of media can be determined by the preferences of governments or sponsoring groups rather than by the preferences of the audience. In this situation, the way media outlets operate and the mechanisms through which media outlets can affect people's behavior work differently, as compared with the case of a perfectly competitive media market. There are several implications from this literature for the understanding of the role of mass media.

First, captured media outlets are different from independent media outlets in terms of their content, sometimes dramatically. Second, governments use a multitude of methods for media control, including censorship, sponsorship via direct ownership or advertising, or media regulation. Third, captured media might still affect people's behavior. In other words, propaganda works, at least sometimes. Fourth, independent media are especially important in environments where other media outlets are captured. Finally, there are limits to propaganda, as well as limits to the power of independent media.

REFERENCES

Acemoglu, D., Hassan, T., Tahoun, A., 2015. The Power of the Street: Evidence from Egypt's Arab Spring. Working paper.

Adena, M., Enikolopov, R., Petrova, M., Santarosa, V., Zhuravskaya, E., 2015. Radio and the rise of the Nazis in Prewar Germany. Q. J. Econ. 130 (4), 1885–1939.

Alston, L.J., Libecap, G.D., Mueller, B., 2010. Interest Groups, Information Manipulation in the Media, and Public Policy: The Case of the Landless Peasants Movement in Brazil. NBER working paper No. 15865.

Bai, J., Golosov, M., Qian, N., Kai, Y., 2014. Understanding the Influence of Government Controlled Media: Evidence from Air Pollution in China. Working paper.

Baldasty, G.J., 1992. The Commercialization of News in the Nineteenth Century. University of Wisconsin Press, Madison, WI.

Baron, D., 2006. Persistent media bias. J. Public Econ. 90, 1–36.

Barone, G., d'Acunto, F., Narciso, G., 2014. Telecracy: testing for channels of persuasion. Am. Econ. J. Econ. Policy 7, 30–60.

Besley, T., Prat, A., 2006. Handcuffs for the grabbing hand: media capture and government accountability. Am. Econ. Rev. 96, 720–736.

Bignon, V., Flandreau, M., 2014. The price of media capture and the debasement of the French newspaper industry during the interwar. J. Econ. Hist. 74 (3), 799–830.

Burguet, R., Caminal, R., Ellman, M., 2015. In Google we trust? Int. J. Ind. Organ. 39, 44–55.

DellaVigna, S., Gentzkow, M., 2010. Persuasion: empirical evidence. Annu. Rev. Econ. 2 (1), 643–669.

DellaVigna, S., Hermle, J., 2014. Does Conflict of Interest Lead to Biased Coverage? Evidence from Movie Reviews. Working paper.

DellaVigna, S., Enikolopov, R., Mironova, V., Petrova, M., Zhuravskaya, E., 2014. Cross-border effects of foreign media: Serbian radio and nationalism in Croatia. Am. Econ. J. Appl. Econ. 6 (3), 103–132.

Di Tella, R., Franceschelli, I., 2011. Government advertising and media coverage of corruption scandals. Am. Econ. J. Appl. Econ. 3 (4), 119–151.

Djankov, S., McLiesh, C., Nenova, T., Shleifer, A., 2003. Who owns the media? J. Law Econ. 46 (2), 341–382.

Dougal, C., Engelberg, J., García, D., Parsons, C.A., 2012. Journalists and the stock market. Rev. Financ. Stud. 25 (3), 639–679.

Durante, R., Knight, B., 2012. Partisan control, media bias, and viewer responses: evidence from Berlusconi's Italy. J. Eur. Econ. Assoc. 10 (3), 451–481.

Egorov, G., Guriev, S., Sonin, K., 2009. Why resource-poor dictators allow freer media: a theory and evidence from panel data. Am. Polit. Sci. Rev. 103 (4), 645–668.

Ellman, M., 2010. How to Subsidize the News. Working paper.

Ellman, M., Germano, F., 2009. What do the papers sell? Econ. J. 119, 668–704.

Enikolopov, R., Petrova, M., Zhuravskaya, E., 2011. Media and political persuasion: evidence from Russia. Am. Econ. Rev. 111 (7), 3253–3285.

Enikolopov, R., Makarin, A., Petrova, M., 2015a. Social Media and Protest Participation: Evidence from Russia. Working paper.

Enikolopov, R., Petrova, M., Sonin, K., 2015b. Social Media and Corruption. Working paper.

Fergusson, L., Vargas, J.F., Vela, M.A., 2013. Sunlight Disinfects? Free Media in Weak Democracies. Working paper.

Gal-Or, E., Geylani, T., Yildrim, T.P., 2012. The impact of advertising on media bias. J. Mark. Res. 49 (1), 92–99.

Galvis, Á.F., Snyder Jr., J.M., Song, B.K., 2013. Newspaper Market Structure and Behavior: Partisan Coverage of Political Scandals in the U.S. from 1870 to 1910. Working paper.

Gambaro, M., Puglisi, R., 2012. What do Ads Buy? Daily Coverage of Listed Companies on the Italian Press. Working paper.

Gentzkow, M., Shapiro, J.M., 2008. Competition and truth in the market for news. J. Econ. Perspect. 22 (2), 133–154.

Gentzkow, M., Glaeser, E., Goldin, C., 2006. The rise of the fourth estate: how newspapers became informative and why it mattered. In: Glaeser, E., Goldin, C. (Eds.), Corruption and Reform: Lessons from America's Economic History. NBER/University of Chicago Press, Chicago, IL.

Gentzkow, M., Shapiro, J.M., Sinkinson, M., 2010. The effect of newspaper entry and exit on electoral politics. Am. Econ. Rev. 101 (7), 2980–3018.

Gentzkow, M., Petek, N., Shapiro, J.M., Sinkinson, M., 2015. Do newspapers serve the state? Incumbent party influence on the US press, 1869–1928. J. Eur. Econ. Assoc. 13 (1), 29–61.

Germano, F., Meier, M., 2013. Concentration and self-censorship in commercial media. J. Public Econ. 97, 117–130.

Hainmueller, J., Kern, H.L., 2009. Opium for the masses: how foreign media can stabilize authoritarian regimes. Polit. Anal. 17, 377–399.

King, G., Pan, J., Roberts, M.E., 2013. How censorship in China allows government criticism but silences collective expression. Am. Polit. Sci. Rev. 107 (2), 326–343.

King, G., Pan, J., Roberts, M.E., 2014. Reverse-engineering censorship in China: randomized experimentation and participant observation. Science 345 (6199), 1–10.

Malesky, E., Schuler, P., Tran, A., 2012. The adverse effects of sunshine: a field experiment on legislative transparency in an authoritarian assembly. Am. Polit. Sci. Rev. 106 (4), 762–786.

McMillan, J., Zoido, P., 2004. How to subvert democracy: Montesinos in Peru. J. Econ. Perspect. 18 (4), 69–92.

Petrova, M., 2008. Inequality and media capture. J. Public Econ. 92 (1–2), 183–212.

Petrova, M., 2011. Newspapers and parties: how advertising revenues created an independent press. Am. Polit. Sci. Rev. 105 (4), 790–808.

Petrova, M., 2012. Mass media and special interest groups. J. Econ. Behav. Organ. 84, 17–38.

Qian, N., Yanagizawa-Drott, D., 2015. Government Distortion in Independently Owned Media: Evidence from U.S. Cold War News Coverage of Human Rights. Working paper.

Qin, B., Wu, Y., Strömberg, D., 2014. Determinants of Media Capture in China. Working paper.

Reuter, J., 2009. Does advertising bias product reviews? An analysis of wine ratings. J. Wine Econ. 4 (2), 125–151.

Reuter, J., Zitzewitz, E., 2006. Do ads influence editors? Advertising and bias in the financial media. Q. J. Econ. 121 (1), 197–227.

Shapiro, J., 2014. Special Interests and the Media: Theory and an Application to Climate Change. Working paper.

Stanig, P., 2015. Regulation of speech and media coverage of corruption: an empirical analysis of the Mexican press. Am. Polit. Sci. Rev. 59 (1), 175–193.

Starr, P., 2004. The Creation of the Media: Political Origins of Modern Communications. Basic Books, New York, NY.

Strömberg, D., 2015. Media and politics. Ann. Rev. Econ. 7, 173–205.

VonDoepp, P., Young, D.J., 2013. Assaults on the fourth estate: explaining media harassment in Africa. J. Politics 75 (1), 36–51.

Yanagizawa-Drott, D., 2014. Propaganda and conflict: theory and evidence from the Rwandan Genocide. Q. J. Econ. 129 (4), 1947–1994.

CHAPTER 18

The Role of Media in Finance

Paul C. Tetlock
Columbia University, New York, NY, USA

Contents

18.1. Introduction	702
18.2. Theory	703
18.3. Media as a Reflection of the Information Environment	705
18.3.1 Information Release and Market Activity	706
18.3.2 Information Content and Valuation	708
18.3.3 Attention and Valuation	711
18.4. Causal Role of Media	712
18.4.1 Case Studies	713
18.4.2 Media Impact on Volume and Volatility	713
18.4.3 Media Impact on Stock Prices	714
18.5. Corporate Finance Applications	715
18.5.1 Media and Firm Performance	715
18.5.2 Media and the Cost of Capital	716
18.6. Discussion and Directions for Future Research	716
Acknowledgments	717
References	718

Abstract

This chapter reviews and synthesizes a rapidly growing subfield that analyzes the relation between media and financial markets. Research in this area identifies novel data sources, such as newspaper articles, Internet search queries, and posts on social networks, and employs inventive empirical methods, notably textual analysis, to quantify the rich information environment in modern financial markets. Such data and methods enable powerful tests of theories and have the potential to address longstanding puzzles in finance, such as why trading volume and stock price volatility are so high.

Keywords

Media, Attention, Behavioral finance, Event studies, Textual analysis

JEL Codes

G02, G12, G14

Handbook of Media Economics, Volume 1B
ISSN 2213-6630, http://dx.doi.org/10.1016/B978-0-444-63685-0.00018-8

18.1. INTRODUCTION

Investors in financial markets vigorously hunt for information about publicly traded companies, but even the most well-informed can sharply disagree about firm values. In 2012 and 2013, hedge fund managers fiercely debated the merits of Herbalife Ltd's network marketing business model. After establishing a $1 billion short position in Herbalife, the manager of Pershing Square Capital, Bill Ackman, publicly proclaimed: "This is the highest conviction I've ever had about any investment I've ever made."[1] At the same time, the manager of Third Point, Dan Loeb, purchased a $200 million stake in Herbalife and dismissed Ackman's view as "preposterous," arguing instead that the firm's business is "performing well" and the shares are "available at an attractive discount."[2] Such investors with great confidence in their beliefs can trade vast sums of money and exert a significant influence on asset prices.

Differences in opinion could come from private information or differential abilities to process information. Testing theories in finance that feature these elements requires rich data on the information environment. This chapter reviews and synthesizes a rapidly growing literature that analyzes media to measure the information environment and thereby shed light on financial markets. Research in this area identifies novel data sources, such as newspaper articles, Internet search queries, and posts on social networks, and employs inventive empirical methods, notably textual analysis, to quantify the information environment in modern financial markets.[3] Such data and methods enable powerful tests of asset pricing theories and have the potential to address longstanding puzzles in finance, such as why there is so much trading and why stock prices move so much.

This chapter focuses on three central themes. First, media reporting can exert a large causal influence on financial markets. Second, even when there is no causal channel, media content can be a useful window into investors and managers' beliefs. Third, theories of media and communication can help guide empirical research. In a companion article (Tetlock, 2014), I discuss these themes from the perspective of information transmission. The ideas and studies discussed in this chapter overlap considerably with those in the companion article.

Empirical studies of media in finance investigate diverse phenomena in asset pricing, such as market reactions to news and non-news and investors' portfolio choices, and in corporate finance, such as merger activity and executive compensation. One of the main findings in asset pricing is that the link between information arrival and stock price movement is surprisingly weak. Underreaction of market prices to informative media content and overreaction to uninformative content partly explains this weak

---

[1] *Source*: Interview with Bill Ackman on "*Money Moves*" on Bloomberg TV on December 21, 2012.

[2] *Source*: Dan Loeb's letter to investors on January 9, 2013.

[3] Li (2010), Das (2011), and Kearney and Liu (2014) provide reviews of textual analysis in finance and accounting.

link. As a result, manipulating media content can affect asset prices, distorting incentives to information providers.

The evidence further indicates that overreaction (underreaction) to content increases (decreases) with investor attention. Attention increases are associated with increases in asset prices, followed by partial price reversals. As a result, the manipulation of attention can also affect asset prices. Finally, in addition to its impact on asset prices, news reporting can cause significant increases in trading volume.

Although the literature on media in corporate finance is still developing, two key findings have already emerged. First, media coverage can enhance firm performance by attracting customers or by reducing the costs of monitoring corrupt and inefficient manager behavior. Second, media coverage, especially positive news, can help firms raise capital by increasing investor awareness and optimism.

In this chapter, I adopt the following taxonomy of studies. In Section 18.2, I discuss selected theories relating to media. In Section 18.3, I examine studies that test whether media activity and content relate to asset market activity. Section 18.4 analyzes studies evaluating the causal impact of media reporting on market activity. Section 18.5 surveys studies of media in the context of corporate finance. Section 18.6 concludes and suggests promising directions for future research.

18.2. THEORY

Theoretical models provide the framework for understanding the role of media in financial markets. Media reflects and shapes investors' and managers' expectations, which affect the supply and demand for securities as well as firms' financial policies. Investors' expectations of firm values are the primary determinant of prices and trading volume in asset markets. Rational investors cannot disagree about firm values if public information, such as the market price, fully reveals traders' beliefs (Aumann, 1976). Milgrom and Stokey (1982) show that this logic implies there will be no trading at all in asset markets inhabited solely by rational agents with purely speculative motives. Grossman and Stiglitz (1980) show that rational agents will collect information only if prices do not fully reveal traders' beliefs, which only happens if factors other than genuine information affect asset prices. Because much trading takes place and many traders collect information in practice, these results suggest that factors other than genuine information are important for explaining observed market activity.

The release of information typically causes some investors' beliefs to converge while others diverge for reasons that may or may not be rational. Several models highlight the importance of investor disagreement for understanding asset pricing and trading volume. Models based on rational disagreement, such as He and Wang (1995) and Tetlock (2010), typically predict that public information causes trade only insofar as it resolves information asymmetry and leads to a convergence in traders' beliefs.

An alternative modeling approach is to allow investors to hold different prior beliefs and interpret information differently. Early models based on differences in opinion include those by Miller (1977), Harris and Raviv (1993), Kim and Verrecchia (1994), and Kandel and Pearson (1995). Kandel and Pearson (1995) argue that such models can explain variation in stock analysts' expectations, asset prices, and trading volume around the release of public information—particularly the fact that analysts' earnings forecasts often diverge or change rank ordering around earnings announcements. The static model of Miller (1977) and the dynamic models of Scheinkman and Xiong (2003) and Banerjee and Kremer (2010) convey the intuition from difference-in-opinion models:

- differences in investors' trading positions reflect the level of disagreement;
- trading volume reflects changes in investor disagreement;
- asset prices represent investors' average beliefs about valuation; and
- with short sale constraints, prices equal or exceed optimistic investors' beliefs.[4]

Whereas most of these models remain agnostic about the origin of investor disagreement and which investors' beliefs are correct, recent models in behavioral finance propose specific belief biases and examine their impact on asset prices and trading volume. If media content reflects or influences these biases, as suggested by Mullainathan and Shleifer (2005a,b), content and biases should exhibit similar relationships with market activity. De Long et al. (1990) characterize equilibrium in a model with random belief biases—i.e., noise trading driven by investor sentiment—and limits to arbitrage. They show that innovations in sentiment affect asset returns, and absolute sentiment innovations determine trading volume between noise traders and rational agents. One can use media content to test these predictions assuming that content is an empirical proxy for investor sentiment.

Media can also affect market activity by directing investor attention. Merton (1987) analyzes a model of incomplete information in which certain investors are unaware of a subset of securities and do not use them in constructing their portfolios. He shows that firms with small investor bases exhibit relatively low stock prices and high expected returns. In his theory, media visibility could increase a firm's investor base, thereby increasing its market value and lowering its expected return. Merton's (1987) static model does not make clear predictions of how a stock's price adjusts to a sudden increase in demand resulting from heightened investor recognition. Duffie (2010) provides a dynamic model of slow-moving capital that predicts prices increase sharply and subsequently reverse over a longer period in response to positive demand shocks. The extent and duration of overshooting depends on trading impediments, such as short-run search frictions and capital constraints.

---

[4] In Scheinkman and Xiong's (2003) model, differences in opinion vary over time. Price "bubbles" can arise because prices embed an option to resell the asset to other investors who may become optimistic in the future.

Studies by Hirshleifer and Teoh (2003) and Peng and Xiong (2006) model how limits on investor attention affect reactions to information. In these setups, investors attend to general information that tends to be salient and widely applicable, while ignoring detailed information that tends to be costly to process. For example, investors attend to summary statistics, such as a firm's total earnings, rather than specific components, such as cash flows and accruals. As a result, asset prices overreact to general information and underreact to detailed information.

Several models consider how the sequential release of information to different investors affects market activity. Hirshleifer et al. (1994) and Brunnermeier (2005) focus on implications for trading volume and informational efficiency. Both studies show that early informed traders can exploit information before and after public information arrival. Such staggered information release can have detrimental consequences for informational efficiency. Tetlock (2011) proposes that investors may not realize the extent to which others have already traded on information in a given news story, leading them to confuse fresh and stale news. In a model with limited arbitrage, this bias causes asset prices to underreact initially and overreact eventually to the sequential release of overlapping information.

Some recent models feature investors who receive similar information within social networks. Colla and Mele (2010) and Ozsoylev and Walden (2011) prove that information linkages among traders increase trading volume by increasing competition and reducing information asymmetry across traders. Traders near each other in a network exhibit positively correlated trades, whereas those far from each other exhibit negatively correlated trades. Han and Hirshleifer (2012) provide a model in which the way investors transmit ideas affects beliefs and market activity. They assume investors prefer to discuss their investment successes and others do not fully account for this tendency. This conversational bias increases the popularity of active investing strategies, such as frequently trading stocks with high volatility and skewness.

18.3. MEDIA AS A REFLECTION OF THE INFORMATION ENVIRONMENT

Early empirical studies establish basic facts about the relation between the media's release of information and asset market activity. Most studies measure information release using newspaper articles and market activity using stock market outcomes because these measures are important and widely available. To demonstrate the types of newsworthy events in financial markets, I analyze data on news stories from 2000 to 2010, building on a categorization of Dow Jones newswires by the firm Ravenpack. Only 31% of newswires about firms relate to firm earnings (22%) or stock analysts (9%); many of these stories include earnings guidance events and stock analyst news that typical analyses of earnings announcements and forecast revisions do not consider. Other important types of news includes stories about firm revenues (15%), insider ownership (12%), mergers and acquisitions (6%), corporate executives (5%), business contracts (4%), cash distributions (3%), product information (2%), investment and liquidation (2%), credit quality (2%), labor issues (1%), security issuance (1%), and legal issues (1%). Neuhierl et al. (2013) analyze market reactions to firms' press releases by news event category.

18.3.1 Information Release and Market Activity

Roll's (1988) presidential address of the American Finance Association is an important early attempt to link stock price changes to identifiable publicly available information, which he measures using news stories about specific firms. Roll (1988) documents that systematic economic influences, such as the market and other factors, account for only 21% of daily fluctuations in firms' returns from 1982 to 1986. In theory, market reactions to public firm-specific news could explain much of the remaining 79% of return variation. Roll (1988) tests this theory by identifying all days in which each of 96 large firms are featured in either *Dow Jones News Service* (*DJNS*) or the *Wall Street Journal* (*WSJ*), two comprehensive sources. After excluding the 24% of days with such news, the explanatory power (R^2) of systematic influences for firm stock returns increases by only 2% (from 21% to 23%). By the process of elimination, Roll's (1988) results point to the importance of private information, sentiment-driven trading, or high-frequency changes in risk premiums in explaining stock returns.

Cutler et al. (1989) examine whether major fundamental news is associated with large market-wide stock price movements. They focus on the 50 days with the most extreme stock price movements and the 49 days with the most important world events between 1941 and 1987. They define important events as those featured in the *World Almanac*, chosen as the lead story in the *New York Times* (*NYT*), and deemed relevant for the stock market by the *NYT* reporter. Their main finding is that it is difficult to link major market moves to economic or other information. On days with major price moves, "the information that the press cites as the cause of the market move is not particularly important" and there are no subsequent "convincing accounts of why future profits or discount rates might have changed" (p. 9). Cornell (2013) extends the Cutler et al. (1989) analysis of major price movements to include the 1988–2012 period and reports strikingly similar results.

Mitchell and Mulherin (1994) and Berry and Howe (1994) relate aggregate stock market volume and volatility to broad measures of news about firms and the economy. Mitchell and Mulherin (1994) analyze the number of *DJNS* and *WSJ* stories per day, while Berry and Howe (1994) measure hourly news items from *Reuters News Service*. Both studies find weak correlations of less than 0.12 between market volatility and the number of news items. The correlation between the number of news stories and trading volume is considerably higher (e.g., 0.37 at the daily frequency). The higher explanatory power of news for trading volume suggests the presence of non-informational trading linked to news, a theme in later studies.

Market inefficiency could partly explain why stock prices do not react strongly to public information and move even in the absence of such information. Chan (2003) examines whether long-run market reactions to a broad sample of firm-specific news and non-news events are efficient. He defines news as a month in which a firm appears in the headline of *DJNS* news data spanning 1980–2000. Chan (2003) analyzes 1-month price momentum within groups of firms with and without news by constructing long–short portfolios based on firms' monthly returns—e.g., the news momentum portfolio consists of long (short) positions in the subset of firms with news that have relatively high (low) monthly returns. His primary result is that the news momentum portfolio outperforms the no-news momentum portfolio by a significant margin of 5% in the year after formation. A key reason is that firms with low returns in news months experience no price reversal, whereas firms with low returns in non-news months experience large price rebounds.

Studies by Tetlock (2010) and Griffin et al. (2011) find qualitatively similar results at the daily frequency in the United States and international data respectively. The news–momentum relation is strongest for news stories that coincide with high trading volume and for small and illiquid firms. These findings suggest significant non-informational trading occurs on news days. Such trading could arise because public news resolves information asymmetry, resulting in the accommodation of long-lived liquidity shocks, as proposed by Tetlock (2010). Consistent with reductions in asymmetric information, bid–ask spreads are lower and market depth is higher around earnings announcements that receive press coverage (Bushee et al., 2010).

A complementary explanation for the news–momentum relation is that investors do not adequately attend to firm-specific news arrival, as predicted by models of limited attention. Although few studies directly measure attention to news, some provide evidence that market reactions to information events increase with news about the event. Klibanoff et al. (1998) assess market reactions to information by comparing closed-end country fund prices to their fundamental values, as measured by net asset value (NAV). They show that fund prices move only 50% as much as NAV in non-news weeks, but prices react to 80% of NAV changes in weeks with front-page *NYT* news about the country. Peress (2008) shows that market underreaction to earnings announcements decreases with *WSJ* media coverage of the event, lending further support to theories of limited attention. [5] However, an earlier study by Vega (2006) finds that firms receiving more media coverage in the 40 days prior to earnings announcements experience increases in post-announcement stock price drift, suggesting investor inattention does not fully account for the well-known drift phenomenon.

---

[5] Similarly, Rogers et al. (2013) examine a regime change in *DJNS* reporting of insider trades, as filed in the Securities and Exchange Commission's Form 4. They find that 3-min stock price increases after events in which insiders purchase stocks are almost twice as large in the regime in which *DJNS* reports insider news.

18.3.2 Information Content and Valuation

Several studies measure the content of news to evaluate directional market responses to the information reflected in news. Niederhoffer's (1971) analysis of news and stock prices introduces key methods and previews basic findings. He identifies 432 world events from 1950 to 1966 as days in which the width of an *NYT* front-page headline exceeds five columns. Human readers categorize these headlines into 19 groups, such as US war developments, US discoveries, political elections, and changes in foreign leadership, and rate each headline's tone on a seven-point good–bad scale. Niederhoffer (1971) finds positive autocorrelation in news arrival and in headline tone, indicating news occurs in streaks. He also shows that sequences of related world events, such as Korean War events, are contemporaneously associated with extreme stock price movements. He notes that cumulative stock returns in days 2 to 5 after the 34 "extremely bad" world events are +1.14%. This apparent price reversal suggests that investors overreact to bad news, but generalizing from so few data points is difficult.

Tetlock (2007) is one of the first studies to apply automated content analysis to the text of news articles about the stock market. He hypothesizes that one can measure investor sentiment using textual analysis, enabling direct tests of behavioral finance theories, such as De Long et al. (1990). Tetlock's (2007) proposed measure is based on the linguistic tone of a popular daily *WSJ* column called "Abreast of the Market" (AM) from 1984 through 1999. The AM column consists of colorful *post-hoc* depictions of traders' moods and expectations from the prior day. This column could reflect and perhaps influence investor sentiment because the *WSJ* is a respected source with the largest circulation among daily financial publications in the United States.

Tetlock (2007) first computes the relative frequencies of AM words in 77 predetermined categories from the Harvard psychosocial dictionary, such as Strong, Weak, Active, and Passive words. He considers all categories but ultimately focuses on a composite category of words with a negative outlook, such as "flaw" and "ruin," because it captures a large fraction of common (time-series) variation in the word frequencies across all 77 categories. Intuitively, a low (high) frequency of negative words could represent investor optimism (pessimism). The notion that negative words are more important than positive words is consistent with the psychology literature. Baumeister et al. (2001) and Rozin and Royzman (2001), among others, argue that negative information has more impact and is more thoroughly processed than positive information in many contexts. Many studies now employ similar dictionary-based textual analysis procedures to those used by Tetlock (2007).[6]

---

[6] Recent studies propose several improvements beyond the simple word-counting methodology, including adapting the dictionary technology to a financial context, as in Loughran and McDonald (2011), inferring word importance from market reactions, as in Jegadeesh and Wu (2013), applying machine learning techniques, as in Antweiler and Frank (2004) and Das and Chen (2007), and using proprietary algorithms, such as Ravenpack's tools used in Beschwitz et al. (2013), Reuters' tools used in Grob-Klubmann and Hautsch (2011), and the Stock Sonar used in Boudoukh et al. (2013).

If negative words in the AM column represent investor sentiment, their frequent occurrence should be associated with temporarily low stock prices that bounce back when either there is sufficient arbitrage capital or noise traders realize their mistake. On the other hand, if negative words in the AM column constitute genuinely unfavorable information about firm values, stock prices should fall and should not reverse their course. A third possibility is that stock prices may not react to negative words if the AM column merely recapitulates information that market participants already know. Empirically, Tetlock (2007) demonstrates that negative words in the AM column are associated with lower same-day stock returns and predict lower returns the following day. Moreover, within a week of an AM column with highly negative tone, stock prices completely recover to their initial level on the day of the column. These results are consistent with the interpretation that negative tone in the AM column represents pessimistic sentiment, which temporarily influences stock prices as in De Long et al. (1990).

García (2013) builds on these results in a study of positive and negative words from two *NYT* columns spanning 1905–2005. He also finds that linguistic tone predicts market returns one day in advance and that there is a partial reversal of this price movement within 1 week. He demonstrates that these patterns vary with the business cycle, becoming stronger in recessions. He argues that this business cycle variation is consistent with the idea that investors are more sensitive to sentiment in downturns.

Bollen et al. (2011) and Karabulut (2013) propose measures of investor sentiment based on content from Internet postings on the social networks Twitter and Facebook respectively. These studies design their sentiment measures to capture investor moods. Bollen et al. (2011) argue that the "Calm" and "Happiness" dimensions of public mood extracted from Twitter have strong predictive power for weekly Dow Jones Index returns in 2008. Karabulut (2013) shows that Facebook's Gross National Happiness index—constructed from textual analysis of status updates—positively predicts next-day stock market returns, followed by a partial price reversal. These results highlight the promise of proxies for sentiment based on social network data.

Whereas researchers typically interpret the linguistic tone of media content about the market as a measure of investor sentiment, most interpret the tone of content about individual firms as an informative measure of a stock's value. Busse and Green (2002), Antweiler and Frank (2004), and Tetlock et al. (2008) conduct early studies of firm content from television, Internet chat rooms, and newspapers respectively.

Busse and Green (2002) analyze the content from 322 analyst reports about individual stocks aired on CNBC's popular *Morning Call* and *Midday Call* segments from June to October of 2000. The authors subjectively rate the tone of each report as positive (280 cases) or negative (42 cases). They find that positive abnormal stock market returns occur within 1 min of a stock's positive mention on CNBC; most predictability in abnormal returns dissipates within 5 min. Prices seem to incorporate most information in negative CNBC reports within 15 min, though this inference is less clear because of the small number of such reports. The authors conclude that the market responds quite efficiently to TV reports.

Antweiler and Frank (2004) study the frequency and tone of stock message-board posts on Yahoo! Finance and Raging Bull about 45 large US stocks in the year 2000. Their main finding is that message-board posting frequency positively predicts stock return volatility and trading volume, even controlling for the frequency of *WSJ* stories. The authors use an algorithm called Naïve Bayes to classify posts as bullish, neutral, or bearish based on the pattern of word occurrences. They report only weak relationships between posting tone and market activity.[7]

Tetlock et al. (2008) analyze the tone of firm-specific newspaper stories. In contrast to studies of selected columns about the market, the authors analyze a comprehensive sample of *WSJ* and *DJNS* news stories focussed on individual firms in the S&P 500 index. On average, these firm-specific stories contain more mundane and detailed information and receive less investor attention than the entertaining and widely-read AM column. The researchers use a common metric—the fraction of negative words in firm-specific news—to examine the directional impact of all newsworthy events.

Tetlock et al. (2008) show that negative words predict negative information about firm earnings, beyond quantifiable traditional measures of firm performance. The forecasting power of textual information for future earnings is comparable to that of stock returns, which in theory should be a very strong predictor of firm earnings. The study also tests whether stock market prices rationally reflect the effect of negative words on firms' expected earnings. It finds that stock market prices immediately incorporate over 80% of the information from negative words, though the one-day delayed reaction is also significant. This evidence suggests linguistic media content captures otherwise hard-to-quantify aspects of firms' fundamentals. Market prices respond to this information with a slight delay, consistent with models of limited investor attention such as Hirshleifer and Teoh (2003) and Peng and Xiong (2006).

Engelberg (2008) relates the findings in Tetlock et al. (2008) to those in the post-earnings announcement drift literature. He measures qualitative earnings information as the fraction of negative words in news about a firm on the day of its earnings announcement. He shows that qualitative earnings information has incremental predictive power for future returns above and beyond quantitative earnings surprises. The predictive power of qualitative earnings information is particularly strong at long horizons. One interpretation is that investors experience difficulty processing qualitative information.

Another challenge for investors with limited cognitive abilities is distinguishing new information from old information. News stories about stocks typically convey a combination of genuinely novel facts and older well-established facts that provide context. Market prices should already reflect these older facts and thus should only react to new information. Investors with limited attention, however, may not recognize which

---

[7] Das and Chen (2007) compare alternative approaches to classifying text from Internet stock message boards and examine the relations between message tone and stock market activity.

facts are old and the extent to which other market participants have already traded on previously released information. As a result, such investors could overreact to old or "stale" information.

Tetlock (2011) uses *DJNS* data from 1996 to 2008 to test the hypothesis that investor overreaction to financial news increases with the staleness of information. He defines the staleness of a news story as its textual similarity to the previous stories about the same firm. The similarity between two texts is a simple [0,1] measure, originally proposed by Jaccard (1901): the number of unique words present in the intersection of the two texts divided by the number of unique words present in the union of the two texts. This measure identifies news stories that contain a greater proportion of textual information that overlaps with previously known facts. The measure of market overreaction is the extent of stock price reversals, as measured by a firm's initial daily return around a news event negatively predicting its return in the week after the event. Tetlock's (2011) main finding is that market reactions to news are better negative predictors of future returns when news is stale.[8] His interpretation is that investors with limited attention overreact to stale information, causing temporary movements in firms' stock prices.

18.3.3 Attention and Valuation

Many of the above studies support the idea that news releases are associated with increases in investor attention to asset markets. This subsection reviews studies that relate media attention or spin to market valuations. Merton's (1987) theory predicts that attention could increase market valuations directly by alleviating informational frictions that prevent investors from holding lesser-known assets. Barber and Odean (2008) hypothesize that unsophisticated investors are prone to buying salient stocks because of limits on attention and short sales. They provide direct evidence that individual investors are net buyers of stocks featured in *DJNS* articles. Both theories predict increases in valuation and low future returns following positive shocks to investor attention. Short-run price dynamics, such as the extent and duration of any price reversal, depend on trading frictions (Duffie, 2010).

Fang and Peress (2009) test whether investor awareness of stocks increases valuations, using firm-specific media coverage in the *NYT*, *USA Today*, *WSJ*, and *Washington Post* as a proxy for investor attention. They find that stocks without media coverage in the prior month earn 3% higher annualized returns than stocks with above-average media coverage from 1993 to 2002. The return differential is as high as 8−12% among stocks with low market capitalizations, low analyst coverage, high individual investor ownership, and high idiosyncratic volatility. These results are broadly consistent with Merton's (1987) theory in which media coverage could make everyday investors aware of certain

---

[8] This result echoes earlier evidence from Davies and Canes (1978) and Barber and Loeffler (1993), who find partial price reversals of market reactions to second-hand analyst recommendations reported in the *WSJ*.

relatively obscure stocks. Stocks with lower investor recognition must offer higher expected returns to compensate their owners for being imperfectly diversified.

Da et al. (2011) provide complementary evidence in an analysis of Internet searches for information about stocks. The authors propose that the frequency of Google searches (Search Volume Index or SVI) for a stock's ticker is a measure of investor attention to the stock—e.g., the SVI of "AMZN" reflects investor attention to Amazon's stock. Using a sample of US stocks from 2004 to 2008, they show that SVI positively predicts three empirical proxies for attention: news stories, trading volume, and the absolute value of stock returns. Their main result is that increases in SVI predict increases in stock prices in the next 2 weeks followed by a partial price reversal within the year.

Several studies use television content to test whether shocks to investor attention predict increases in stock prices, as Merton (1987) hypothesizes. Fehle et al. (2005) examine firms featured in Super Bowl commercials, Meschke and Kim (2011) analyze the firms of chief executive officers (CEOs) interviewed on CNBC, and Engelberg et al. (2012) study stocks recommended on CNBC's popular *Mad Money* show. These three studies provide large-scale evidence that strongly supports theories in which investor attention increases stock prices. Each study uses direct attention measures, such as Nielsen viewership ratings, and shows that stock price reactions increase with viewership. The studies by Meschke and Kim (2011) and Engelberg et al. (2012) find evidence of a partial reversal of the initial spike in stock prices, consistent with Duffie's (2010) theory of slow-moving capital.

Media coverage could also affect market valuation by influencing investors' beliefs. Studies by Tumarkin and Whitelaw (2001), Dewally (2003), and Bhattacharya et al. (2009) suggest that media touting of Internet stocks during the boom of the late 1990s increased investor sentiment, but it had a muted impact on stock prices. Several studies examine the relation between email endorsements of stocks, commonly called "stock spam," and stock market activity. Stock spam consists of unsolicited emails recommending particular stocks; these messages can reach one million email accounts and cost only hundreds of dollars to send (Böhme and Holz, 2006). Studies by Böhme and Holz (2006), Frieder and Zittrain (2007), Hanke and Hauser (2008), and Hu et al. (2010) provide evidence on hundreds of stock spam messages touting small stocks traded on the Pink Sheets from 2004 to 2006. These studies document dramatic increases in daily trading volume of the order of 50% and significant stock price increases up to 2%. The increases in stock prices appear to be temporary, consistent with investor overreaction to non-information and limits to arbitrage.

18.4. CAUSAL ROLE OF MEDIA

Although many of the above studies establish Granger causality between media content and market activity, few studies distinguish market reactions to media reporting *per se* from reactions to the underlying information event reported. Suppose one seeks an estimate of the causal impact of media reporting of earnings announcements on market activity. One could compare market activity around earnings announcements with media coverage to market activity around announcements without media coverage—e.g., as in Peress (2008). The observed difference in average market activity between these events could be a biased estimator of the impact of reporting because the media decision to report on an announcement may depend on the nature of the event—for example, coverage could be more likely for surprising events and perhaps for positive events. This section reviews several clever studies that identify plausibly exogenous variation in media reporting in order to analyze the causal impact of reporting.

18.4.1 Case Studies

Huberman and Regev (2001) analyze a striking instance in which a news article in the *NYT* about promising new anti-cancer drugs causes the stock of EntreMed, a small biotechnology firm, to increase by over 600% within a day. The *NYT* reporting is plausibly exogenous because disclosure of the underlying information event, EntreMed's promising research, occurred 5 months earlier in *Nature*. Although EntreMed's stock experiences a partial price reversal, its price remains elevated by over 150% in the next 3 weeks. These results are consistent with Merton's (1987) hypothesis in which media reporting increases investor attention and hint that the magnitude of media-induced attention could be enormous. However, it is difficult to distinguish media's impact on temporary irrational exuberance from its impact on attention.

Another remarkable anecdote studied by Carvalho et al. (2011) and Marshall et al. (2014) highlights the influence of media reporting on investor beliefs. In 2008, a 6-year-old news story about United Airlines' 2002 bankruptcy mistakenly appeared on several websites as news. Within minutes of the article's posting on Bloomberg news, United's stock price fell by 76%. Soon thereafter, United denied the story, exposing the news to be stale and irrelevant. Although the firm's stock price rebounded, it remained down by 11% at the close of trading. This episode demonstrates that reporting influences investor beliefs beyond its effect on attention.

18.4.2 Media Impact on Volume and Volatility

While these anecdotal studies illustrate the potential magnitude of media effects, only large-scale evidence on the causal impact of media indicates the practical importance of media effects. The challenge is that natural experiments in which media reporting varies for exogenous reasons may not produce meaningful variation in reporting. Furthermore, by design, reporting in these cases is uncorrelated with the information being reported. If reporting influences investors most when it reinforces their preexisting prejudices and tendencies, evidence from natural experiments provides a lower bound on the causal impact of media.

Engelberg and Parsons (2011) compare the trading behavior of investors exposed to different local media coverage of the same information event, namely firm earnings announcements. Local newspaper coverage of an earnings announcement increases the daily trading activity of individual investors in nearby zip codes by 48%. Peress (2014) examines the effect of reductions in media coverage caused by newspaper strikes in different countries. Strikes reduce daily trading volume by 14% and return volatility by 9% in a country's stock market. The impact of strikes is largest for small stocks, which have high individual ownership. Both studies provide impressive evidence that reporting causes significant increases in trading activity. However, neither study distinguishes media impact on attention from its impact on beliefs.

18.4.3 Media Impact on Stock Prices

Studies of the directional impact of media on stock prices may be able to disentangle attention and belief effects. Dyck and Zingales (2003) analyze how the type of earnings emphasized in newspaper stories—either official accounting earnings or unofficial pro forma earnings—relates to stock price changes around earnings announcements. They show that stock prices react more to the type of earnings reported in newspapers—particularly credible ones, such as the *WSJ*—suggesting newspaper reporting influences beliefs.

An alternative strategy for isolating the impact of media on beliefs is to examine variation in media incentives to report favorable news about an asset. Reuter and Zitzewitz (2006) show that personal finance publications, such as *Money Magazine*, are more likely to positively recommend mutual funds from companies that buy advertisements in these publications. These positive mentions of funds are associated with fund inflows, consistent with an influence on investor beliefs. Solomon (2012) tests whether stock price reactions to news depend on whether firms hire investor relations (IR) firms, who can spin their clients' news. Firms with IR spin enjoy higher average returns around non-earnings news events, but they exhibit significantly lower returns around earnings announcements, perhaps because earnings news is more difficult to spin. One interpretation is that IR firms exert a temporary impact on investor beliefs.[9]

Dougal et al. (2012) exploit exogenous rotation of *WSJ* writers of the AM column, who differ in their writing styles. They find that journalist fixed effects have significant predictive power for next-day aggregate stock market returns, increasing the R^2 of a forecasting regression from 2.8% to 3.8%. A positive (negative) fixed effect estimate indicates that a journalist exerts a bullish (bearish) influence on stock prices. On one hand, the

---

[9] In a similar vein, Ahern and Sosyura (2015) argue that media coverage of merger rumors unduly influences investors' beliefs about merger likelihood, causing temporary increases in the stock prices of potential target firms.

impact of writing style is modest; on the other, it is surprising that the writing style of the writer of a single newspaper column about yesterday's market activity has any measurable impact. Presumably this effect operates through investor beliefs.

A recent study by Schmidt (2013) suggests that the attention channel is also important. He uses Google searches for international sporting events to test Peng and Xiong's (2006) theory in which distracted investors prioritize market news over firm-specific news.[10] He shows that a standardized increase in investor attention to sports—implying inattention to stocks—reduces dispersion in firms' stock prices by 13%. In addition, investor attention to sports reduces market volatility by 8% and trading activity by 4%. Although this evidence ostensibly supports the attention mechanism, attention is a prerequisite for media content to influence beliefs.

18.5. CORPORATE FINANCE APPLICATIONS

The above studies indicate that media coverage exhibits strong correlations and causal relations with asset prices. Given the importance of capital markets for managerial decisions, it is natural to examine whether media coverage is linked to firm behavior and the real economy. This section reviews studies that use media data to analyze the relation between corporate finance and information environment.

18.5.1 Media and Firm Performance

Media coverage could improve firm performance in two ways. First, coverage could serve as advertising that increases consumer awareness of the firm and improves attitudes toward its products, thereby increasing firm revenues and profits. As a result, firm decisions that influence media coverage, such as disclosure or financing policies, could affect performance. For example, Demers and Lewellen (2003) argue that initial public offering (IPO) events and IPO underpricing attract media attention and generate valuable publicity for firms going public. The authors demonstrate that first-day IPO returns positively predict website traffic growth for Internet firms and media coverage for non-Internet firms, suggesting significant marketing benefits.

Second, coverage could enhance firm performance by reducing the costs of monitoring corrupt or inefficient managerial behavior. Dyck et al. (2008) analyze media coverage of corporate governance violations by Russian firms from 1999 to 2002. They document that international media coverage increases the probability that a firm reverses a corporate governance violation, presumably motivated by external social and shareholder pressure. Kuhnen and Niessen (2012) examine media coverage of CEO pay in the US and show that negative coverage predicts reductions in stock option grants. Enikolopov et al. (2014) investigate the effects of blog postings about corruption in Russian state-controlled

---

[10] Eisensee and Strömberg (2007) is the first study to identify distraction using "news pressure" from other events.

firms and find that postings positively predict management turnover. Collectively, these results are consistent with the theory that media play an important monitoring role.

18.5.2 Media and the Cost of Capital

If media coverage influences the price at which firms raise or acquire capital, managers have incentives to take actions that affect coverage. Actions that could improve media coverage include issuing more press releases, hiring an IR firm, or increasing advertising expenditures. Bushee and Miller (2012) document that hiring an IR firm increases media coverage, analyst following, and institutional investor holdings. Gurun and Butler (2012) find that firms' advertising expenditures in local media outlets positively predict the linguistic tone of local news about the firms.

Media coverage, particularly positive coverage, can help firms raise capital by increasing investor awareness or by increasing investor sentiment. Cook et al. (2006) and Liu et al. (2014) test this idea in analyses of media coverage prior to firms' IPOs. Cook et al. (2006) find that a firm's pre-IPO publicity positively predicts its stock return on the day of its IPO and retail investor trading on the IPO date. Liu et al. (2014) show that pre-IPO media coverage positively predicts a stock's long-term valuation, liquidity, analyst coverage, and institutional ownership. Both studies conclude that media coverage reduces firms' cost of capital.

Media coverage could also affect the cost of acquiring capital. Ahern and Sosyura (2014) analyze mergers in which firms use their stock as currency for acquiring another firm. They show that bidders in stock mergers issue more press releases during merger negotiations and that the temporary run-up in bidder stock price associated with such stories decreases the effective cost of acquiring the target firm's stock.

The success of a mutual fund depends critically on the willingness of investors to provide capital. In an analysis of mutual funds' disclosed stock holdings, Solomon et al. (2014) show that funds' holding stocks with high past returns attract inflows of capital only if these stocks have appeared recently in major newspapers. Such investors' portfolio choices give fund managers an incentive to hold stocks featured in the news. Consistent with this incentive, Falkenstein (1996) finds that mutual funds tend to hold stocks that appear in the news. Fang et al. (2014) show that fund managers who buy stocks with high media coverage tend to underperform relevant benchmarks by up to 2% per year, suggesting these fund managers behave inefficiently.

18.6. DISCUSSION AND DIRECTIONS FOR FUTURE RESEARCH

The growing literature on the media in finance investigates a wide array of mechanisms for transmitting information, a broad set of informative events, and measures of information content based on non-numeric information. Two sets of findings provide especially fertile ground for further study. First, anecdotal studies suggest the impact of media on asset prices could be enormous, with the publication of single articles causing prices to rise or fall by factors of three to six. But the large-scale evidence from studies using instruments for exogenous changes in media reporting reveals impacts that are smaller by an order of magnitude. One can reconcile these facts by arguing either the anecdotes are unusual or the instruments are weak. Future research should determine the merits of these explanations.

Second, an especially important and unsettling finding in the literature is the weak link between information arrival and price movement. Part of the explanation seems to be that market prices underreact to information and overreact to non-information. A complementary possibility is that high-frequency changes in risk premiums influence prices and volume. However, the properties of measurable firm-level risk and market returns noted by Lewellen and Nagel (2006) cast doubt on the quantitative importance of this risk-based explanation. The importance of the two remaining classes of explanations remains debatable. Private information could be critical for explaining market activity, as suggested by French and Roll (1986). Alternatively, current measures of public information may be inadequate.

The abundance of public data in modern society presents opportunities for testing these competing theories, but it also makes identifying, parsing, and analyzing implications for market activity challenging. Given the potential importance of quasi-public information, such as widely dispersed word-of-mouth communication and Internet chatter, allocating more resources to the collection and analysis of such data seems worthwhile. In this spirit, a flurry of recent studies by Bollen et al. (2011), Giannini et al. (2014), Heimer and Simon (2012), Karabulut (2013), and Chen et al. (2014) undertakes the challenge of analyzing data from social networks of investors, including Facebook, Seeking Alpha, and Twitter.

These data, along with data on individuals' media viewership and search activity, can help researchers understand the role of attention and active information gathering in financial markets. For example, by measuring how many potential investors view specific content at specific times, we could analyze how information diffusion across investors affects trading behavior and asset price adjustment. Then researchers could test the growing number of theories of information diffusion within investor networks. Continued improvements in access to data and computing power are likely to propel this line of research for years to come.

ACKNOWLEDGMENTS

In a companion article (Tetlock, 2014), I discuss many of the themes in this chapter from the perspective of information transmission. This chapter reuses portions of the earlier article with permission from the *Annual Review of Financial Economics*.

REFERENCES

Ahern, K., Sosyura, D., 2014. Who writes the news? Corporate press releases during merger negotiations. J. Financ. 69, 241–291.

Ahern, K., Sosyura, D., 2015. Rumor has it: sensationalism in financial media. Rev. Financ. Stud. 28, 1849–1873.

Antweiler, W., Frank, M.Z., 2004. Is all that talk just noise? The information content of internet stock message boards. J. Financ. 59, 1259–1294.

Aumann, R.J., 1976. Agreeing to disagree. Ann. Stat. 4, 1236–1239.

Banerjee, S., Kremer, I., 2010. Disagreement and learning: dynamic patterns of trade. J. Financ. 65, 1269–1302.

Barber, B.M., Loeffler, D., 1993. The 'Dartboard' column: second-hand information and price pressure. J. Financ. Quant. Anal. 28, 273–284.

Barber, B.M., Odean, T., 2008. All that glitters: the effect of attention and news on the buying behavior of individual and institutional investors. Rev. Financ. Stud. 21, 785–818.

Baumeister, R.F., Bratslavsky, E., Finkenauer, C., Vohs, K.D., 2001. Bad is stronger than good. Rev. Gen. Psychol. 5, 323–370.

Berry, T.D., Howe, K.M., 1994. Public information arrival. J. Financ. 49, 1331–1346.

Beschwitz, B.V., Keim, D.B., Massa, M., 2013. Media-Driven High Frequency Trading: Implications of Errors in News Analytics. Working Paper, INSEAD.

Bhattacharya, U., Galpin, N., Ray, R., Yu, X., 2009. The role of the media in the internet IPO bubble. J. Financ. Quant. Anal. 44, 657–682.

Böhme, R., Holz, T., 2006. The Effect of Stock Spam on Financial Markets. Working Paper, Dresden University of Technology.

Bollen, J., Mao, H., Zeng, X., 2011. Twitter mood predicts the stock market. J. Comput. Sci. 2, 1–8.

Boudoukh, J., Feldman, R., Kogan, S., Richardson, M., 2013. Which News Moves Stock Prices? A Textual Analysis. National Bureau of Economic Research, Working Paper No. 18725.

Brunnermeier, M.K., 2005. Information leakage and market efficiency. Rev. Financ. Stud. 18, 417–457.

Bushee, B.J., Miller, G.S., 2012. Investor relations, firm visibility, and investor following. Account. Rev. 87, 867–897.

Bushee, B.J., Core, J.E., Guay, W., Hamm, S.J.W., 2010. The role of the business press as an information intermediary. J. Account. Res. 48, 1–19.

Busse, J.A., Green, T.C., 2002. Market efficiency in real time. J. Financ. Econ. 65, 415–437.

Carvalho, C., Klagge, N., Moench, E., 2011. The persistent effects of a false news shock. J. Empir. Finance 18, 597–615.

Chan, W.S., 2003. Stock price reaction to news and no-news: drift and reversal after headlines. J. Financ. Econ. 70, 223–260.

Chen, H., De, P., Hu, Y., Hwang, B., 2014. Wisdom of crowds: the value of stock opinions transmitted through social media. Rev. Financ. Stud. 27, 1367–1403.

Colla, P., Mele, A., 2010. Information linkages and correlated trading. Rev. Financ. Stud. 23, 203–246.

Cook, D.O., Kieschnick, R., Van Ness, R.A., 2006. On the marketing of IPOs. J. Financ. Econ. 82, 35–61.

Cornell, B., 2013. What moves stock prices: another look. J. Portf. Manag. 39, 32–38.

Cutler, D.M., Poterba, J.M., Summers, L.H., 1989. What moves stock prices? J. Portf. Manag. 15, 4–12.

Da, Z., Engelberg, J., Gao, P., 2011. In search of attention. J. Financ. 66, 1461–1499.

Das, S.R., 2011. News analytics: framework, techniques, and metrics. In: Mitra, G., Mitra, L. (Eds.), The Handbook of News Analytics in Finance, vol. 2. John Wiley & Sons, Chichester.

Das, S.R., Chen, M.Y., 2007. Yahoo! for Amazon: sentiment extraction from small talk on the web. Manag. Sci. 53, 1375–1388.

Davies, P.L., Canes, M., 1978. Stock prices and the publication of second-hand information. J. Bus. 51, 43–56.

De Long, J.B., Shleifer, A., Summers, L.H., Waldmann, R.J., 1990. Noise trader risk in financial markets. J. Polit. Econ. 98, 703–738.

Demers, E., Lewellen, K., 2003. The marketing role of IPOs: evidence from internet stocks. J. Financ. Econ. 68, 413–437.

Dewally, M., 2003. Internet investment advice: investing with a rock of salt. Financ. Analysts J. 59, 65–77.

Dougal, C., Engelberg, J., García, D., Parsons, C.A., 2012. Journalists and the stock market. Rev. Financ. Stud. 25, 639–679.

Duffie, D., 2010. Asset price dynamics with slow-moving capital. J. Financ. 65, 1237–1267.

Dyck, A., Zingales, L., 2003. The Media and Asset Prices. Working Paper, Harvard Business School.

Dyck, A., Volchkova, N., Zingales, L., 2008. The corporate governance role of the media: evidence from Russia. J. Financ. 63, 1093–1135.

Eisensee, T., Strömberg, D., 2007. News droughts, news floods, and U.S. disaster relief. Q. J. Econ. 122, 693–728.

Engelberg, J., 2008. Costly Information Processing: Evidence from Earnings Announcements. Working Paper, Northwestern University.

Engelberg, J., Parsons, C.A., 2011. The causal impact of media in financial markets. J. Financ. 66, 67–97.

Engelberg, J., Sasseville, C., Williams, J., 2012. Market madness? The case of mad money. Manag. Sci. 58, 351–364.

Enikolopov, R., Petrova, M., Sonin, K., 2014. Social Media and Corruption. Working Paper, New Economic School.

Falkenstein, E.G., 1996. Preferences for stock characteristics as revealed by mutual fund portfolio holdings. J. Financ. 51, 111–135.

Fang, L.H., Peress, J., 2009. Media coverage and the cross-section of stock returns. J. Financ. 64, 2023–2052.

Fang, L.H., Peress, J., Zheng, L., 2014. Does media coverage of stocks affect mutual funds' trading and performance? Rev. Financ. Stud. 27, 3441–3466.

Fehle, F., Tsyplakov, S., Zdorovtsov, V., 2005. Can companies influence investor behaviour through advertising? Super Bowl commercials and stock returns. Eur. Financ. Manag. 11, 625–647.

French, K.R., Roll, R., 1986. Stock return variances: the arrival of information and the reaction of traders. J. Financ. Econ. 17, 5–26.

Frieder, L., Zittrain, J., 2007. Spam works: evidence from stock touts and corresponding market activity. Hast. Commun. Entertain. Law J. 30, 479–520.

García, D., 2013. Sentiment during recessions. J. Financ. 68, 1267–1300.

Giannini, R., Irvine, P., Shu, T., 2014. Do Local Investors Know More? A Direct Examination of Individual Investors' Information Set. Working Paper, University of Georgia.

Griffin, J.M., Hirschey, N.H., Kelly, P.J., 2011. How important is the financial media in global markets? Rev. Financ. Stud. 24, 3941–3992.

Grob-Klubmann, A., Hautsch, N., 2011. When machines read the news: using automated text analytics to quantify high frequency news-implied market reactions. J. Empir. Finance 18, 321–340.

Grossman, S.J., Stiglitz, J.E., 1980. On the impossibility of informationally efficient markets. Am. Econ. Rev. 70, 393–408.

Gurun, U.G., Butler, A.W., 2012. Don't believe the hype: local media slant, local advertising, and firm value. J. Financ. 67, 561–597.

Han, B., Hirshleifer, D., 2012. Self-Enhancing Transmission Bias and Active Investing. Working Paper, UC Irvine.

Hanke, M., Hauser, F., 2008. On the effects of stock spam e-mails. J. Financ. Mark. 11, 57–83.

Harris, M., Raviv, A., 1993. Differences of opinion make a horse race. Rev. Financ. Stud. 6, 473–506.

He, H., Wang, J., 1995. Differential information and dynamic behavior of stock trading volume. Rev. Financ. Stud. 8, 919–972.

Heimer, R.Z., Simon, D., 2012. Facebook Finance: How Social Interaction Propagates Active Investing. Working Paper, Brandeis University.

Hirshleifer, D., Teoh, S.H., 2003. Limited attention, information disclosure, and financial reporting. J. Account. Econ. 36, 337–386.

Hirshleifer, D., Subrahmanyam, A., Titman, S., 1994. Security analysis and trading patterns when some investors receive information before others. J. Financ. 49, 1665–1698.

Hu, B., McInish, T., Zeng, L., 2010. Gambling in penny stocks: the case of stock spam e-mails. Int. J. Cyber Criminol. 4, 610–629.

Huberman, G., Regev, T., 2001. Contagious speculation and a cure for cancer: a nonevent that made stock prices soar. J. Financ. 56, 387–396.

Jaccard, P., 1901. Étude comparative de la distribution florale dans une portion des Alpes et des Jura. Bull. Soc. Vaudo. Sci. Nat. 37, 547–579.

Jegadeesh, N., Wu, A.D., 2013. Word power: a new approach for content analysis. J. Financ. Econ. 110, 712–729.

Kandel, E., Pearson, N.D., 1995. Differential interpretation of public signals and trade in speculative markets. J. Polit. Econ. 103, 831–872.

Karabulut, Y., 2013. Can Facebook Predict Stock Market Activity? Working Paper, Goethe University.

Kearney, C., Liu, S., 2014. Textual sentiment in finance: a survey of methods and models. Int. Rev. Financ. Anal. 33, 171–185.

Kim, O., Verrecchia, R.E., 1994. Market liquidity and volume around earnings announcements. J. Account. Econ. 17, 41–67.

Klibanoff, P., Lamont, O., Wizman, T.A., 1998. Investor reaction to salient news in closed-end country funds. J. Financ. 53, 673–699.

Kuhnen, C.M., Niessen, A., 2012. Public opinion and executive compensation. Manag. Sci. 58, 1249–1272.

Lewellen, J., Nagel, S., 2006. The conditional CAPM does not explain asset-pricing anomalies. J. Financ. Econ. 82, 289–314.

Li, F., 2010. Textual analysis of corporate disclosures: a survey of the literature. J. Account. Lit. 29, 143–165.

Liu, L.X., Sherman, A.E., Zhang, Y., 2014. The long-run role of the media: evidence from initial public offerings. Manag. Sci. 60, 1945–1964.

Loughran, T., McDonald, B., 2011. When is a liability not a liability? Textual analysis, dictionaries, and 10-Ks. J. Financ. 66, 35–65.

Marshall, B.R., Visaltanachoti, N., Cooper, G., 2014. Sell the rumour, buy the fact? Account. Finance 54, 237–249.

Merton, R.C., 1987. A simple model of capital market equilibrium with incomplete information. J. Financ. 42, 483–510.

Meschke, F., Kim, Y.H., 2011. CEO Interviews on CNBC. Working Paper, University of Kansas.

Milgrom, P., Stokey, N., 1982. Information, trade, and common knowledge. J. Econ. Theory 26, 17–27.

Miller, E., 1977. Risk, uncertainty, and divergence of opinion. J. Financ. 32, 1151–1168.

Mitchell, M.L., Mulherin, J.H., 1994. The impact of public information on the stock market. J. Financ. 49, 923–950.

Mullainathan, S., Shleifer, A., 2005a. The market for news. Am. Econ. Rev. 95, 1031–1053.

Mullainathan, S., Shleifer, A., 2005b. Persuasion in Finance. Working Paper, Harvard University.

Neuhierl, A., Scherbina, A., Schlusche, B., 2013. Market reaction to corporate press releases. J. Financ. Quant. Anal. 48, 1207–1240.

Niederhoffer, V., 1971. The analysis of world events and stock prices. J. Bus. 44, 193–219.

Ozsoylev, H.N., Walden, J., 2011. Asset pricing in large information networks. J. Econ. Theory 146, 2252–2280.

Peng, L., Xiong, W., 2006. Investor attention, overconfidence and category learning. J. Financ. Econ. 80, 563–602.

Peress, J., 2008. Media Coverage and Investors' Attention to Earnings Announcements. Working Paper, INSEAD.

Peress, J., 2014. The media and the diffusion of information in financial markets: evidence from newspaper strikes. J. Financ. 69, 2007–2043.

Reuter, J., Zitzewitz, E., 2006. Do ads influence editors? Advertising and bias in the financial media. Q. J. Econ. 121, 197–227.

Rogers, J.L., Skinner, D.J., Zechman, S.L.C., 2013. The Role of Media in Disseminating Insider Trading News. Working Paper, University of Chicago.

Roll, R., 1988. R-squared. J. Financ. 43, 541–566.

Rozin, P., Royzman, E., 2001. Negativity bias, negativity dominance, and contagion. Personal. Soc. Psychol. Rev. 5, 296–320.

Scheinkman, J.A., Xiong, W., 2003. Overconfidence and speculative bubbles. J. Polit. Econ. 111, 1183–1219.

Schmidt, D., 2013. Investors' Attention and Stock Covariation: Evidence from Google Sport Searches. Working Paper, INSEAD.

Solomon, D.H., 2012. Selective publicity and stock prices. J. Financ. 67, 599–637.

Solomon, D.H., Soltes, E.F., Sosyura, D., 2014. Winners in the spotlight: media coverage of fund holdings as a driver of flows. J. Financ. Econ. 113, 53–72.

Tetlock, P.C., 2007. Giving content to investor sentiment: the role of media in the stock market. J. Financ. 62, 1139–1168.

Tetlock, P.C., 2010. Does public news resolve asymmetric information? Rev. Financ. Stud. 23, 3520–3557.

Tetlock, P.C., 2011. All the news that's fit to reprint: do investors react to stale information? Rev. Financ. Stud. 24, 1481–1512.

Tetlock, P.C., 2014. Information transmission in finance. Annu. Rev. Financ. Econ. 6, 365–384.

Tetlock, P.C., Saar-Tsechansky, M., Macskassy, S., 2008. More than words: quantifying language to measure firms' fundamentals. J. Financ. 63, 1437–1467.

Tumarkin, R., Whitelaw, R.F., 2001. News or noise? Internet message board activity and stock prices. Financ. Analysts J. 57, 41–51.

Vega, C., 2006. Stock price reaction to public and private information. J. Financ. Econ. 82, 103–133.

CHAPTER 19

Economic and Social Impacts of the Media

Stefano DellaVigna*, Eliana La Ferrara†
*University of California, Berkeley and NBER, Cambridge, MA, USA
†Bocconi University and IGIER, Milano, Italy

Contents

19.1. Introduction	724
19.2. Methodological Issues	728
19.3. Outcomes	731
19.3.1 Education	731
19.3.2 Family Outcomes	737
19.3.3 Labor Markets and Migration	741
19.3.4 Environmental Economics	743
19.3.5 Health	744
19.3.5.1 Suicide	*744*
19.3.5.2 Smoking	*744*
19.3.5.3 HIV/AIDS	*745*
19.3.6 Crime	746
19.3.7 Public Economics	751
19.3.8 Attitudes	754
19.3.9 Consumption and Savings	756
19.3.10 Development Economics	757
19.4. Policy and Conclusion	758
Acknowledgments	766
References	766

Abstract

In this survey, we review the literature on the impact of exposure to the media. We cast a wide net and cover media impacts on education, family choices, labor and migration decisions, environmental choices, health, crime, public economics, attitudes, consumption and savings, and development economics. We stress five themes. First, the demand for entertainment plays a key role, with the economic impacts emerging largely as by-products. Second, to understand the media effects, one cannot just focus on the direct effect of exposure but one needs to take into account the crowding out of alternative activities (substitution effect). Third, the sources of identification play a critical role in determining what is known: credible estimates of short- and long-run effects are available for some topics and some media but not for others. Fourth, most of the evidence on social and economic impacts is for exposure to the entertainment media such as television, as opposed to the printed press. Fifth, for the policy impacts, both the substitution effect of media exposure and the demand for entertainment play important roles.

Handbook of Media Economics, Volume 1B
ISSN 2213-6630, http://dx.doi.org/10.1016/B978-0-444-63685-0.00019-X

Keywords

Media economics, Imitation, Persuasion, Edutainment, Television, Radio, Internet

JEL Codes

A13, D01, D10, H4, I10, I20, J00, K42, L82, L96, O10

19.1. INTRODUCTION

Does television exposure impair educational achievement? Does violence in the media trigger arousal and violent crime? Can media content affect deep-seated decisions like fertility choices? Is there consistent evidence of imitation of media behavior?

Questions such as these, of relevance to both researchers and policymakers, have motivated the literature on the impacts of media exposure. In this survey, we review this literature, covering a wide range of economic and social outcomes and summarizing key studies within each area. To maximize readability, we structure the content by field of study, including the topics of education, health, crime, consumption, and family choices. Table 19.1 provides a summary of the studies we review.

We delineate the content for the survey along three boundaries: outcomes, methodology, and media. In terms of outcomes, while we cast a wide net, the survey will not cover the evidence on the impact of media on politics, covered in Strömberg (2015) and Enikolopov and Petrova (2015), nor the impact of advertising, covered in Wilbur (2015). We also refer to Tetlock (2015) for the analysis of financial choices.

Regarding methodology, we examine a variety of evidence from the field, including natural experiments, field experiments, and observational data. We do not instead cover evidence from laboratory experiments or pure survey evidence, methods common in media studies in psychology, political science, and sociology.

Regarding the media covered, we provide evidence on a wide variety of media outlets, from the more traditional ones (radio, movies, and television) to the more modern ones (Internet and video games). We do not instead cover the fast-growing literature using text messages and smartphones to deliver content, given the difference in themes.[1]

While we cannot succinctly summarize the results in each of the different fields in this introduction, we do want to emphasize five recurring themes emerging from the survey: (i) *demand for entertainment*, (ii) *direct versus substitution effects*, (iii) *identification and time horizon*, (iv) *the role of entertainment media*, and (v) *policy impacts*.

The first one is the key role of the *demand for entertainment*. In nearly all the settings we consider, the consumer demand for media content is largely due to demand for entertainment, with the economic impacts emerging as a by-product. Children watch

---

[1] While the demand for entertainment plays a key role for the applications we survey, SMS messages are typically used to provide information and reminders.

television for its fun value, likely not thinking of possible impacts on education. Adults choose to watch a violent movie or to follow a soap opera for entertainment value, disregarding possible effects on aggression or on family values. This implies that selection into a particular media is likely unrelated to the preference for particular economic outcomes—say, education, violent crime, or fertility. The overarching role of the demand for entertainment is reflected in the fact that people spend a large share of time on media entertainment: in the United States, the average amount of time spent watching television (which is just one form of media entertainment) is 2.7 h per day, half of leisure time (Aguiar et al., 2013).

The demand for entertainment differentiates the applications we survey from the analysis of political or financial impacts of the media. The exposure to political information often reflects a direct demand for political content as Strömberg (2015) and Gentzkow et al. (2015) stress. The exposure to financial-themed media like CNBC also reflects a direct interest in investment advice.

In Section 19.2, we incorporate this insight into a simple model of media choice, building on the model in Dahl and DellaVigna (2009). We assume that consumers choose the optimal use of time between several activities, some of which are media activities and some are not. For example, the consumers decide whether to follow a soap opera or to go out with friends. The value of the media activities takes into account the entertainment value as well as cost factors. Similarly, there are utility shifters for the value of alternative uses of time. The activities chosen impact relevant economic outcomes, like education, violent crime, and fertility, but these effects are *not* considered as part of the utility-maximizing choice, simplifying the analysis. We then derive comparative statics of parameters capturing some of the identifying variation in the media studies.

This takes us to the second key theme, *direct versus substitution effects*. We stress that there are two main sources of variation of media effects in this entertainment setting. The first one is a shock to the entertainment value of a channel, or to its cost, which affects the audience for a media. For example, violent movies are of higher quality on a particular weekend (a positive demand shock), or soap operas become more widely available in a given year (a positive cost shock). In both cases, as the comparative statics indicates, the resulting media effect estimates incorporate both a *direct* effect and a *substitution* effect. The release of a movie like *Hannibal* at the theater implies that more people will be watching a (violent) movie and thus will be doing less of the second-best alternative activity. The net effect of this shock on crime depends on the *comparative* effect of violent movies on crime *relative* to the effect of the alternative activity on crime. Similarly, to understand the impact of introduction of a soap opera, we need to consider the activity and content that it substituted for. Thinking of the substitute activities and evaluating the estimated impact as a net impact relative to substitutes is a key lesson from the studies. Indeed, Strömberg (2015) stresses that a similar direct-versus-substitution effect applies to the interpretation of media effects on politics.

The model also highlights a second source of variation, which is a direct shock to the content of the media. Suppose that an episode of an ongoing soap opera features a gay couple, or an occurrence of suicide. This change in content is likely to leave the utility-maximizing choice of media entertainment mostly unaffected, especially if the content of the episode is unanticipated. Still, the content may affect economic behavior, say through imitation. In this case, the estimated media effect captures the *direct* impact of the media, since the consumption of substitute activities is held constant.

The third key theme for the survey is the role played by *identification and time horizon*. Take the analysis of imitation of media behavior. A first question of interest is whether there is a short-run imitation effect after a media episode features a particular behavior. A second question is if there are long-term imitative effects of prolonged exposure to the media. To identify the first question, high-frequency variation in the content of a widely seen media outlet is sufficient. But for the identification of long-run effects, one needs plausibly exogenous variation across places and over time in the introduction of a media outlet which carries unique content. The variation in identification determines the type of media effects one can credibly estimate.

For family choices, we have evidence of imitation in both the short run and long run. Kearney and Levine (2014) estimate, among other outcomes, the short-run impact of the United States show *16 and Pregnant* on Google searches for keywords related to fertility choices. Conversely, La Ferrara et al. (2012) estimate the long-term effects on fertility rates in Brazil of exposure to telenovelas, taking advantage of the staggered introduction of Globo, which largely introduced telenovelas in Brazil.

In most other cases, however, it is not possible to estimate both short-term and long-term effects. In their research on media violence and violent crime, Dahl and DellaVigna (2009) exploit the natural experiment induced by the idiosyncratic release of violent movies to estimate the short-run effects of exposure to media violence. Their design, however, does not lend itself to the analysis of long-term effects. Indeed, to our knowledge, there is no study providing credible estimates of the long-run impact of exposure to media violence. The difficulty is that violent content on the media has been pervasive for a long time, making identification of long-term exposure near impossible, at least in the United States. In cases such as this, it is tempting to look for alternative evidence on long-term effects: indeed, even the American Academy of Pediatrics cites correlational evidence between television usage and violent behavior to support its policy recommendations. Unfortunately, this evidence is plagued by bias—taste for violence is likely to drive both behaviors—and should in our mind be disregarded. In these settings, we have credible estimates of short-term effects but are left in the dark regarding long-term effects. In other cases, like the impact of video game consumption on crime, even short-run effects are problematic to estimate because high-frequency variation in video game consumption is very limited.

The fourth theme is the *role of entertainment media*. A striking feature apparent from Table 19.1 is the scarcity of evidence about print media: newspapers and periodicals.

To put things in perspective, variation in newspaper circulation plays a key role in the identification of political impacts of the media, as local papers provide critical information on local politics (Strömberg, 2015). And yet, when it comes to the impact on outcomes such as education, health, crime, or family choices, most of the available evidence concerns the entertainment media—television, movies, and Internet.[2]

Even within the entertainment media, the evidence available depends also on the ability to find identifying variation in exposure, as we stressed above. It is easier to find geographic variation in radio wave penetration or penetration of specific TV channels as driven by geography, cable programming, or content of movies released. It is harder to find credible variation of the penetration of television overall (as opposed to a particular channel), of the Internet, or of video games. Thus, we tend to have more evidence on the impact of the first group of media than the second group of media.

The fifth key theme is *policy impacts*. A number of the topics we examine reflect policy concerns, like the impact of television and of violent media. Yet the research papers suggest policy implications which can appear surprising. A first example is that the studies reviewed do not find consistent evidence of a negative effect of television on education (the evidence in this respect is mixed), and find that the availability of violent movies in the short run leads to reductions, not increases, in crime. The key insight here goes back to the substitution effects: television or violent movies may be substituting other activities that are not better for the relevant outcomes. A second example is that one of the most clearly documented policy objectives achieved by media exposure—the reduction of the fertility rate in developing countries (e.g., Brazil in the 1970s and 1980s)—was attained as a by-product of the success of telenovelas, and was not a goal in the design of the entertainment material. This second example brings us back to the first theme, the overarching role of demand for entertainment.

A more recent set of studies takes stock of the primacy of demand for entertainment for policy purposes, and takes it one step further: why not attempt to incorporate policy goals into the entertainment material? The parallel with advertising is clear: marketing companies have for decades used product placement to sell products, suggesting a natural path for the use of entertainment to "sell" policies. Still, this strategy faces thorny issues, as one may legitimately worry about its use for propaganda purposes. We return to the issue of "educational entertainment" (or "edutainment"), discussed in more depth in La Ferrara (2015), in Section 19.4.

---

[2] This is possibly due to the non-obvious way in which newspaper content on social issues may be coded, compared to political content. For example, measures of ideological bias in newspaper coverage have been proposed comparing the terminology used in the articles to that used by congressmen (e.g., Groseclose and Milyo, 2005), but no similar strategy has been developed for themes related to education, health, etc.

19.2. METHODOLOGICAL ISSUES

To focus thoughts on the interpretation of media effects, we propose a simple framework highlighting the different channels for the media effects. This model builds on Dahl and DellaVigna (2009).

Consider a discrete-choice model where an audience is choosing between activities $x_1, x_2, \ldots, x_n$. Some of these activities are media choices, such as watching a television show, listening to the news on the radio, or reading a newspaper. Other activities instead represent alternative uses of time, such as attending a group meeting in a village, reading a book, or traveling to a nearby concert.

Assume a standard discrete-choice framework with activity x_i yielding utility

$$u(x_i) = X_i - \gamma c_i + \varepsilon_i,$$

where ε_i has a type I extreme distribution. This specification allows for both (i) shocks to demand X_i for a medium, like the fact that a show becomes very popular, and (ii) shocks to the supply of a medium, such as the introduction of a new show, captured by a change in costs c_i.

The standard logit derivation implies that the share of time spent on activity i will be

$$s_i = \frac{\exp\left(X_i - \gamma c_i\right)}{\sum_j \exp\left(X_j - \gamma c_j\right)}. \tag{19.1}$$

Expression (19.1) provides intuitive comparative statics for the utility-maximizing consumption of activity x_i: the consumption s_i will be increasing in its value X_i, decreasing in its cost c_i and decreasing in the quality of the other media X_j (for $j \neq i$).

The emphasis of this chapter, however, is not on the consumption s_i of media activity *per se*, but on its impact on some outcome of interest y. For example, we may be interested in how consumption of telenovelas may affect fertility, how watching television may affect educational attainment, or how watching violent movies may affect crime. We thus consider the outcome variable y (family decisions, education, crime) which is related to the activity choice. For simplicity, we assume a linear relationship:

$$y = \sum_j \alpha_j s_j.$$

That is, each activity x_i contributes to the outcome y with a "direct-effect" coefficient α_i. For example, say that activity x_1 is watching a soap opera while activity x_2 is socializing with friends. We may assume that exposure to telenovelas tends to reduce fertility ($\alpha_1 < 0$) while interaction with friends increases it ($\alpha_2 > 0$). The direct effect α_i could capture, for example, an imitation effect of the behavior in the media, say because of persuasion (DellaVigna and Gentzkow, 2010).

A key assumption is that the individual does *not* take into account the impact on y in choosing the utility-maximizing activity x_i. For example, when choosing a soap opera, the person is not thinking that watching the soap opera will affect his attitudes toward fertility. This is often a plausible assumption, at least in cases in which the outcome is an incidental and plausibly unanticipated by-product.

The assumption on y implies

$$y = \frac{\sum_j \alpha_j \exp\left(X_j - \gamma c_j\right)}{\sum_j \exp\left(X_j - \gamma c_j\right)}.$$

This expression allows us to derive a set of comparative statics of determinants of activity choice on the economic outcome y, which are the modeling counterpart to the estimates of media effects. The first comparative static is the impact of a shift in value X_i, such as the case in which a media outlet x_i has become more popular. We derive

$$\frac{\partial y}{\partial X_i} = s_i \sum_j \left(\alpha_i - \alpha_j\right) s_j = s_i(\alpha_i - \overline{\alpha}), \tag{19.2}$$

where $\overline{\alpha} = \sum_j \alpha_j s_j$ is the average α across all activities, with weights given by the utility-maximizing choices s_j.

Expression (19.2) highlights three important features. First, the sign of the effect does not depend on the "direct-effect" coefficient α_i *per se*, but rather on the *comparison* between the direct-effect α_i and the substitution effect, the average α across all other activities, $\overline{\alpha}$. That is, what matters is not whether activity x_i *per se* would trigger behavior y, but whether it triggers behavior y *more* than the alternative activities. The reason is that an increase in the attractiveness X_i of activity x_i crowds out activities x_j, and thus affects y through that substitution channel. We are thus going to label this channel the "substitution" channel: the impact of increased exposure to a channel on some outcome y must be evaluated with respect to whatever it substitutes in its time use. So, for example, if a soap opera becomes more popular, its effect on family outcomes must be considered with respect to the activities that it substitutes, like meeting with friends in a social context.

The second related point is that the substitution effect depends on the *optimal* alternative use of time. That is, the net effect depends on $\overline{\alpha} = \sum_j \alpha_j s_j$, which is the average of the effect of the activities x_j, with weights given by the utility-maximizing choices s_j. So when comparing the effect of a media shift, one must pay attention to the preferences of the people affected by that shift, since that determines the weights s_j. For example, in the case of violent movies, the effect of the release of a blockbuster violent movie on crime must be compared relative to the effect of the activities that the relevant group would have chosen otherwise. For people with a taste for violent movies, these alternative activities may be tilted toward other activities with a potential violent component, like getting drunk at a bar. Furthermore, that implies that an increase in exposure to media activity

i can have different effects for two different groups, even if all the α parameters are the same, as long as the groups differ in their activity choices s_i, since that affects the relevant $\bar{\alpha}$ for the group.

The third point stressed by expression (19.2) is that the effect of an increase in attractiveness of a channel is going to be proportionately larger the larger the share of time s_i devoted to activity x_i. Intuitively, a demand shift to a media outlet will have a larger effect the more significant the consumption of the media outlet was. In light of this point, we track as much as possible the intensity of exposure to the media outlet.

We can similarly derive the comparative statics with respect to shifts in the price of a media c. We obtain

$$\frac{\partial \gamma}{\partial c_i} = -\gamma s_i (\alpha_i - \bar{\alpha}).$$

The response to price changes is parallel to the response to demand increases, just with the opposite sign.

The third instance of comparative statics which we consider is with respect to a change in α_i. This comparative static is relevant when there is a temporary shock to the media programming or content which does *not* affect consumer demand or cost. Consider, for example, a popular TV show which features a gay couple in a particular episode. In this case, the unusual programming does not lead to a change in s_j given that it is unanticipated, but it may have a direct effect on, say, attitudes toward same-sex relationships (the relevant γ variable in this case). Another example would be the news coverage of a prominent suicide case, with the outcome variable being the incidence of suicide cases in the following days. We assume that activity x_i on this particular occasion is associated with a different impact α_i compared to its normal impact. The comparative static in this case is

$$\frac{\partial \gamma}{\partial \alpha_i} = s_i. \tag{19.3}$$

An increase in the "direct-effect" coefficient α_i has a bigger effect the larger the share of time allocated to the program. In this case there is no substitution effect, as individuals are not reoptimizing their choices.

We use this framework to highlight plausible interpretations of the media effects for a number of the papers. We stress, though, that for most of the papers it is difficult to disentangle the channels lacking all the relevant information. For a shifter increasing demand for a media, for example, one needs to know the activities that the audience substitutes away from. Such evidence is rarely available in quantitative format. Nevertheless, we believe that this framework can provide guidance on the interpretation of the media effects.

19.3. OUTCOMES

We review the impact of media exposure on a series of outcomes. We separate the outcomes broadly by field of study so as to facilitate the access to researchers interested in a particular topic. We start with the impact of television on education, highlighting lessons on identification as well as on the direct versus substitution channel.

The next topic, family choices, provides the clearest evidence on imitation of media role models, whereas the following three topics—the study of migration, environmental impacts, and health—provide interesting caveats to the imitation effects. The study of crime provides evidence both on the emotional impact of the media and, once again, on the importance of the substitution effect.

Next, we turn to considering the effect on public economics outcomes, first on social capital where the substitution effect plays a key role, and then on attitudes toward taxation and government. Continuing on attitudes, we present evidence on the impact of the media on beliefs regarding other groups in society or the sources of economic success. Finally, we consider the impact on consumption and savings.

Throughout, a number of examples come from developing countries; instead of grouping these examples under a separate "development" section, we weave in the development economics examples in the relevant topic.

19.3.1 Education

We start by reviewing studies that have explored the relationship between media exposure and education. We consider in depth the education topic to illustrate two of the themes discussed in the introduction: the channels of the effect and in particular the importance of substitution effects; and the key role for identification.

Television (TV) plays a double role with regard to educational outcomes: it provides content but also competes with other activities for time use. Regarding the direct effect, to the extent that TV programs embed useful information and a rich enough language, exposure to this media may increase individuals' knowledge and proficiency with the language. The substitution effect, however, implies that watching TV crowds out activities such as study, social interaction, etc., and thus can be detrimental to cognitive and non-cognitive development. A higher amount of time spent in front of the TV at an early stage of childhood or adolescence thus could induce negative consequences on cognitive development, which is crucial to human capital formation in later years. As Heckman (2000) observes, "success or failure at this stage feeds into success or failure in school which in turn leads to success or failure in post-school learning." The potential negative effect in terms of time use is perceived most acutely for children and adolescents, so many of the studies investigating these issues focus on exposure to television for these age categories.

Zavodny (2006) examines the impact of the amount of time spent in front of the TV by young adults on their performance in standardized exams in the United States. The author uses three sources of data, the National Longitudinal Survey of Youth 1979 (NLSY79), the High School and Beyond survey (HSB), and the National Education Longitudinal Study (NELS). She finds a negative correlation between the number of hours spent watching TV and test scores, although the magnitude of the effect is rather small. Furthermore, the above correlations may reflect endogeneity in TV watching, for example if children with less parental support in their studies prefer to spend time watching television. The author tries to address this concern using a twofold strategy: on the one hand, she includes individual and family fixed effects; on the other hand, she performs siblings and twins regression, in order to eliminate unobserved household characteristics. Once fixed effects are considered, no significant effect is found: comparisons across siblings, including twins, do not reveal a negative relationship between performance on standardized exams and TV viewing.

While additional controls and sibling fixed effects certainly help, they cannot ultimately fully control for the possibility of selection into television use. If the individuals who watch television more often have characteristics associated with worse educational outcomes, selection biases the outcome. This issue with unobservables plagues the large majority of the early literature on effects of the media, and particularly on the impact of television on educational outcomes, since this literature simply compared individuals who *self-select* to watch a medium to others who do not.

To address this important confound, the literature on the economics of the media has achieved identification largely through natural experiments affecting the demand or availability of a particular medium. The idea is to find plausibly exogenous reasons which affect media consumption. The first papers using natural experiments in media availability examined the impact on political outcomes: Strömberg (2004) explored the natural variation in radio exposure, and Besley and Burgess (2001) used variation in newspaper penetration to test for the effect of the media on responsiveness of politicians to citizen demands. Following up on these papers, Gentzkow (2006) uses the roll-out of the television to test whether it affects turnout to the polls, while DellaVigna and Kaplan (2007) exploit the idiosyncratic availability of Fox News across cable towns to test for a political impact of media bias.

In all of these examples, the identifying assumption is that the *availability* of a particular medium in a location and time is exogenous in a way that selection into listening to a medium is not. The papers above use a combination of historical arguments, geographic factors, and documenting selection on observables to make their case. For example, Strömberg uses geographical factors in the availability of radio during the New Deal for identification, while DellaVigna and Kaplan use the fact that the timing of adoption of Fox News by the local cable companies since its inception in 1996 appears to have been largely idiosyncratic.

A relevant case for educational outcomes is the identification strategy used by Gentzkow (2006), which exploits the fact that television licenses were granted in waves with interruptions in the licensing process. The licensing started in 1941, was put on hold between 1942 and 1945 during World War II, restarted after the War and slowed down again from 1948 until 1952. The timing of access to television for a metropolitan area is thus plausibly idiosyncratic. Indeed, the paper documents that the timing of licensing appears to be uncorrelated with a set of demographic variables, conditional on population, income, previous turnout, and region dummies. Gentzkow (2006) then shows that the arrival of television led to a change in the pattern of news consumption, and a corresponding decrease in turnout, especially in the off-year congressional elections. The finding is likely explained, as in the model above, by a substitution effect: the spread of television led to a decrease in consumption of local papers, which carry the information about congressional candidates. The spread of TV led to less information about the candidates, and lower electoral participation.

We do not dwell in detail on the political effects of the spread of television; these are summarized in Strömberg (2015). Still, we summarize the Gentzkow (2006) paper because Gentzkow and Shapiro (2008) use the same identification strategy to study the effect of exposure to television during early childhood on later educational outcomes. The staggered provision of television licenses provides a rare natural experiment guaranteeing variation in television exposure which is not immediately correlated with confounding variables.

It is worthwhile stressing how valuable this particular natural experiment is. A vast literature on the public health effects of television exposure concludes that television generally has adverse effects on child development (American Academy of Pediatrics, 2001; Gentile et al., 2004). Unfortunately, the large majority of these studies relies on comparing individuals that differ in television consumption, a comparison that very likely is plagued with confounds. Researchers have looked for natural variation in television, but it is hard to come across. Television waves travel across the air over a vast expanse, and nearly all of the United States and most other Western countries have had access to television for decades. There is, simply put, no exogenous variation in overall television exposure in the United States for the recent decades that can be used as a natural experiment.

And yet, going back in time, that variation existed, back in the days when television was still in its infancy. That means that, while it is not possible to quantify the impact of *today*'s television on test scores, it is possible to quantify the impact of television on test scores half a century ago. In fact, the variation is more limited than that. By the time test score data is available for a large enough swath of the population (the educational data from the 1965 Coleman study), there is essentially no variation in television exposure left: all metropolitan areas have good access to television. And yet there is variation in the length of exposure: for some areas it is just 10 years, for other areas nearly 20 years. Thus, it is possible to compare two groups of ninth graders as of 1965: one group was (potentially) exposed to television since birth, while the second group was not exposed during pre-school, though it also had exposure during elementary school. This design can help us address the question: does exposure to television during the pre-school year have a lasting impact on elementary school achievement?

This is the only question that this strategy allows us to address but, luckily, it is also an important question. Indeed, much of the recent interest in learning in the pre-school years centers on whether early exposure to stimuli has a lasting effect. Gentzkow and Shapiro address this question using data from the Coleman Study—a 1965 survey of standardized test scores for over 300,000 American students in grades 6, 9, and 12—and variation in television exposure in the years before.

The first main result is that, on average, exposure to television during pre-school does not have an adverse impact on educational scores, as one may have worried. Importantly, the results are not due to imprecision of the estimates: the authors can reject an adverse effect of 0.03 standard deviations or more. This contrasts with the common belief that early exposure to television could be a powerful negative force.

The second main result is that there is important heterogeneity in this effect. Among minorities and children of immigrants, in fact television leads to an *improvement* in educational test scores in English, though not in Mathematics. This key result lends itself to a natural interpretation in terms of the *substitution* effect in (19.2). Assume that the direct effect of television α_1 on English test scores (the y variable) of children is the same for natives and for immigrants and is positive, given that television exposes children to spoken English. Still, the two groups differ in that they have a very different mix of other activities s_j, and thus a different $\bar{\alpha}$. For the natives, television is likely to substitute verbal interactions in English, associated with a relatively high $\bar{\alpha}$—thus the null net effect. But for the children of immigrants, television (in English) substitutes interactions mostly in other languages, which would have a null (or negative) $\bar{\alpha} < \alpha_1$. When evaluated against this alternative option, television is a real improvement with regard to building English skills for the immigrants. This argument is clearer for English skills than for math skills, consistent with the data.

The key point here is that in asking what television does to education, one need not ask the question, "is television good or bad?" Instead, one should ask the question, "is television *better or worse* than the alternative option?" This is a key point that we stress at other points in this review and that gets lost surprisingly often.

We are not aware of other papers that provide evidence on educational impacts of the media using equally clear natural variation in media exposure. Still, a number of other papers use observational data to aim to understand the relationship between television and education under a set of identifying assumptions. We discuss this evidence with a caveat about the difficulty of controlling for selection in these cases.

The relationship between television and learning outcomes should not be regarded as a static one: exposure to television can influence cognitive development, which in turn may affect the amount of TV watched in the future. To provide some evidence on this issue, Huang and Lee (2010) develop a two-stage procedure and estimate a "dynamic causal effect." They use the National Longitudinal Survey of Youth 1979 (NLSY79) and estimate the effect of TV watching on child cognitive development, measured through standardized mathematics and reading scores. Once they take into account the dynamic nature of the relationship, Huang and Lee estimate that watching TV for any amount of time during the ages of 6–7 and 8–9 has a negative impact on math test scores at ages 8–9, with the negative effects of TV watching at younger ages 6–7 being much larger. In addition, panel data econometric approaches using continuous-response variables suggest that around 2 h spent watching television per day are associated with an improvement in reading scores, while the effects of TV watching on math scores are usually negative. Overall, this paper is consistent with the non-univocal effect of television on education mentioned before: the final impact varies depending on the age at which TV is watched and the subject in which performance is assessed; it is nonlinear and its magnitude is relatively small. Still, one should keep in mind that the evidence used in this paper is based on observational data and cannot take advantage of a natural experiment as in Gentzkow and Shapiro (2008).

At this point, one may wonder what should be the optimal allocation of children's time for the purpose of improving their cognitive and non-cognitive development. An attempt to answer this question is provided by Keane and Fiorini (2014), who investigate how the allocation of children's time among several activities influences cognitive and non-cognitive development. They use the Longitudinal Study of Australian Children (LSAC), which includes 24-hour diaries that allow the authors to measure time inputs such as time spent with parents versus time spent with other relatives, time devoted to educational activities versus time using media, etc. The production function of children's cognitive and non-cognitive skills is allowed to depend on time inputs and parental background characteristics, and the controls include child fixed effects, lagged inputs, and lagged test scores. Potential endogeneity of the time inputs, however, remains an issue. The main conclusions of this study are that (i) educational activities like being talked to or reading a story are the most productive for cognitive skill development, especially when they are performed together with parents; (ii) non-cognitive skills appear insensitive to alternative time allocations—they are influenced especially by the mother's parenting style (which is captured by two indices of mother warmth and effective mother discipline, using parents' answers to the LSAC questionnaire). Focusing specifically on time devoted to the media, the authors find that media time is not worse than other non-educational activities (like time in before/after school care) for skills development.

The fact that exposure to television could be exploited for educational purposes was recognized early on, giving rise to popular programs such as *Sesame Street*. *Sesame Street* can probably be considered one of the largest (and possibly the cheapest) early childhood interventions, although it is not typically considered as such. This show was introduced in 1969 with the aim of improving first-grade readiness and reducing the gap between disadvantaged children and better-off ones in terms of pre-school experience. A recent paper by Kearney and Levine (2015) estimates the effects of this program on educational and labor market outcomes. To identify these effects, they exploit the fact that *Sesame Street* was initially aired by PBS-affiliated stations, which broadcast on UHF in about half of the cases. Because many TV sets at the time did not receive UHF, and because distance from transmitters also reduced access, about one-third of the population did not have access to the show initially. The authors thus exploit variation in coverage across counties and among cohorts (with children younger than 7 in 1969 considered as "treated" and older ones as "control" and adopt a difference-in-differences strategy using data from three Census waves (1980—2000).

They find evidence of sizeable and significant impacts during school years: children living in counties with better reception had a higher probability of attending the right grade for their age, especially so if they were boys, non-Hispanic blacks, and living in disadvantaged areas. On the other hand, the evidence is mixed for educational attainment and labor market outcomes: no significant impact is found on high school dropout rates or college attendance, and the effects on employment and wages, albeit marginally significant, are quantitatively very small. Overall, these results suggest that the main impact of the program was in improving school readiness, with more nuanced effects in the long run.

Another channel through which media exposure may affect education is not directly through exposure of the children, but rather exposure of their parents or teachers. Using survey data, Keefer and Khemani (2011) study the effects of exposure to community radios in Benin on children's school performance. In Benin, radio is widely used as means of communication and there is a high degree of variation in access across villages. A first channel of the radio effect is through accountability: radio may provide information that households then use to organize collective action and demand better services from the government. In this respect, Benin represents a good setting to explore the accountability channel since it has a relatively long tradition of competitive elections and peaceful turn-overs of political power. A second channel for impact comes from the focus of community radios on educational content. Exposure to programming on the importance of education may generate higher parental investments in children's education. In this regard, the radio content in this case is an exception to the general preponderance of entertainment content.

The identification of the effects relies on variation in access to radio generated by accidental features of the topography and signal strength, most notably of out-of-commune radio stations. The results indicate a substantial effect of media exposure on education performance: access to one additional radio station increases the share of literate children by 8 percentage points. If this effect were driven by increased accountability, villages with greater access should see higher government provision of those inputs that are closely related to child literacy (e.g., textbooks per pupil, teacher—pupil ratio, teacher absentee-ism, number of classrooms). This does not seem to be the case. Also, access to community radios is not associated with better knowledge by parents of government education policies (e.g., of a massive program to hire new teachers, of test requirements to pass primary school examinations, etc.). Accountability thus seems to play a relatively limited role in the effects on literacy. On the other hand, households with greater exposure to community radios invest more in their children's education (e.g., they buy more books for their children), suggesting that parents' exposure to educational messages leads to positive changes in private behaviors.

To conclude, the empirical evidence on the effect of media exposure on educational outcomes is not univocal. Media can be an important vehicle for sensitizing individuals on the importance of education and hence can stimulate parental investments, but when it comes to children's direct exposure to media (especially television), the crowding out of alternative activities can have counteracting effects. Particularly notable in this respect are the differing effects of TV exposure on mathematics versus language test scores found in some of the literature.

19.3.2 Family Outcomes

In the previous section on education outcomes, we considered mainly the effect of exposure to television, compared to alternative uses of time. In this section, we consider a more detailed channel, and in particular the exposure to role models embedded in the entertainment content on television. To what extent do these role models lead to imitation of their behavior?

We consider the imitation of role models in the media with respect to family outcomes, such as fertility, family planning, age at marriage, and attitudes toward domestic violence. This is an important setting on at least two grounds. First, family choices are of first-order importance for both research and policy, especially in developing countries, where the reduction of fertility rates is often a policy target. Even setting aside the policy importance, family choices are an ideal setting to test for the importance of imitation: since family choices stem from deep-seated preferences and cultural factors, to the extent that exposure to peer effects from the media leads to changes in behavior, it constitutes a particularly compelling case of media imitation.

We consider the impact of the media on family outcomes mainly in the context of developing countries. In these countries, media exposure vastly increases the availability of information about the outside world and exposure to different ways of life. This is especially true for remote and rural areas, where television is one of the primary sources through which households acquire information on the life outside their village (Fernandes, 2000; Johnson, 2001; Scrase, 2002). The majority of popular TV programs feature urban settings, whose lifestyles are in stark contrast with those of rural regions. Importantly, the main characters of many soap operas broadcast in developing countries have smaller families, marry later, and usually have higher educational attainment than the average viewer. Furthermore, many female characters work outside the home and have significant decision-making power within the household. To the extent that these characters act as implicit role models, exposure to these characters and their ways of life may affect marital outcomes and fertility choices.

La Ferrara et al. (2012) estimate the effect of soap operas on fertility rates in Brazil. Brazil is an interesting case study for two reasons. First, fertility has declined dramatically in a very short time: the total fertility rate decreased from 6.3 in 1960 to 2.9 in 1991, without any specific government policy to encourage population control. Second, soap operas (or *novelas*, as they are called in Brazil) are by far the most popular TV program, and they are broadcast by the media giant Rede Globo, which has basically preserved a monopoly in this sector. Interestingly, the timing of expansion of Rede Globo across the country largely coincided with the fertility transition. The authors combine these two aspects and advance the hypothesis that the diffusion of television and the lifestyles portrayed by soap operas may have contributed to the fertility decline. This hypothesis is supported by the content of Rede Globo's telenovelas, which between 1965 and 1999 overwhelmingly showed female characters with no children or one child, in marked contrast with the fertility rates prevalent in society.

To identify the effects of exposure to these programs on fertility, La Ferrara et al. use a difference-in-differences strategy, exploiting the staggered entry of Globo into different municipal areas. Combining Census data with data on antenna location of Globo stations, they find that exposure to the Globo signal decreases the probability of giving birth by 0.5 percentage points (a 5% reduction over the mean), which is comparable in magnitude to the effect of increasing a woman's education by 1.6 years. This effect is not driven by pre-trends, and the reduction in fertility begins exactly 1 year after the entry of Globo in the area. Furthermore, the impact is larger for women of lower socioeconomic status, as one would expect given that these women are less likely to have been exposed to written information on these aspects, and for women who are in the middle and late phase of their childbearing life. These estimates suggest that in the decade 1980–1991 the expansion of Globo accounted for about 7% of the reduction in the probability of giving birth.

An interesting aspect of the study by La Ferrara et al. is the attempt to provide direct evidence on the role played by the content of the soap operas leading to imitative behavior. A first piece of evidence is that children born in areas covered by Globo have a significantly higher probability of being named after the main characters of the novela broadcast during the year in which they were born.[3] Second, the authors exploit variation in the plots over the years, as well as variation in the potential empathy and identification between characters and viewers based on individual factors. They find that fertility decreases by more in years when the plot features upward social mobility, and for women whose age is closer to that of the main female character.

---

[3] This probability is 33% for areas covered by Globo and 8.5% for those not covered, a significant difference.

In a separate paper, Chong and La Ferrara (2009) investigate the impact of Brazilian *novelas* on a different family outcome: divorce. In addition to showing small families, the content of Rede Globo's *novelas* promoted the circulation of modern ideas, such as women's empowerment and emancipation. Using the same diff-in-diff strategy as the paper above, the authors estimate the effect of exposure to Globo on the probability of marital dissolution. They find that separation and divorce rates increase in municipalities covered by the Globo signal in the years after the arrival of the network.

An influential study on the impact of television on women's emancipation is that by Jensen and Oster (2009). These authors study the effect of the introduction of cable television on women's status in rural India. They use a 3-year panel covering 180 villages in five Indian states from 2001 to 2003 and their empirical strategy relies on comparing changes in attitudes toward women between survey rounds across villages, based on whether and when they introduced cable TV: 21 of the 180 sample villages introduced cable during 2001–2003. Given this framework, a crucial empirical issue could be the presence of unobserved factors (such as income or attitude toward "modernity") that determine cable television access and are also correlated with women's socioeconomic status. In order to rule out this concern, the authors adopt a twofold strategy. On the one hand, they show that there are no pre-existing differential trends in women's conditions for villages with and without cable TV and that the timing of changes in the outcomes of interest is closely related to the introduction of cable. On the other hand, they show that outcomes are not correlated with cable access in the future. They find that exposure to cable is associated with a significant reduction in the number of reported situations in which it is acceptable for a man to beat his wife and a decrease in son preference. In addition, getting cable TV significantly improves women's bargaining power within the household, as measured by autonomy in decision-making, and it decreases the likelihood of being pregnant. Finally, they also find benefits for younger children, since the introduction of cable encourages their enrollment in school, an effect that may be driven by the higher participation of women in household decision-making.

Decision-making and children's educational outcomes have been found to be influenced by the media also in other settings. Cheung (2012) uncovers a media effect in Cambodia, where women's decision-making power within the household and children's primary school attendance increase within the signal range of Women's Station FM 102. This is a popular radio station launched by the Women's Media Center of Cambodia (WMC) in order to change the stereotypes of women in traditional gender roles using an "educational entertainment" approach. To obtain credible causal evidence, two complementing identification strategies are employed. The first one exploits the variation in over-the-air signal strength between radio transmitters and villages within a district due to topographical characteristics (such as the presence of mountains) and it performs a cross-section analysis using individual data from the Cambodia Demographic and Health Survey 2005. The second approach exploits the fact that the radio coverage is gradually expanded over time and across regions to perform a difference-in-differences estimation. Irrespective of the identification strategy, the author observes that radio exposure improves women's bargaining power within the household and children's primary school attendance. The empirical investigation also aims at dealing with possible trends in other factors that might confound the results and potential correlation between the outcome of interest and future radio coverage, concluding that these are not a concern for the identification strategy. Finally, this work provides suggestive evidence on the impact of radio exposure on attitudes toward domestic violence and son preference and this is in line with previous findings presented in this section.

The persuasion effect of the media when it comes to family outcomes is not confined to the developing world. Kearney and Levine (2014) examine the impact of the widely viewed MTV show *16 and Pregnant* (16P), which follows the lives of teenagers during pregnancy and early days of motherhood, on teenage fertility in the United States. The authors employ four distinct sources of data: Google Trends, to capture changes in searches on Google; Twitter, used to analyze all "tweets" made by individuals; Nielsen ratings data to capture geographic variation in TV viewership; and the Vital Statistics Natality Microdata, to measure changes in teen births. The key variation exploited in the paper is the differential viewership across designated market areas, as measured by Nielsen ratings. This creates a potential endogeneity problem, since viewers' interest in 16P is presumably higher in areas where teenagers are prone to getting pregnant. To address this problem, the authors perform an instrumental variable (IV) estimation, instrumenting the show's ratings with ratings for all shows that aired on MTV in the four sweeps months preceding the introduction of 16P. The underlying assumption is that ratings obtained before 16P was created should be orthogonal to subsequent trends in teen pregnancies.

The authors offer three sets of results. First, they document a significant interest in the show: during the weeks in which 16P is showing, there are clear spikes in Google searches and tweets containing the terms "16 and Pregnant." Second, there is suggestive evidence that the show triggers information seeking on birth control and abortion: on the day a new episode is released, there is a spike in Google searches and Twitter messages containing the term "birth control" and "abortion." Third, the show leads to a 5.7% reduction in teen births in the 18 months following its introduction, an effect size explaining around one-third of the total decline in teen births in the country over that period. When they split the sample into different age groups, they find that the effect is similar in magnitude and significant up to age 24, while it becomes insignificant for older age groups, consistent with the fact that the viewership of 16P is relatively young.

To conclude, there is robust evidence that exposure to a particular behavior on television changes behavior in the audience. In most cases, the generally positive media portrayal of a role model leads to imitation, as in the case of Brazilian soap operas leading to lower fertility and higher divorce rates. In other cases, the media portrayal of a difficult situation leads to the opposite behavior, as in the case of *16 and Pregnant.* The persuasion effect is consistent across different settings and applies to decisions as consequential as fertility and divorce. Furthermore, the research designs allow us to detect evidence of role model effects not only in the short run but also in the long run, after years of exposure. The effect on family outcome is one of the clearest cases of substantial media impacts.

This literature also highlights an important point on identification. In contrast to the effects of television on education where there is little credible evidence, we have quite extensive and detailed evidence on the imitation of family choices seen on television. From a methodological point of view, the key difference is in the variation in media access needed. To examine the impact of television overall (say, on education), one needs credible variation in exposure to television, which is hard to find. Conversely, to document the impact of imitation of a particular behavior seen on television, one needs variation in a particular show with unique content, which is easier to find.

19.3.3 Labor Markets and Migration

In the same way that television delivers information on family choices, it also exposes viewers to information regarding labor market opportunities, both domestically and abroad. Especially in developing countries or lower-income areas within a country, television exposes viewers to higher standards of living. The imitation hypothesis holds that exposure to these lifestyles induces attempts to emulate them, including migrating to higher-income areas and countries. The evidence on this topic turns out to be more nuanced than that.

A first piece of evidence is provided by Braga (2007), who investigates the impact of Italian television on individual migration decisions in Albania. The Albanian case is emblematic, since both economic and political contacts with the rest of the world were absent during the communist regime. From 1941 to the late 1980s, the media and broadcasting system was strictly controlled by the Communist party and there was only one national television channel, broadcasting propaganda and politicized documentaries. However, although foreign TV was forbidden, Albanians could easily watch Italian TV starting from the early 1960s, due to geographical proximity between the two countries.

Italy has experienced a large inflow of immigrants from Albania in recent decades. To test if this can at least in part be attributed to Italian television, Braga (2007) uses data from the Albanian Living Standard Measurement Survey and estimates individual migration status as a function of a number of controls plus foreign media exposure. Exposure to foreign television is measured by the shortest distance between the location of Italian transmitters and the place of residence of the respondent (in Albania). The results show that the probability of migrating significantly increases the shorter the distance from Italian transmitters (0.7 percentage points for every additional kilometer). This is a large effect, considering that the baseline rate of international migration is 8%. Furthermore, exposure to Italian media increases migration not only to Italy but also to other countries, suggesting that images on Italian television favored Albanians' openness towards other countries.

Interestingly, Farré and Fasani (2013) reach an opposite conclusion for the case of Indonesia. Using the Indonesian Family Life Survey (IFLS) and The Village Potential Statistics (PODES), they investigate the effect of media exposure on internal migration in Indonesia. In particular, they exploit the differential introduction of private TV throughout the country and the variation in signal reception across districts due to topography. They consider both "early" exposure to television during adolescence and "current" exposure. The first variable is motivated by the fact that migration movements usually occur at a young age, thus individuals may be substantially influenced by expectations formed early in life. The second variable captures the fact that individuals also update their expectations when new information becomes available. The authors uncover a negative effect of both early and current TV exposure on the propensity to migrate: a one standard deviation increase in exposure to television decreases the overall migration rate by 8–15% of a standard deviation, depending on the model specification.

How does one reconcile the two findings? As Farré and Fasani suggest, the imitation hypothesis is somewhat simplistic: one should not expect that *all* role models presented in the media would lead individuals to attempt to imitate them. In many circumstances, it is reasonable for media audiences to update on a particular behavior in the direction of the role model. In other cases, however, the updating could go the opposite way: exposure to a behavior on television could lead audiences to change their beliefs in a way leading to behavior opposite to the role model. In the Indonesian case, it is possible that Indonesian citizens prior to the expansion of private TV broadcasting were too optimistic in assessing the potential gains from moving, and that television helps to correct this optimism.

This is an important caveat to keep in mind when studying the impact of media role models: the effect of what people see on television or hear on the radio depends on content not only in "absolute" terms, but relative to the baseline values and beliefs held by the individuals. It is thus very helpful if information on baseline beliefs and values is available so as to accurately interpret the empirical findings.

Another dimension in which exposure to the media can affect labor market outcomes is by influencing occupational choice. Bjorvatn et al. (2015) analyze a field experiment with around 2000 secondary school students from Dar es Salaam, Tanzania. The experiment consisted of encouraging students and their families to watch an educational TV show about entrepreneurship, business skills, and financial literacy. A total of 21 schools were randomly assigned to watch this show, while 22 schools were assigned to a control non-educational movie. The educational show consisted of 11 weekly episodes on the lives of six young entrepreneurs (males and females). The authors estimate both short-term and long-term (2 years after the end of the show) effects' impact on a number of variables. In the short term, the show is effective in increasing ambition and some entre-preneurial traits (measured through lab experiments), and this maps into a differential propensity to starting a business which persists in the long run: 2 years later, the probability of having started a business is about 9 percentage points higher for the treatment group, representing a 30% increase relative to the mean for the control. Interestingly, there is no impact on business knowledge in the short run. An important result in the paper is that the show has a negative impact on school performance in the long run: treated students are less likely to pass the final exam and to continue studying beyond secondary school. While this result may be specific to the Tanzanian context, where the quality of formal education may have been considered by the participants to be relatively low, it does caution us about possible unintended effects of the instrumental use of television for "educational" purposes.

19.3.4 Environmental Economics

In this section, we examine the extent to which documentaries, which often have the purpose of changing behavior, achieve their goals by triggering imitation of a desirable behavior. Within the field of environmental choices, a good example is the documentary *An Inconvenient Truth* by Al Gore, which presents in dramatic fashion the evidence on global warning and suggests the need to act. Did it then affect environmental choices? Notice that this example differs from the "edutainment" examples, since *An Inconvenient Truth* was not conceived as entertainment, but rather as a content-packed exhortation to action.

Jacobsen (2011) examines the impact of exposure to this movie on a form of environmentalism, the purchase of carbon offsets. For identification, the author exploits closeness to the nearest movie theater that showed *An Inconvenient Truth*. The difference-in-difference specification shows an increase in carbon offset purchases of about 50% relative to the baseline for individuals living within 10 miles of a movie theater showing the movie. Still, it is quantitatively a relatively small increase given that the baseline purchases are quite limited, and it is a transitory effect, with no evidence of persistence a few months later.

There is a natural comparison between the effect of a documentary intended to persuade versus the evidence from entertainment options like telenovelas, which are not intended to change behavior *per se*. Documentaries can indeed have an impact on behavior as the Jacobsen (2011) paper stresses; however, this impact is likely to be limited given that the audience interested in documentaries is relatively small and mostly consists of individuals already embracing a cause. In contrast, entertainment shows reach millions of individuals across all walks of life: the large and persistent impact documented on family choices by La Ferrara et al. (2012) is particularly striking given the cultural values associated with choices such as the number of children.

19.3.5 Health

As for the case of family choices, migration, and environmental choices, researchers have considered the effect of media exposure on health. Most papers examine the impact of information about desirable (or undesirable) health behavior contained in media programming. Surprisingly given the interest in health economics, the evidence is limited and mostly comes from outside economics, such as health and communication studies. The estimates often lack a convincing design, document only short-run effects of exposure, or employ an outcome variable that is an indirect measure, such as the number of calls to a hotline, as opposed to the ultimate variable of interest.

19.3.5.1 Suicide

The literature on suicide provides an example of the promise and limitations of the existing health evidence. A motivation for the studies on suicides is the worry that media coverage of the suicide of a celebrity may lead to a wave of suicides among vulnerable individuals in a copycat effect.

In a prominent series of early papers, David Phillips and coauthors find that the occurrence of suicides appears to increase after major suicide episodes are in the news. In a representative paper, Bollen and Phillips (1982) use the Vanderbilt dataset of television news stories on ABC, CBS, and NBC to code all stories under the heading "suicide" broadcast between 1972 and 1976. They then link the data to the US daily suicide statistics. In a time series regression with seasonality controls, the authors find evidence of a significant increase in suicides occurring on the first 2 days and on days 6–7 after the story. The coefficients, which are significant at the 5% level in a one-tailed test, imply an overall increase of 28 suicides for each suicide story, a large imitation effect.

In a follow-up study, however, Baron and Reiss (1985) show that the evidence in Bollen and Phillips (1982) and in other related papers is not reliable. First, the imitation effect is not statistically significant if one considers all lags jointly, rather than focusing only on the significant ones. Second, the effects appear due to improper controls for seasonality. Indeed, when running a placebo regression which lags the suicide story by exactly 1 year and thus keeps constant the seasonality structure, the authors find similar imitation effects, pointing to problems in the econometric specification.

Follow-up studies in the 30 years since number in the dozens in sociology and medical journals. Still, in our reading the evidence on imitation of media portrayals of suicide is not convincing. A comprehensive study with attention to the channels and to confounding factors is missing.

19.3.5.2 Smoking

Smoking remains the most important avoidable public health risk in the United States and in a number of countries. What do we know about the impacts of exposure to media content on smoking? Since advertising by cigarette companies has been severely limited in the United States in the recent past, most media studies focus on the impact of anti-smoking media campaigns on smoking.

Bauman et al. (1991) examine a field experiment on smoking cessation messages broadcast via radio in the US South. Two metropolitan statistical areas (MSAs) served as treatment groups and four as control MSAs, and in these MSAs about 2000 adolescents were surveyed one and a half years after the exposure to the radio messages. The evidence suggests that the messages affected the self-reported valuation of smoking, but not smoking rates.

While the previous paper examined randomized exposure on a small sample, Farrelly et al. (2009) evaluate the exposure to the national "truth" smoke-prevention campaign that was launched in 2000 in the United States. The roll-out of the "truth" campaign, however, was not randomized, so the analysis is based on comparisons across media markets controlling for observables. Using NLSY data on smoking initiation, the authors estimate that the media campaign significantly reduced smoking initiation by as much as 20%.

These two representative papers in a vast literature provide suggestive evidence on the impact of anti-smoking campaigns. While the evidence is in our reading of higher quality than the evidence on suicide imitation, we are not aware of a study that combines the strengths of the two papers above—a clear design for identification and large-scale evidence—without the respective weaknesses.

19.3.5.3 HIV/AIDS

As a third outcome, we consider the impact of media exposure on HIV prevention. In this case, the two papers we review examine the impact of educational messages embedded within entertainment content.

A first piece of evidence is provided in a study on HIV prevention in Tanzania by Vaughan et al. (2000). They evaluate the effects of an educational-entertainment radio soap opera, *Twende na Wakati* (*Let's Go with the Times*), on knowledge, attitudes, and behaviors toward HIV. HIV rates in Tanzania are among the highest in the world, and radio is one of the most important sources of information regarding AIDS in the country. Radio Tanzania, together with the government and UNFPA (United Nations Population Fund), produced this soap opera to convey messages regarding HIV prevention, family planning, gender equity, and other health-related themes. The program was broadcast twice a week for 30 min from 1993 to 1999. To evaluate its effects, Vaughan et al. exploit the fact that the soap opera was not broadcast by the Dodoma regional transmitter from 1993 to 1995, allowing the use of this region as a "control group." The authors compare outcomes before and after exposure to the radio program across treatment and control locations, and find that it was effective in promoting HIV-responsible behaviors, e.g., reducing the number of sexual partners by both men and women and increasing condom adoption.

Additional evidence in a different setting is provided by Kennedy et al. (2004). In their work, media impact is measured by the total number of calls received by the CDC National STD and AIDS Hotline after the introduction of a subplot regarding AIDS in the soap opera *The Bold and The Beautiful* in the United States. Calling this hotline is employed as a proxy for health information-seeking behavior. After two of the episodes—when a character was diagnosed with HIV and when he told his partner—the toll-free number of the hotline was displayed on screen. The study reports a large increase in the number of attempted calls on the days of the two episodes, in the time slot during and immediately after the soap opera broadcast. This suggests that the soap opera is effective in sensitizing viewers toward HIV/AIDS.

While the above studies provide suggestive evidence that TV and radio soap operas can be effective in sensitizing people to health issues, more work is needed to credibly establish a causal link and to understand if the positive effects found shortly after the exposure persist in the long run. The recent work by Banerjee et al. (2015), which we briefly discuss in the conclusion, is an attempt to make progress in both directions.

19.3.6 Crime

For our sixth topic, we consider the impact of the media on crime, and especially violent crime. A leading research hypothesis akin to the imitation hypothesis studied in the context of family choices and immigration is that exposure to violence leads to arousal, triggering further violence. The converse hypothesis also has followers: exposure to media violence has a cathartic effect, freeing potential aggressiveness and lowering real-life violence.

Whether media violence triggers violent crime has clear policy implications. Indeed, in 2000, the American Medical Association, together with five other public-health organizations, issued a joint statement on the risks of exposure to media violence (Cook et al., 2000). The evidence cited in these reports, surveyed by Anderson and Bushman (2001) and Anderson et al. (2003), however, does not establish a causal link between media violence and violent crime. The evidence on the topic is of two types, experimental and correlational.

The experimental literature consists of exposing subjects in the laboratory (typically children or college students) to short, violent video clips. An example is Josephson (1987), who randomizes exposure to short violent clips versus clips with action scenes, but no violence. After the media exposure, the subjects play a game of hockey, and the group exposed to violent clips is more likely to engage in aggressive play. These experiments typically find a sharp increase in aggressive behavior immediately after the media exposure, compared to a control group exposed to non-violent clips, supporting the arousal hypothesis. This literature provides causal evidence on the short-run impact of media violence on aggressiveness. However, this evidence does not address whether this translates into higher levels of violent crime in the field.

A second literature (e.g., Johnson et al., 2002) documents that survey respondents who watch more violent media are substantially more likely to be involved in self-reported violence and criminal behavior. This correlational evidence, while indeed linking media violence and crime, has the standard problems of endogeneity and reverse causation. The individuals who watch more violent television are not comparable to the ones who do not, confounding the correlation.

Dahl and DellaVigna (2009) propose a different strategy to capture the impact of violent media on actual violent crime without the confounds of endogeneity. Namely, they exploit the natural experiment induced by time-series variation in the violence of movies shown in theaters. Using a violence rating system from *kids-in-mind.com* and daily movie revenue data, they generate a daily measure of national-level box office audience for strongly violent (e.g., *Hannibal*), mildly violent (e.g., *Spider-Man*), and non-violent movies (e.g., *Runaway Bride*). Since blockbuster movies differ significantly in violence rating, and movie sales are concentrated in the initial weekends after release, there is substantial variation in exposure to movie violence over time. The audience for strongly violent and mildly violent movies respectively is as high as 12 million and 25 million people on some weekends, and is close to zero on others. This variation creates the conditions for identification using time-series variation. The authors match this data to crime data from the National Incident Based Reporting System (NIBRS) to estimate the short-run impact of exposure to violent media on violent crime. Notice that the short-run (as opposed to long-run) impact is what the laboratory experiments also capture, and is the relevant variation to identify the arousal hypothesis.

The results appear to contradict the laboratory evidence supporting the arousal hypothesis: on days with a high audience for violent movies, violent crime is *lower*, even after controlling flexibly for seasonality, weather, and other potential confounds. Breaking down the effects into time blocks, which is possible given the granularity of the crime data, helps assess the channel of the findings. There is no effect in the morning or in the afternoon before movie exposure, as one would expect. In the evening hours (6 p.m.–12 a.m.), for each million people watching a strongly or mildly violent movie, respectively, violent crimes decrease by 1.3% and 1.1%, a statistically and economically significant impact. In the nighttime hours following the movie showing (12 a.m.–6 a.m.), the delayed effect of exposure to movie violence is even more negative.

Is the negative effect then evidence of a cathartic effect? Not so fast. Returning to the model in Section 19.2, the relevant variation for identification is in the quality X of violent versus non-violent movies, leading to sharply different audiences on different weekends. As the model makes clear, this variation identifies the *net* effect on crime of exposure to violent movies versus the next best alternative use of time (that is, $\alpha_v - \overline{\alpha}$). Even if violent movies trigger crime (that is, $\alpha_v > 0$), the estimated impact on violent movies will be negative if alternative activities trigger crime at an even higher rate (that is, $\alpha_v < \overline{\alpha}$). With this in mind, the negative effect in the evening hour reflects the voluntary incapacitation of individuals into the movie theaters, a low-crime setting compared to almost any alternative: thus, $\alpha_v - \overline{\alpha}$ is clearly negative.

In the night hours, though, the theaters are closed: how should one interpret the results? The findings indicate that spending an evening at the movie theater leads to less violent behavior in the night thereafter compared to the alternative activity that the (potentially violent) audience of the movies would have chosen. A natural channel is alcohol: individuals who spend two or more hours at the movie theater in the evening are more likely to be sober by midnight compared to spending the evening at a bar or drinking with friends. Dahl and DellaVigna (2009) provide some direct evidence on this channel: if alcohol is a key channel, the effect of movie exposure should be larger for people who are barely of drinking age (21- to 24-year-olds) compared to people who are barely below drinking age (17- to 20-year-olds), since drunkenness is significantly less likely in this second group. Notice that the comparative statics here exploit variation in $\overline{\alpha}$, the impact of the alternative option, across the two groups, holding constant α_v. This comparison is akin to the comparison in the effects of television between natives and immigrants in Gentzkow and Shapiro (2008). Consistent with an important role for intoxication, the negative impact of exposure to violent movies on crime is large and negative for individuals aged 21–24, but close to zero for individuals aged 17–20.

What does one learn from a natural experiment of this type? The identification of the impact of violent media relative to the alternative option (that is, $\alpha_v - \overline{\alpha}$) provides some relevant policy counterfactuals. For example, based on these estimates, a policy that would ban violent movies on certain weekends would increase assaults by roughly 1000 occurrences per weekend given the ensuing shift to more dangerous activities.[4] The estimates, however, do not tell us whether exposure to violent media *per se* leads to arousal ($\alpha_v > 0$), catharsis ($\alpha_v < 0$), or neither. One can, however, estimate the direct effect of exposure to violent movies α_v under some assumptions about the effect of alternative activities. Under one such set of assumptions, Dahl and DellaVigna (2009) decompose the observed effect into a direct effect α_v and a substitution effect $\overline{\alpha}$, and find that the evidence is most consistent with the arousal hypothesis: the direct effect of exposure to violent movies is to increase violent behavior ($\alpha_v > 0$). Thus, the field evidence is consistent with the laboratory findings, once one does the proper comparison. Yet this decomposition is more tentative given the additional assumptions needed; additional evidence that is able to parse the different parameters would be very valuable.

A second point is that this evidence does not teach us anything about the long-term effects of exposure to violent media. Given the high-frequency nature of the instruments, the authors can examine the effects within a month of exposure (finding no evidence of

---

[4] More generally, this research is consistent with the hypothesis that other activities with a controlled environment that attract young men, like Midnight Basketball proposed by Bill Clinton in the 1990s, would also reduce crime in the short run.

a delayed impact on crime), but cannot pin down the long-term effects, which is a key question for policy. To identify such effects, one needs variation in prolonged exposure to a medium, as in La Ferrara et al. (2012) or Gentzkow (2006). Unfortunately, we are not aware of any such evidence that plausibly varies the long-term exposure to violent media. We stress that correlational evidence between media use and violence as in Johnson et al. (2002) is no substitute for this evidence, and should not be used for policy recommendations.

Returning to the role of arousal in violent crime, an alternative identification strategy is variation in media content, holding constant the use of time. That is, suppose that individuals are exposed to a particular media program which they choose for entertainment value, but the content of the program varies in its arousing content in unexpected ways. As the model in Section 19.2 details, this direct comparative static on α would uncover the direct effect of media arousal, given that there is no substitution to other activities.

While we are not aware of a paper using this identification for media violence, Card and Dahl (2011) use it to identify the impact of emotions, in particular disappointment and elatedness, on violent crime, and more specifically domestic violence. The motivation for the paper is understanding the role of emotional triggers on domestic violence. In the paper, emotional triggers are the results of football games broadcast via television. The design allows the authors to distinguish between the impact on fans of the winning versus losing team based on the location of the domestic crimes in the NIBRS crime data.

An appealing feature of the research design is that it allows for a measure of expectations, and deviations from such expectations, with the resulting emotional trigger. Namely, the authors use the betting line to measure expectations about outcomes of football matches so they can distinguish between expected and unexpected losses, and between expected and unexpected wins. The authors then measure domestic crimes in the hours surrounding the game.

The results point to the importance of disappointment for violent crime: unexpected losses increase domestic violence by 7%, compared to the expected result (a win). As one would expect, the effect is larger for more important games and it is entirely driven by violence of men on women and not by violence of women on men. Furthermore, the effect disappears within a few hours of game end, consistent with the impact of transient emotions. In comparison, there is no converse effect of a positive surprise: there is no evidence that a surprising win (compared to the expected loss) lowers violent crime.

These results indicate that the triggers of violence originating from the media need not be violent themselves: in this case, the emotional trigger is disappointment from an unexpected loss.

So far, we have discussed the potential impact on crime of exposure to two traditional media outlets, movies and television. Yet access to the Internet and broadband access introduce their own potential for an impact on crime. In particular, access to the Internet introduces access to content that is harder to find in traditional media, such as pornography. As such, some researchers have worried that the spread of the Internet may lead to a spike in sex crimes to the extent that sexual arousal leads to sexual aggression. Alternatively, it is also possible that pornography may be a substitute for sexual assaults, rather than a complement.

There are two main difficulties in documenting the effect of access to pornography via the Internet on outcomes such as crime. First, the Internet provides access to a bundle of content, of which pornography is only a part (if one with heavy traffic); thus, one should speak of the effect of the Internet overall, rather than of its individual components. Second, Internet access in most countries such as the United States expanded in a relatively linear fashion over time, making identification difficult.

Bhuller et al. (2013) provide evidence from Norway where a public program with limited funding rolled out broadband access points in 2000–2008, providing plausibly exogenous variation in Internet use across different municipalities over time. The authors adopt an IV strategy, instrumenting the fraction of households with broadband Internet subscriptions in a given municipality/year with the fraction of households that were covered by the relevant infrastructure in the previous year. They find that exposure to Internet content significantly increased the number of sex crimes, with the impact occurring in the year of the increased coverage, and lasting over the next 2 years. The effect is sizeable: during the sample period about 3.2% of the total number of rapes and 2.5% of the total number of sex crimes and child sex abuses can be attributed to broadband Internet exposure.

To pin down the interpretation of the results, the authors consider additional results. A first possibility is that availability of the Internet changed reporting of sex crimes, with no changes in the underlying occurrence. There is, however, no evidence that the types of reported crimes have changed over time along the lines one would expect if this were the case. A second possibility is that the Internet may have increased the match rate between potential offenders and victims, while a third possibility is that the effect occurs through an arousal effect. While it is difficult to separate the last two channels, an interesting source of variation occurs in the alternative choices available, namely non-Internet pornography. Since pornography is banned in Norway but allowed in Sweden, Norwegians living near the border with Sweden are likely to experience a smaller impact of the Internet, especially if the channel is arousal. Indeed, the impact is larger further from the border.

Bhuller et al. (2013) also stress the importance of identifying the media users who are on the margin of media adoption, or technically the compliers in the IV local average treatment effect. This is the population that is induced to Internet consumption due to the recent expansion of infrastructure. Survey data on Internet consumption shows that young males are overrepresented among the compliers. Similarly, Dahl and

DellaVigna (2009) show that violent movies are more likely to draw an audience of young males compared to other movies. The self-selection into media adoption plays an important role in understanding the media effects. The model stresses this role in that the substitution effect $\bar{\alpha}$ must be evaluated with respect to the activity choice s_i of the relevant individuals, the compliers. This relevant population, with young males overrepresented, could otherwise differ in the crime effects α_i compared to the rest of the population. This becomes particularly relevant when extrapolating the media effects to another population. For example, as the Internet roll-out continues, the marginal users may have a lower propensity to violence compared to young males, or different substitution patterns.

Aside from the Internet, a different modern media with a possible relationship to crime is video games. On the one hand, some experts worry that violent video games may trigger aggression as in the arousal hypothesis. On the other hand, having potentially violent individuals spend much time playing video games may induce substitution away from more dangerous activities, leading to a reduction in crime.

Unfortunately, even setting aside the identification of long-run effects, the identification of short-run effects of exposure to video games is more difficult than the analysis for violent movies, on two grounds. First, while one can obtain weekly measures of the sales of new video games similarly to weekly measures of movie audience, for video games the sale represents just the beginning of a period of play, while for movies purchase equals consumption. This weakens significantly the power of the instrument induced by timing of release. Second, the release of major new video games displays a massive spike around Christmas that is more accentuated than the spikes for releases of movies. This further limits the remaining variation after controlling for seasonality. In this light, the evidence in Cunningham et al. (2011) of a negative relation between video game sales and violent crime should be seen as a tentative assessment. Hopefully, future research will suggest sources of variation to precisely pin down the impact of video games, a topic of real importance given the significant number of hours spent by the youth on video games.

19.3.7 Public Economics

In this section, we review the effect of media coverage on a set of public outcomes, including participation in social organizations and attitudes toward the government. In this respect as well, it is helpful to return to the direct effect and substitution effect of media coverage. The direct effect is such that, if media outlets convey information on politicians' performance, they can affect individuals' trust toward government, tax compliance, and knowledge of public policies. This is a point studied since the seminal papers by Strömberg (2004) and Besley and Burgess (2001) and surveyed in Strömberg (2015). At the same time, through a substitution effect, exposure to mass media can have detrimental effects on social capital, since the large amount of time spent in front of the TV or listening to the radio can crowd out significant social activities.

The latter point was originally made by Putnam (2000) in his influential book *Bowling Alone*. The contention in the book is that the availability of television and other modern entertainment possibilities have contributed to isolate individuals who previously used to spend leisure time in social activities like going bowling together. In turn, this leads to a loss of social capital.

Olken (2009) provides evidence on this in a study of the impact of television and radio on social capital in Indonesia. He exploits two different sources of exogenous variation in the number of television and radio channels that households receive. First, he takes advantage of the differential introduction of private television in the country between the 1990s, when there was just one government TV station, and the mid-2000s, when 11 TV channels were present in Indonesia. Second, he considers the variation in the propagation of the signal due to topographical and geographical conformation of the territory (for instance, the presence of mountains in Central and East Java generates a variation in TV reception that is unrelated to village characteristics). Specifically, he adapts the Irregular Terrain Model of Hufford (2002), which predicts that locations in direct line of sight to a transmitter will receive the strongest signal, while if mountains block sight lines, the signal will diffract around the mountains and signal strength will depend on the frequency of the signal. This approach has since been used in a variety of studies of television and radio effects.

In the first set of results, Olken uses the number of channels received by each sub-district as a proxy for TV and radio exposure. In a first stage, the reception of an additional channel is associated with 14 additional minutes per day spent watching TV and listening to the radio. In the second stage, each additional channel received is associated with about 7% fewer social groups existing in the village and 11% lower attendance at meetings, suggesting a significant negative impact of television on social capital. The author finds similar results when introducing the model of electromagnetic signal propagation to isolate the effect of topography: greater TV reception is associated with lower levels of participation in village development meetings and with lower levels of self-reported trust.

Olken also explores the relationship between media exposure and governance. As a measure of governance, Olken uses attendance at village-level meetings that planned and monitored road construction, the quality of discussion at those meetings, and the percentage of funds used in the project that could not be accounted for by an independent engineering team. Despite finding a negative impact of television access on attendance at village meetings on the road project, he finds no impact on what happens during these meetings and on "missing expenditures" in the road project. Altogether, media exposure can lead to a significant decrease in participation in social activities and in self-reported trust, especially if it appears to substitute group activities. However, the link to government outcomes is unclear, at least in this study.

While Olken's paper is focused on pernicious effects of television, television programming also offers positive opportunities. In particular, entertainment TV programs can be used to convey information regarding a government's action and programs and, under some circumstances, they can encourage support and trust toward the government. In this direction, Trujillo and Paluck (2011) show that a specifically designed soap opera can influence political attitudes and engagement. The authors test the impact of the telenovela *Más Sabe El Diablo* (*The Devil Knows Best*), a Spanish-language soap opera broadcast by Telemundo which portrays Latino characters' involvement with the 2010 Census. The Census has historically had trouble estimating the Latino population living in the United States for two main reasons: the difficulty faced by Spanish-speaking individuals in understanding the information about the Census and completing the forms, and the diffused lack of trust in government authorities, in particular regarding the use of the information collected. The latter reached a peak in 2010, when Latino religious leaders organized a boycott of the Census with the objective of pressing the government into enacting immigration reforms.

Given this scenario, Trujillo and Paluck investigated whether a telenovela could affect Census attitudes and engagement among US Latinos. During the Census collection period, they organized a hybrid lab-field experiment and randomly assigned Latino community members in Arizona, New Jersey, and Texas to watch pro-Census scenes or control scenes that featured the same character but not the Census. The Census clip overall had a positive effect: compared to control viewers, Census viewers expressed more positive attitudes toward the US government and displayed more behavioral support for the Census, for instance by wearing pro-Census stickers and taking informational flyers. This effect is interestingly heterogeneous. In Arizona, which had recently passed anti-immigrant legislation (Senate Bill 1070), the attitudes toward the government were actually worse among the group that watched the Census clip. This suggests that the local context plays a critical role in mediating the effect of media programs on outcomes.

Additional evidence on the effect of media on trust and attitudes toward the government is provided by Kasper et al. (2015). They address the question of how taxpayers' perceptions of government and tax authorities are influenced by media coverage. In order to do so, they randomly assign a sample of 487 employees living in Vienna to a 2×2 media manipulation exercise, randomizing trust in authorities (low/high) and perceived enforcement power of authorities (low/high). The treatment consists of media reports on trust and power. In the high-trust scenario, the political situation in Austria is described as very stable, while in the low-trust scenario, Austria is described as a country with relatively low political stability, referring to frequent premature government terminations. The high-power scenario depicts the Austrian tax authorities as very efficient, punishing tax evasion effectively and severely, while the low-power scenario describes tax authorities as ineffective regarding prosecution and punishment of tax evasion. The authors test the impact of these media reports on three different outcomes: trust in authorities (i.e., belief that they act in a fair way and on behalf of their citizens), perceived ability to detect tax evasion, and intended tax compliance (i.e., self-reported likelihood of paying one's taxes). Overall, media coverage significantly affects the indicated level of trust in tax authorities and the perceived power of governmental institutions. Both these conditions were also effective in inducing a higher self-reported tax compliance.

Dutta et al. (2013) provide an interesting example of how entertainment movies can be used to convey useful information regarding governmental policy. Their goal is to improve public service delivery in the context of India's "Mahatma Gandhi National Rural Employment Guarantee Scheme" (NREGS), which is the country's largest national anti-poverty program. To increase the low participation rates in the state of Bihar, the authors implemented a randomized controlled trial for an information intervention, in the form of a short movie. This movie conveyed information about rights and entitlements under the program, describing how it works, who is eligible, and how to apply. From a sample of 150 villages, 40 were randomly selected for a screening of this movie. Two to four months after the intervention, the authors collected a follow-up survey with a variety of outcomes including knowledge, perceptions, and usage of the scheme. They found that respondents from treatment villages were significantly more likely to know the key features of NREGS (e.g., number of days of work, wage, etc.). They also had more positive perceptions, e.g., regarding increases in employment and decreases in migration due to NREGS, and were more likely to state that economic opportunities had improved for their family in the past year. Interestingly, they were significantly less likely than the control group to believe that women could get work under the scheme—despite this being a feature of the program—possibly because the main character in the movie was male.

The latter point illustrates one of the dangers of conveying information exclusively through entertainment programs, i.e., the possibility that the partial set of information that can fit in a short entertaining product may give a biased perception about complex realities. But the most interesting result in the study by Dutta et al. (2013) is probably the discrepancy between perceived and actual outcomes. In fact, objectively measured employment shows no gain on average, neither on the extensive nor on the intensive margin, suggesting that the movie was effective in changing social perceptions about the scheme but not actual utilization.

19.3.8 Attitudes

In this section, we briefly discuss the relationship between media exposure and individual attitudes, focusing as an example on inter-ethnic attitudes and material aspirations. More specifically, we examine whether exposure to the media can affect deeply rooted prejudice, norms of inter-group cooperation, and individual beliefs about the drivers of success in life.

Studies by Paluck (2009) and Paluck and Green (2009) provide evidence that education entertainment can be effectively used to change perceived social norms. The authors exploit an experiment in Rwanda that used a radio soap opera to promote reconciliation in the country 10 years after the genocide. This program, named *Musekeweya* (*New Dawn*), was explicitly designed to teach listeners about the roots of violence, the importance of independent thought, and the danger of excessive deference to authority. The studies are based on a randomized controlled trial, where treatment consisted of the reconciliation radio program, while the control group was assigned to listen to a radio soap opera about reproductive health and AIDS. The communities in the study were chosen to represent salient political, regional, and ethnic breakdowns of present-day Rwanda: two genocide survivor communities (mostly Tutsi), two Twa communities (the Pygmy minority), two prisons, and eight general population communities. Within each category, each community was matched to the most similar one (on the basis of education, gender ratio, quality of dwellings) and one community in each pair was randomly assigned to treatment. Overall, the radio program proved effective in influencing social norms and behaviors, while no effect was found on beliefs. Compared with listeners in the control group, treated listeners' perceptions of social norms and behaviors changed with respect to intermarriage, open dissent, trust, empathy, cooperation and trauma healing, while the radio soap opera did little to change listeners' personal beliefs.

An important question is whether positive effects on attitudes found in the short run persist in the medium or long run. After all, norms and attitudes are deeply rooted and one may suspect that the effects uncovered in experimental evaluations may be short-lived. Hennighausen (2015) tries to address this concern by investigating if the information provided by mass media has the power to persistently affect individual beliefs about the drivers of success in life. Similar to Bursztyn and Cantoni (forthcoming), she exploits a natural experiment on West German television reception in former East Germany to analyze its impact on East Germans' beliefs before reunification and up to one decade after. While most citizens of East Germany had access to West German television already before reunification, 15% of the inhabitants in the Northeastern and Southeastern areas did not, due to geographic characteristics such as distance from transmitters or presence of mountains. This variation allows her to use survey data from the 1980s and test whether exposure to West German programs affected the beliefs of East Germans before reunification. Living in a district without access to Western TV decreases the probability of believing that effort matters for success by 7 percentage points, from a mean of 60% in other parts of Germany. The authors then use data from the German Socio-Economic Panel (GSOEP) during 1994–1999 to test if the effects of pre-reunification exposure persist a decade later. She finds that they do: respondents from districts that did not receive West German programs are 3–5 percentage points more likely to believe that success in life is a matter of luck.

These findings suggest that Western TV programs vehicled important messages on the relationship between effort and success in life and had a long-lasting effect on the corresponding beliefs of East Germans. Given that beliefs about the determinants of success in life are also correlated with voters' preferences for redistribution (e.g., Alesina and La Ferrara, 2002; Fong, 2001), these findings can have important policy implications: media exposure may affect redistributive preferences and other policy outcomes even if these effects are not intended.

19.3.9 Consumption and Savings

Another set of outcomes which can be affected by media exposure include consumption and savings decisions. While we do not cover the substantial literature on the impact of the media on financial choices of investors (see Tetlock, 2015), we summarize two papers on the impact of the media on household consumption and financial choices.

Bursztyn and Cantoni (forthcoming) study the exposure to Western television during the communist regime in East Germany, with a focus on the impact on household consumption. Similar to Hennighausen (2015), they take advantage of the natural experiment created by differential reach of Western signal broadcast across regions of the former German Democratic Republic (GDR) during the communist era. The authors' hypothesis is that exposure to Western TV during the communist regime affected preferences for different consumption goods but, because of rationing, the impact on preferences could not translate into consumption choices. However, after reunification, citizens in East Germany have access to the same stores and consumption goods as West Germans, so if television had an impact we would expect differences in consumption for citizens exposed to Western TV after 1990.

Using a difference-in-differences strategy, Bursztyn and Cantoni find that West German TV did not affect aggregate consumption and savings, but rather the composition of consumption. In particular, product categories with high intensity of advertising during the decade before reunification were purchased in higher proportions by East German citizens who had been exposed to Western TV. This result is consistent with long-lasting effects of media exposure, ultimately resulting in imitative behavior as in other papers surveyed in this review.

While the above study examines the effect of "unintentional" exposure to consumption messages, a recent study in South Africa explores the possibility of intentionally embedding information in entertainment programs to affect savings behavior. Berg and Zia (2013) analyze the impact of financial education messages on debt management delivered through the soap opera *Scandal!*. This soap opera had been running for over

8 years, with four weekly episodes, and was broadcast by the second most popular TV station in South Africa. In 2012, a sub-plot was included for a period of 2 months to show the consequences of debt mismanagement and advise on how to avoid debt traps and get out of debt. To address possible concerns related to self-selection into watching the soap opera, the authors adopted a symmetric encouragement design. From a sample of about 1000 individuals, a randomly selected group was encouraged to watch *Scandal!*, while the remaining group was encouraged to watch a comparable soap opera that overlapped with *Scandal!* in television prime time. The encouragement took the form of financial incentives: participants were informed that they would be called on the phone during the weeks in which the soap opera was showing and would be asked some questions about the plot, receiving a monetary compensation in the case of mostly correct answers. A follow-up questionnaire was added 3 months later. Berg and Zia found encouraging results: treated individuals had significantly better financial knowledge of the specific issues presented in the soap opera storyline (not better general financial knowledge). Concerning behaviors, viewers of *Scandal!* were almost twice as likely to borrow from formal sources, less likely to engage in gambling, and less prone to enter hire purchase agreements compared to the control group.

These two papers suggest that information and behaviors portrayed on TV can affect consumption and savings choices in ways that are not purely mediated by the advertising role that has traditionally been attributed to television.

19.3.10 Development Economics

We have not kept a separate discussion of impacts of the media in developing countries because indeed some of the best evidence comes from these settings, as Table 19.1 shows. One of the earliest empirical papers on the economics of the media was indeed focused on India (Besley and Burgess, 2001). Up to today, important sections of our knowledge on media effects come from studies set in these countries. Notable examples from the contributions discussed in the previous sections include Jensen and Oster (2009) and La Ferrara et al. (2012) for family outcomes in India and Brazil, respectively; Olken (2009) on social capital in Indonesia; Paluck (2009) on inter-ethnic attitudes in Rwanda; and Berg and Zia (2013) on financial choices in South Africa.

Without re-summarizing the impact in developing-country contexts, it is worth emphasizing three natural reasons for the richness of media evidence in these contexts. The first is the wealth of identifying variation. The uneven speed of development in these economies implies that access to media often arrives suddenly, monopolies of content are not uncommon, and geographic factors, such as those that affect radio reception, provide natural variation in access. In high-income countries, instead, media markets are saturated, and competition between media outlets is so stiff that idiosyncratic variation in exposure or content across places and over time is hard to find.

A second reason has to do with the scope for impact. Exposure to the media often outlines role models and portrays societies that are particularly different from local behavior. This difference implies that the potential for behavior change is larger. The impact of telenovelas on fertility is a case in point. Telenovelas are common not just in developing countries but in the developed world, and they often involve similar plots and role models. The behavior of such role models, for example with respect to fertility, is, however, more similar to the typical behavior of the audience in developed countries than in developing countries. In turn, this implies that, to the extent that there are peer effects from the role models, these effects will be felt much more in developing countries than in developed settings.

A third reason is that media such as radio and television play an even more important role in countries with low literacy rates, in which print media have limited diffusion. In these countries there is a particular interest, as we stress in the concluding section, in the role that radio and television can play for educational purposes.

19.4. POLICY AND CONCLUSION

Having reviewed the impact of media exposure across a variety of settings, we return to the policy implications briefly outlined in the Introduction. In particular, what are the perspectives for the use of media programming for social policy?

As we discussed, an important opportunity emerges from the complementarity between entertainment and education in the "educational entertainment" (or "edutainment") combination: entertainment shows that incorporate role-model lessons. A precedent for this combination is the case of product placement, in which a particular product, such as a particular beer, is consumed by a character during a movie or television show. In the case of *edutainment*, the content placed is not a product, but a social behavior, presented so that it will be imitated, or the opposite. La Ferrara (2015) discusses the underpinnings of this approach from the social psychology literature and its applications to anti-poverty policies.

The studies above on family outcomes highlight the potential of such combination: soap operas played an important role in lowering fertility rates in a country with very high fertility like Brazil. Importantly, this policy impact occurred with no apparent loss of audience. Indeed, the role models in the soap operas were not explicitly designed, as far as we know, to affect social change, but were a by-product of the entertainment plot. The examples of such success stories stress the potential of such interventions.

Other points, however, suggest a cautionary note. We discussed an example regarding migration in which media exposure had the opposite effect of what one may have thought: exposure to a higher standard of living reduced, rather than increased, migration. In other cases, exposure to edutainment just had no impact on behavior.

While scattered examples of evaluations exist, it seems that more systematic and rigorous evaluations could greatly help in assessing the effectiveness of edutainment policies across different contexts. Specifically designing evaluations to understand through what channels these programs affect behavior is an exercise still relatively rare in this field. A recent example is the work by Banerjee et al. (2015), who have implemented a randomized controlled trial to estimate the impact of the MTV series *Shuga 3* on risky sexual behavior, gender norms, and domestic violence in Nigeria. A key feature of this evaluation is that it embeds in the design the estimation of spillovers and the role that individual *ex ante* beliefs play in shaping reactions to the program. Future evaluations of edutainment productions would ideally foresee variations in the design, e.g., in the content delivered, to improve our understanding of this potential policy tool.

A different, delicate issue concerns the ethics of the interventions: what are the limits of using commercial television for social development? (Brown and Singhal, 1990). Some interventions, like the placement of ethnic examples designed to lead to ethnic reconciliation, are unlikely to be controversial. Yet other cases are likely to spur controversies. After all, a major motivation for the study of media effects was understanding the exploitation of the media for propaganda purposes by autocratic governments. As part of this manipulation, dictators such as Hitler and Mussolini embedded political messages in entertainment content provided by the state, an early example of edutainment. Which of the modern edutainment applications cross the line from contribution to society to controversial propaganda? More debate on the topic, together with further evidence on the effectiveness of the placed media content, is surely in order.

It is important to add that the policy implications are not limited to the placement of content within entertainment. A general message throughout this chapter is the importance of the substitution channel for the media effects: so much time is spent on media entertainment that even moderate shifts in the time allocated to media consumption can crowd out, or crowd in, activities with policy relevance. A first example is the study of effects on social capital: the expansion of television takes time away from activities that we tend to think of as having high value added: social interactions and participation in groups providing public goods.

An opposite example emerges from the finding that releases of violent movies lower violent crime because they reduce the allocation of time to even more pernicious activities. This is a surprising policy impact for a media genre that generally is seen very critically. This finding is not likely isolated. More generally, media entertainment that attracts groups with violent inclinations has the potential to play an important positive role.

All in all, the study of the economic and social impacts of the media is an area in transition that exhibits great potential. The large majority of what we know in the area did not even exist 10 years ago. That only leads one to imagine what breakthroughs lie ahead for the field.

Table 19.1 Summary of papers on the economic and social effects of the media

Paper	Main outcome	Media	Country	Empirical strategy	Identification
Economics of education					
Zavodny (2006)	Scores in standardized tests	TV	USA	Correlation	Fixed effects and restriction to twins
Gentzkow and Shapiro (2008)	Cognitive and non-cognitive outcomes	TV	USA	Natural experiment	Variation in years of television introduction across media markets
Huang and Lee (2010)	Cognitive outcomes—math and reading scores	TV	USA	Correlation	Dynamic panel data model with feedback
Keane and Fiorini (2014)	Ranking of productivity of different activities	Media	Australia	Correlation	Econometric modeling and exclusion restrictions
Kearney and Levine (2015)	Educational and labor market outcomes	Exposure to *Sesame Street* on PBS (TV)	USA	Natural experiment	Variation in signal coverage across counties due to technological features and distance, and in exposure among cohorts
Keefer and Khemani (2011)	Share of literate children in the village	Radio	Benin	Natural experiment	Variation in radio coverage across villages
Economics of the family					
La Ferrara et al. (2012)	Fertility rates	Telenovelas (TV)	Brazil	Natural experiment	Geographic and temporal variation in access to Rede Globo network telenovelas
Chong and La Ferrara (2009)	Divorce rates	Telenovelas (TV)	Brazil	Natural experiment	Geographic and temporal variation in access to Rede Globo network telenovelas
Jensen and Oster (2009)	Acceptability of domestic violence, degree of preference for male children, female autonomy/decision-making ability, female school enrollment, fertility	TV	India	Natural experiment	Geographic and temporal (2001–2003) variation in access to cable television

Study	Outcome	Medium	Country	Method	Identification strategy
Cheung (2012)	School enrollment, women status: ideal number of sons, acceptability of domestic violence, sole final say	Radio	Cambodia	Natural experiment	Geographic and temporal variation in access to radio
Kearney and Levine (2014)	Talking about related topics: Twitter and Google searches; rates of teen childbearing; birth certificates information	*16 and Pregnant* (TV)	USA	Correlation/ IV	Panel data/variation in searching trends/ instrumental variables

LABOR/migration decisions

Braga (2007)	Individual migration decisions	TV	Albania	Natural experiment	Variation in distance from Italian television transmitters due to topographic characteristics
Farré and Fasani (2013)	Migration	TV	Indonesia	Natural experiment	Variation in reception due to the topography of the terrain
Bjorvatn et al. (2015)	Entrepreneurship	Show on enterpreneurship (TV)	Tanzania	Randomized controlled trial	Randomized encouragement to watch TV show on entrepreneurship

Environmental economics

Jacobsen (2011)	Environmental friendly behavior: carbon offsets purchase	Documentary movie *An Inconvenient Truth*	USA	Natural experiment	Spatial variation in film release to theaters

Health

Suicide

Bollen and Phillips (1982)	Suicide incidence	TV	USA	Event study	Compares day/week following the news about celebrity suicide to other periods

Continued

Table 19.1 Summary of papers on the economic and social effects of the media—cont'd

Paper	Main outcome	Media	Country	Empirical strategy	Identification
Baron and Reiss (1985)	Suicide incidence, homicide incidence	TV	USA	Event study	Compares day/week following the news about celebrity suicide to other periods. Relative to Bollen and Phillips, Baron and Reiss include additional controls
Smoking					
Bauman et al. (1991)	Adolescents: subjective expected utility for smoking, friends approval, friends encouragement, smoking intentions	Anti-smoking advertisement via radio	USA	Field experiment	Two MSAs in US South allocated as treatments, four MSAs as controls
Farrelly et al. (2009)	Smoking initiation among adolescents aged 12–17 years	Anti-smoking advertisement	USA	Natural experiment	As proxy of exposure gross rating points—indicators of reach and frequency of a campaign in each media market—are used
HIV/AIDS					
Vaughan et al. (2000)	Communication about HIV, HIV awareness, prevention behaviors, number of partners	Radio soap opera	Tanzania	Natural experiment	Exposure to radio soap opera with content on HIV prevention
Kennedy et al. (2004)	Number of calls received by the CDC National STD and AIDS Hotline's English service	TV soap opera *The Bold and the Beautiful*	USA	Interrupted time series design	HIV related episode in soap opera + message with hotline number

Crime

Josephson (1987)	Boys' aggression (as reported by teachers completing the nine-item Rip van Winkle Peer Rated Index of Aggression)	Short video	Canada	Experiment	Random assignment to one of six treatment groups—two orders of frustration (before/after TV-watching) crossed with three TV violence exposure conditions
Dahl and DellaVigna (2009)	Violent crime	Violent movies	USA	Natural experiment	Day-to-day variation in the movie audiences of strongly violent, mildly violent, and non-violent movies
Card and Dahl (2011)	Family violence	Football game shown on TV	USA	Natural experiment	Variation in football score, compared to the predicted score of the game (Las Vegas bookmakers), comparing locals fans to other viewers
Bhuller et al. (2013)	Sex crime and rape and child sex abuse	Internet	Norway	Natural experiment	Spatial and temporal variation in access to Internet due to implementation of National Broadband Policy
Cunningham et al. (2011)	Weekly crime	Video games	USA	Instrumental variables	Instrument: ratings of video games by a video games rating agency, exploiting the variation in game sales correlated with the variation in quality

Continued

Table 19.1 Summary of papers on the economic and social effects of the media—cont'd

Paper	Main outcome	Media	Country	Empirical strategy	Identification
Public economics					
Olken (2009)	Social capital: trust, participation to social groups, number of activities in the village; governance: attendance at village meetings, quality of discussion, percentage of funds used in the project	Radio and TV	Indonesia	Instrumental variables	Variation in propagation of signal due to topographical and geographical conformation of the territory
Trujillo and Paluck (2011)	Support for the US census and attitudes toward government amongst US latinos	Telenovela *Más Sabe El Diablo* (*The Devil Knows Best*)	USA	Randomized controlled trial	Random assignment of subjects into treatment group exposed to pro-census messaging in a latino soap opera or into control group exposed to an episode of the same soap opera not involving the census
Kasper et al. (2015)	Government trust and power; tax compliance	TV	Austria	Randomized controlled trial	Assignment to four conditions: high-versus low-trust scenarios and high-versus low-power scenarios
Dutta et al. (2013)	Knowledge of BREGS; perceptions that BREGS increase employment, reduce migration, enhance infrastructures; actual or desired participation, wage rates or days worked	Movie about rights under an entitlement program	India	Randomized controlled trial	Random assignment of villages to screening of movie

Attitudes

Paluck and Green (2009)	Beliefs regarding prejudice, violence and trauma; norms regarding how to behave in situations related to prejudice, conflict and trauma; behaviors: speak, dissent and cooperate	Radio soap opera *Musekaweya* (or *New Dawn*)	Rwanda	Randomized controlled trial	Randomized assignment to radio soap opera versus control programming
Hennighausen (2015)	Beliefs about the drivers of success	TV	Eastern Germany	Natural experiment	Variation in access to western television due to geographical and topographical characteristics of the territory

Consumption and savings

Bursztyn and Cantoni (forthcoming)	Disposable income, total private consumption, and savings; use of financial instruments; consumption choices	TV	Eastern Germany	Natural experiment	Variation in access to western television due to geographical and topographical characteristics of the territory
Berg and Zia (2013)	General and specific financial literacy, borrowing from formal banks, borrowing for investment purposes, saving propensity, likelihood of using money for gambling and hire expenses, seek for financial advice	TV soap opera *Scandal!*	South Africa	Randomized controlled trial	Randomized encouragement to watch soap opera

ACKNOWLEDGMENTS

We are grateful to Gordon Dahl, Matthew Gentzkow, Magne Mogstad, Ben Olken, Jesse Shapiro, and David Stromberg for comments on the draft. We thank Benedetta Brioschi, Yizhuang Alden Cheng, Brian Wheaton, Martina Zanella, Jeffrey Zeidel, and Michael Zhang for excellent research assistance.

REFERENCES

Aguiar, M., Hurst, E., Karabarbounis, L., 2013. Time use during the great recession. Am. Econ. Rev. 103 (5), 1664–1696.

Alesina, A., La Ferrara, E., 2002. Who trusts others? J. Public Econ. 85 (2), 207–234.

American Academy of Pediatrics, 2001. American academy of pediatrics: children, adolescents, and television. Pediatrics 107 (2), 423–426.

Anderson, C.A., Bushman, B.J., 2001. Effects of violent video games on aggressive behavior, aggressive cognition, aggressive affect, physiological arousal, and prosocial behavior: a meta-analytic review of the scientific literature. Psychol. Sci. 12, 353–359.

Anderson, C.A., Berkowitz, L., Donnerstein, E., Huesmann, L.R., Johnson, J.D., Linz, D., Malamut, N.M., Wartella, E., 2003. The influence of media violence on youth. Psychol. Sci. Public Int. 4, 81–110.

Banerjee, A., La Ferrara, E., Orozco, V., 2015. Changing Norms and Behavior of Young People in Nigeria: An Evaluation of Entertainment TV. Bocconi University, Mimeo.

Baron, J.N., Reiss, P.C., 1985. Same time, next year: aggregate analysis of the mass media and violent behavior. Am. Sociol. Rev. 50, 347–363.

Bauman, K.E., LaPrelle, J., Brown, J.D., Koch, G.G., Padgett, C.A., 1991. The influence of three mass media campaigns on variables related to adolescent cigarette smoking: results of a field experiment. Am. J. Public Health 81 (5), 597–604.

Berg, G., Zia, B., 2013. Harnessing Emotional Connections to Improve Financial Decisions: Evaluating the Impact of Financial Education in Mainstream Media. World Bank Policy Research Working Paper No. 6407.

Besley, T., Burgess, R., 2001. Political agency, government responsiveness and the role of the media. Eur. Econ. Rev. 45, 629–640.

Bhuller, M., Havnes, T., Leuven, E., Mogstad, M., 2013. Broadband internet: an information superhighway to sex crime? Rev. Econ. Stud. 80, 1237–1266.

Bjorvatn, K., Cappelen, A., Helgesson Sekeiz, L., Sørensen, E., Tungodden, B., 2015. Teaching Through Television: Experimental Evidence on Entrepreneurship Education in Tanzania. NHH Norwegian School of Economics, Mimeo.

Bollen, K.A., Phillips, D.P., 1982. Imitative suicides: a national study of the effects of television news stories. Am. Sociol. Rev. 47, 802–809.

Braga, M., 2007. Dreaming Another Life: The Role of Foreign Media in Migration Decision—Evidence from Albania. World Bank Working Paper.

Brown, W.J., Singhal, A., 1990. Ethical dilemmas of prosocial television. Commun. Q. 38 (3), 1990.

Bursztyn, L., Cantoni, D., forthcoming. A tear in the iron curtain: the impact of Western Television on consumption behavior. Rev. Econ. Stat. doi: 10.1162/REST_a_00522. Available at http:// www.mitpressjournals.org/doi/pdf/10.1162/REST_a_00522.

Card, D., Dahl, G.B., 2011. Family violence and football: the effect of unexpected emotional cues on violent behavior. Q. J. Econ. 126, 1–41.

Cheung, M., 2012. Edutainment Radio, Women's Status and Primary School Participation: Evidence from Cambodia. Stockholm University, Working Paper.

Chong, A., La Ferrara, E., 2009. Television and divorce: evidence from Brazilian novelas. J. Eur. Econ. Assoc. Pap. Proc. 7 (2–3), 458–468.

Cook, D.E., Kestenbaum, C., Honaker, L.M., Anderson Jr., E.R., 2000. Joint Statement on the Impact of Entertainment Violence on Children. Congressional Public Health Summit, http://www2.aap.org/advocacy/releases/jstmtevc.htm.

Cunningham, S., Engelstätter, B., Ward, M.R., 2011. Understanding the Effects of Violent Video Games on Violent Crime. ZEW Discussion Papers, No. 11-042.

Dahl, G., DellaVigna, S., 2009. Does movie violence increase violent crime? Q. J. Econ. 124 (2), 677–734.

DellaVigna, S., Gentzkow, M., 2010. Persuasion: empirical evidence. Annu. Rev. Econ. 2, 643–669.

DellaVigna, S., Kaplan, E., 2007. The Fox news effect: media bias and voting. Q. J. Econ. 122 (2), 807–860.

Dutta, P., Ravallion, M., Murgai, R., van de Walle, D., 2013. Testing Information Constraints on India's Largest Antipoverty Program. World Bank, Policy Research Working Paper No. 6598.

Enikolopov, R., Petrova, M., 2015. Media capture: empirical evidence. In: Anderson, S.P., Strömberg, D., Waldfogel, J. (Eds.), Handbook of Media Economics, vol. 1B. Elsevier, Amsterdam.

Farré, L., Fasani, F., 2013. Media exposure and internal migration: evidence from Indonesia. J. Dev. Econ. 102 (C), 48–61.

Farrelly, M.C., Nonnemaker, J., Davis, K.C., Hussin, A., 2009. The influence of the national truth campaign on smoking initiation. Am. J. Prev. Med. 36 (5), 379–384.

Fernandes, L., 2000. Nationalizing 'the global': media images, cultural politics, and the middle class in India. Media Cult. Soc. 22 (5), 611–628.

Fong, C., 2001. Social preferences, self interest, and the demand for redistribution. J. Public Econ. 82 (2), 225–246.

Gentile, D.A., Oberg, C., Sherwood, N.E., Story, M., Walsh, D.A., Hogan, M., 2004. Well-child visits in the video age: pediatricians and the American Academy of Pediatrics' guidelines for children's media use. Pediatrics 114 (5), 1235–1241.

Gentzkow, M., 2006. Television and voter turnout. Q. J. Econ. 121 (3), 931–972.

Gentzkow, M., Shapiro, J.M., 2008. Preschool television viewing and adolescent test scores historical evidence from the Coleman study. Q. J. Econ. 123 (1), 279–323.

Gentzkow, M., Shapiro, J., Stone, D., 2015. Media bias in the marketplace: theory. In: Anderson, S.P., Strömberg, D., Waldfogel, J. (Eds.), Handbook of Media Economics, vol. 1B. Elsevier, Amsterdam.

Groseclose, T., Milyo, J., 2005. A measure of media bias. Q. J. Econ. 120, 1191–1237.

Heckman, J.J., 2000. Policies to foster human capital. Res. Econ. 54 (1), 3–56.

Hennighausen, T., 2015. Exposure to television and individual beliefs: evidence from a natural experiment. J. Comp. Econ. .

Huang, F., Lee, M., 2010. Dynamic treatment effect analysis of TV effects on child cognitive development. J. Appl. Econ. 25 (3), 392–419.

Hufford, G., 2002. The ITS Irregular Terrain Model, Version 1.2.2: The Algorithm. Institute for Telecommunication Sciences, National Telecommunications and Information Administration. http://www.its.bldrdoc.gov/media/50674/itm.pdf.

Jacobsen, G.D., 2011. The Al Gore effect: an inconvenient truth and voluntary carbon offsets. J. Environ. Econ. Manag. 61, 67–78.

Jensen, R., Oster, E., 2009. The power of TV: cable television and women's status in India. Q. J. Econ. 124 (3), 1057–1094.

Johnson, K., 2001. Media and social change: the modernizing influences of television in rural India. Media Cult. Soc. 23 (2), 147–169.

Johnson, J.G., Cohen, P., Smailes, E.M., Kasen, S., Brook, J.S., 2002. Television viewing and aggressive behavior during adolescence and adulthood. Science 295, 2468–2471.

Josephson, W.L., 1987. Television violence and children's aggression: testing the priming, social script, and disinhibition predictions. J. Pers. Soc. Psychol. 53, 882–890.

Kasper, M., Kogler, C., Kirchler, E., 2015. Tax policy and the news: an empirical analysis of taxpayers' perceptions of tax-related media coverage and its impact on tax compliance. J. Behav. Exp. Econ. 54, 58–63.

Keane, M., Fiorini, M., 2014. How the allocation of children's time affects cognitive and non-cognitive development. J. Labor Econ. 32 (4), 787–836.

Kearney, M.S., Levine, P.B., 2014. Media Influences on Social Outcomes: The Impact of MTV's 16 and Pregnant on Teen Childbearing. NBER Working Paper No. 19795.

Kearney, M.S., Levine, P.B., 2015. Early Childhood Education by MOOC: Lessons from Sesame Street. NBER Working Paper No. 21229.

Keefer, P., Khemani, S., 2011. Mass Media and Public Services: The Effects of Radio Access on Public Education in Benin. Policy Research Working Paper Series 5559, The World Bank.

Kennedy, M.G., O'Leary, A., Beck, V., Pollard, W.E., Simpson, P., 2004. Increases in calls to the CDC national STD and AIDS hotline following AIDS-related episodes in a soap opera. J. Commun. 54 (2), 287–301.

La Ferrara, E., 2015. Mass Media and Social Change: Can We Use Television to Fight Poverty? JEEA-FBBVA Lecture.

La Ferrara, E., Chong, A., Duryea, S., 2012. Soap operas and fertility: evidence from Brazil. Am. Econ. J. Appl. Econ. 4 (4), 1–31.

Olken, B.A., 2009. Do TV and radio destroy social capital? Evidence from Indonesian villages. Am. Econ. J. Appl. Econ. 1 (4), 1–33.

Paluck, E.L., 2009. Reducing intergroup prejudice and conflict using the media: a field experiment in Rwanda. J. Pers. Soc. Psychol. 96, 574–587.

Paluck, E.L., Green, D.P., 2009. Deference, dissent, and dispute resolution: a field experiment on a mass media intervention in Rwanda. Am. Polit. Sci. Rev. 103 (4), 622–644.

Putnam, R.D., 2000. Bowling Alone: The Collapse and Revival of American Community. Simon & Schuster, New York, NY.

Scrase, T.J., 2002. Television, the middle classes and the transformation of cultural identities in West Bengal, India. Int. Commun. Gaz. 64 (4), 323–342.

Strömberg, D., 2004. Radio's impact on public spending. Q. J. Econ. 119 (1), 189–221.

Strömberg, D., 2015. Media coverage and political accountability: theory and evidence. In: Anderson, S.P., Strömberg, D., Waldfogel, J. (Eds.), Handbook of Media Economics, vol. 1B. Elsevier, Amsterdam.

Tetlock, P., 2015. The role of media in finance. In: Anderson, S.P., Strömberg, D., Waldfogel, J. (Eds.), Handbook of Media Economics, vol. 1B. Elsevier, Amsterdam.

Trujillo, M., Paluck, E.L., 2011. The devil knows best: experimental effects of a televised soap opera on Latino trust in government and support for the 2010 census. Anal. Soc. Issues Public Policy 12 (1), 113–132.

Vaughan, P., Rogers, E., Singhal, A., Swalehe, R., 2000. Entertainment-education and HIV/AIDS prevention: a field experiment in Tanzania. J. Health Commun. 5 (1), 81–100.

Wilbur, K., 2015. Recent developments in mass media: digitization and multitasking. In: Anderson, S.P., Strömberg, D., Waldfogel, J. (Eds.), Handbook of Media Economics, vol. 1A. Elsevier, Amsterdam.

Zavodny, M., 2006. Does watching television rot your mind? Estimates of the effect on test scores. Econ. Educ. Rev. 25 (5), 565–573.

INDEX

Note: Page numbers followed by *f* indicate figures and *t* indicate tables.

A

Abreast of the Market (AM), 708–709
Advertisers, 545–546, 553, 567
Advertising
  privacy and, 544–552
  social, 553
Advertising-avoidance tools, 546
Advertising-supported internet, privacy and, 551–552
Agenda-setting effects, 654
Agenda setting power, 664
Alternative modeling approach, 704
AM. *See* Abreast of the Market (AM)
Amazon and Barnes & Noble's platforms, 571
AngiesList, 582, 585
An Inconvenient Truth (documentary), 743
Attention, and valuation, 711–712
Attitudes, 754–756
Audience share bias, 618–619
Audience size effects, 610–611

B

Baseline model, 675
Bayesian framework, 694–695
Behavioral finance, 708
Behavioral price
  discrimination, 546–547
  privacy concerns and, 546–547
Bias, 624–627
  audience share, 618–619
  estimation, 649–658
  explicit, 650–651
  implicit, 651–658
  media access, 619
  newsworthiness, 619
  supply-driven, 630–633
  target group, 620
  and voter behavior, 662–663
  and welfare, 627
Bias, demand-driven, 633–643
  delegation, 634–638
  psychological utility, 638–641
  reputation, 641–643

Biased news, 678–679
Bias, factors correlated with, 659
  demand-side factors, 659
  role of competition, 661–662
  supply-side factors, 659–661
Blackwell, 627, 634–635
Business models, UGC issues, 584–585
Bystanders, 567

C

Capture models, 684
Censorship, 694–695
Competition policy, 683
Consumption, and savings, 756–757
Copycat effect, 744
Corporate finance applications, 715–716
  media and cost of capital, 716
  media and firm performance, 715–716
Credit Mobilier scandal partisan newspapers, 690
Crime, media exposure, 746–751

D

Decision-making, and children's educational outcomes, 739–740
Demand-driven bias, 633–643
  delegation, 634–638
  psychological utility, 638–641
  reputation, 641–643
Demand for entertainment theme, 724–725
Demand-side factors, 659
Designer, UGC platform, 567
Development economics, 757–758
Difference-in-differences approach, 571
Digital exhaust, 586–587
Direct versus substitution effects theme, 725
Dow Jones News Service (DJNS), 706, 710

E

eBay, 573
Economic effects, of media, 760*t*
Economics of privacy, 542–544
Educational entertainment (edutainment), 727, 739–740, 743, 758–759

Education, impact of television on, 731–737
Edutainment (educational entertainment), 727, 743, 758–759
Entertainment media role theme, 726–727
Environmental economics, 743
E-Privacy Directive, 548
Explicit bias measurement, 650–651

F
Facebook, 567, 569, 574
Food & Wine magazine, 564–565

G
Global Trust Barometer, 694–695
Government, privacy and, 557–558

H
Health, media exposure on, 744
    HIV/AIDS, 745–746
    smoking, 744–745
    suicide, 744
HHI. *See* Hirschmann-Herfindahl Index
High School and Beyond survey (HSB), 731–732
Hirschmann-Herfindahl Index (HHI), 676–677, 683–684
HIV/AIDS, media exposure on, 745–746
Hotelling, 633, 637, 640–641

I
Identification and time horizon theme, 726
Ideological bias, 648–649
Imitation
    description, 726, 728
    effect, 744
    hypothesis, 741–742, 746
    of media role model, 731, 737, 740–741
    suicide, 745
Implicit bias measurement, 651–652
    comparison approach, 652–653
    issue intensity approach, 654–656
    measuring tone approach, 656–658
Independent media, 689
    impact, in captured environments, 695–696
Information environment, media as reflection of, 705–712
Information, in politics, 597–599
Information release, and market activity, 706–707
Informative media, on politics, 599

Initial public offering (IPO), 715
Internet
    access, 749–750
    and sex crimes, 750
Investor relations (IR) firms, 714
Investors, rational, 703
Issue intensity approach, 654–656

L
Labor markets, and migration, 741–743
LinkedIn, 588
Longitudinal Study of Australian Children (LSAC), 735

M
Mahatma Gandhi National Rural Employment Guarantee Scheme (NREGS), 754
Market activity, information release and, 706–707
Market for news, model of, 628–629
Market inefficiency, 707
Market provision, of news, 600
    competition, 602–604
    coverage across issues and multitasking, 604–605
    monopoly media, 601–602
    optimal regulation and public provision of news, 605–608
    total coverage of politics, 600–601
Market structure, privacy and, 551
Mass media, 648, 654, 688–689
Measuring tone approach, 656–658
Media
    attention and valuation, 711–712
    causal role of, 712–715
    economic and social effects of, 760*t*
    and firm performance, 715–716
    impact of, on family outcomes, 737–741
    information content and valuation, 708–711
    information release and market activity, 706–707
    persuasion effect of, 740
    as reflection of information environment, 705–712
    role models in, 737–741
    theory for, 703–705
Media access bias, 619
Media bias, 624, 626–627, 629, 658, 676
    forms of, 648–649
Media capture, 669–670, 672–676, 688
    and content, 689–691

determinants of, 693–694
effect of, 689
environments, 695–697
evidence on, 689–693
impact, 694–696
limits of, 697–698
media effects in, 694–697
Media censorship, 694–695
Media competition, 602, 632–633, 640–641, 643
Media concentration, 672, 674–675, 682
Media consumption, 609, 615, 617
Media consumption matrix, 678*t*, 682
Media content, capture and, 689–691
Media control, 694–695
Media coverage, 711–712, 716
Media Diversity Index, 676–677
Media effects, 654
  in Cambodia, 739–740
  in media capture, 694–697
  methodological issues, 728–730
Media exposure
  crime, 746–751
  health, 744
  HIV/AIDS, 745–746
  impact of, on outcomes, 731–758
  smoking, 744
  suicide, 744
Media impact
  on stock prices, 714–715
  on volume and volatility, 713–714
Media, independent, 689
  impact, in captured environments, 695–696
Media outlets, 673
  description, 648, 651–652
  measurement, 648
Media power, 669–670, 676–682
Media power index, 682, 682*t*
Media regulation, 683, 690
  implications for, 682–685
Media transparency, adverse effects of, 696–697
Media visibility, 704
Migration, labor markets and, 741–743
Minimal-bandwidth index, 682, 682*t*
Monopoly media, 601–602
Multitasking
  audience share bias, 618–619
  coverage across issues and, 604–605
  media access bias, 619

newsworthiness bias, 619
target group bias, 620

N
National Education Longitudinal Study (NELS), 731–732
National Incident Based Reporting System (NIBRS), 747
National Longitudinal Survey of Youth 1979 (NLSY79), 731–732, 734–735
Net asset value (NAV), 707
News
  bias, 628–629
  market provision of (*see* Market provision, of news)
  public provision of, 605–608
Newspapers, 650–655
Newsworthiness bias, 619
NREGS. *See* Mahatma Gandhi National Rural Employment Guarantee Scheme (NREGS)

O
Online advertisers, 548
Online advertising, 546–547, 549–550, 556
Online data security, privacy, 555–557
Optimal regulation, and public provision of news, 605–608

P
Persuasion, 663
  effect, 728, 740–741
Polarize platforms, 632
Policy, 758–765
  impacts, 727
  politicians, 616–618
Political economy, 671–672
Politicians policy, 616–618
Politics
  informative media on, 599
  role of information in, 597–599
  total coverage of, 600–601
  volume of coverage, 610–611, 612*f*, 617–618
Potential endogeneity, 735
Privacy
  and advertising, 544
  and advertising-supported internet, 551–552
  and behavioral pricing, 546–547
  economics of, 542–544

Privacy (*Continued*)
    future spheres of, 558–559
    and government, 557–558
    and market structure, 551
    online data security, 555–557
    paradox, 544
    regulation and targeted advertising, 547–551
    and social media, 552–554
    and targeted advertising, 544–546
    theory of, 541–542
    in US legal history, 541–542
    in world of infinitely persisting data, 554–555
Pro-Democratic bias, 654–655
Propaganda, 697
PSB. *See* Public service broadcasting
Public economics, 751–754
Public provision of news, optimal regulation and, 605–608
Public service broadcasting (PSB), 684–685

R
Radio, 727–728, 732, 736–737, 739–740, 745
Rational agents, 703
Rational disagreement model, 703
Rational investors, 703
ReaderShare$_{md}$, 610–611
Reuters News Service, 706
Robinson-Patman Act of 1936, 547
Role models, in media, 737–741

S
Search Volume Index (SVI), 712
The Seattle Times (newspaper), 564–565
Sesame Street program, 735–736
Smoking, media exposure on, 744–745
Social advertising, 553
Social effects
    of media, 760t
    of social media, 573–574
Social media
    platforms, 566–567
    privacy and, 552–554
    social effects of, 573–574
Stock prices, media impact on, 714–715
Substitution effects, 731, 734, 751–752
Suicide, media exposure, 744
Supply-driven bias, 630–633
Supply-side factors, 659–661

T
Targeted advertising
    privacy concerns and, 544–546
    privacy regulation and, 547–551
Target group bias, 620
Television, 731–737
Textual analysis, 702, 708–709
TripAdvisor, 564, 568, 570, 578, 587–588

U
User-centric controls, 549–550
User-generated content (UGC)
    business models, 584–585
    competition and network effects, 585–586
    description, 566, 588–589
    digital exhaust, property rights, and privacy, 586–587
    incentive design and behavioral foundations, 582–584
    information aggregation, 587–588
    novel feature of, 566–567
    platforms, 566–567, 566t
    sample platforms with, 565t
    welfare effects, 588
User-generated content, impact of, 568
    cross-platform comparisons, 570
    data and identification challenges, 568–571
    on demand, 571–573
    field experiments, 570–571
    findings and open questions, 574–575
    platform quirks, 570
    social effects of social media, 573–574
User-generated content quality, 575
    issues, 581–582
    peer effects and social influence, 581
    promotional content, 575–579, 579t
    self-selection, 579–581
User-generated information concept, 564
User reviews, sample platforms with, 565t

V
Volatility, media impact on, 713–714
Voter behavior, bias and, 662–663
Voters
    information, 611–613
    political participation, 614–615
    responsiveness, 613–614

W

Wall Street Journal (WSJ), 706, 710
Welfare, bias and, 627
Wikia, 582–583
Women's Media Center of Cambodia (WMC),
    739–740
World Almanac, 706

Y

Yelp, 567–568, 571–572, 579, 582–585